COLLECTIVE CHOICE PROCESSES

A Qualitative and Quantitative Analysis of Foreign Policy Decision-Making

IRMTRAUD N. GALLHOFER
and WILLEM E. SARIS

Westport, Connecticut
London

Library of Congress Cataloging-in-Publication Data

Gallhofer, Irmtraud N.
    Collective choice processes : a qualitative and quantitative
analysis of foreign policy decision-making / Irmtraud N. Gallhofer
and Willem E. Saris.
       p.   cm.
    Includes bibliographical references and index.
    ISBN 0–275–96029–3 (alk. paper)
    1. International relations—Decision making. 2. International
relations—History. I. Saris, Willem E. II. Title.
JX1391.G266   1997
327—dc21   97–8866

British Library Cataloguing in Publication Data is available.

Library of Congress Catalog Card Number: 97–8866
ISBN: 0–275–96029–3

First published in 1997

Praeger Publishers, 88 Post Road West, Westport, CT 06881
An imprint of Greenwood Publishing Group, Inc.

Printed in the United States of America

The paper used in this book complies with the
Permanent Paper Standard issued by the National
Information Standards Organization (Z39.48–1984).

10 9 8 7 6 5 4 3 2 1

Copyright Acknowledgments

The authors and the publisher gratefully acknowledge permission to use the following:

"From Individual Preferences to Group Decisions in Foreign Policy Decision Making: The Dutch
Council of Ministers," by Irmtraud N. Gallhofer, Willem E. Saris, and Robert Voogt. 1994. *European
Journal of Political Research* 25: 151–170, Tables 1, 2, 4, 5, 6, 7 and Figure 1. © 1994 Kluwer
Academic Publishers. With kind permission of Kluwer Academic Publishers.

Contents

Introduction

In 1914 the cabinet of the Austro-Hungarian monarchy had to decide what their reaction should be to the assassination in Sarajevo of their heir to the throne. They considered whether or not to declare war on Serbia. Their decision led to World War I.

In August 1939 Hitler intended to declare war on Poland. Since Great Britain and France had guaranteed Poland's neutrality and were to declare war on Germany if it attacked Poland, Hitler discussed his plans with his supreme commanders. This decision led to World War II.

In October 1962 President Kennedy and his advisers had to decide how to react to the deployment of Russian missiles in Cuba. They considered various options including a full-scale air attack on Cuba, with its possible consequence, a Third World War using nuclear weapons. In this case a war was avoided.

In 1948 the Dutch cabinet had to decide how to stop the Indonesian independence movement in its East Indian colony. The government considered the alternatives of military action or negotiations. In this case the government decided first to negotiate, but later a military action was initiated.

In all these cases governments had to decide between war and peace. Although the problem was similar, the way the decision in each case was made was very different. This was largely due to the difference in rules the different groups used for decision-making. In this book we discuss the rules that are applied in different decision-making units to make important foreign policy decisions.

These decision-making processes also have something in common. Normally, a decision-making process begins with a problem analysis and an argument for or against an available option.

In another book (Gallhofer and Saris 1996), we studied how individual participants in a decision-making process formulate their arguments in favor of a specific policy option. More precisely, we examined how different individual decision-makers of the Austro-Hungarian monarchy argued to initiate a war with Serbia, how Hitler formulated his choice to begin World War II, how Kennedy and his advisers argued to avoid a nuclear war, and how members of the Dutch government formulated their choice to punish a seceding colony. Since most important political decisions are taken in a group, this volume is a sequel to the first book to the extent that it investigates how the various individual preferences of members participating in a collective decision-making process are combined into a group choice that becomes a binding foreign policy decision.

The first part of this book examines again how Hitler and his supreme commanders came to the conclusion to invade Poland, how President Kennedy and his advisers decided to avoid a nuclear war with the Soviet Union, how the Austro-Hungarian cabinet decided to initiate World War I, and how the Dutch cabinet decided to take military action in Indonesia. Since the settings of these groups are quite diverse, the rules which govern the aggregation process also differ substantially. In Hitler's case, the members of the group were confronted with a dictator who did not really appreciate advice, whereas President Kennedy, although he had the power to make the decision himself, was eager to get advice from different sources. The Austro-Hungarian cabinet had to arrive together at a majority choice, at the least, taking into account the various views of its members. The same was true of the Dutch cabinet, consisting of members with extremely diverse views.

This process does not seem to be too obvious, not even to politicians, if one believes the following comment of an anonymous British statesman:

The great mystery of all conduct is social conduct. I have had to study it all my life, but I cannot pretend to understand it. I may seem to know a man through and through, and still I would not want to say the first thing about what he will do in a group (Hirokawa and Poole 1986, 15).

This book consists of two parts. Part 1 deals with a qualitative study of decision-making processes in different decision-making groups, and Part 2 relates to a quantitative study of decision-making by the Dutch government in this century.

Part 1 begins with an overview of theoretical frameworks for group decision-making (Chapter 1) from which we derive the framework used in this book and the propositions to be tested (Chapter 2). Chapter 3 explains the methodology used, and subsequently the case studies relating to different decision-making groups are presented (Chapters 4 to 8). Part 1 concludes with a summary of findings concerning the practice of collective choice in different decision-making units.

Collective choice in a so-called heterogeneous group, where cabinets are composed of members of different political parties or different groups from society, is much more difficult to achieve, yet it is important to study it because most Western European governments consist of such a unit. Therefore, Part 2 is entirely devoted to a quantitative study of decision-making in such a group. As both authors are living in the Netherlands it seemed convenient to study Dutch cabinet decision-making, because we could get access to documents of meetings. This quantitative study is based on a sample of minutes of meetings of the Dutch cabinet concerning important decisions taken between 1900 and 1955 for which we obtained access. Chapter 9 shows how we intend to study the decision-making process on the basis of the literature and the propositions we developed. Subsequently, the decision-making process (Chapter 10) and the preference aggregation rules are studied (Chapter 11). Part 2 concludes with a summary of the findings and a comparison of the extent to which similar rules govern the decision-making process in the major Western European countries.

ACKNOWLEDGMENTS

This book represents the efforts of many people. Many students have helped to gather the data, but it would not be practical to try to name everyone who has contributed by coding, if only for fear of inadvertently omitting some of the coders. To all of them, our thanks. Special thanks go to Robert Voogt, who, together with the authors of this book, carried out a large part of the quantitative study of Dutch cabinet decisions. We are also grateful for valuable information on substantive matters and comment on some case studies from the late prime minister Willem Drees, Sr., and the late minister of foreign affairs Eelco Van Kleffens. Since most of the documents under investigation were secret and unpublished, we needed access to the archives of the council of ministers, the ministries of foreign affairs, economics, and defense, and to several collections in the state archives. We therefore wish to express our gratitude to those officials who gave us access, and especially to Mr. M. de Graaff at the state archives, who helped us on several occasions in the most pleasant way to find the required documents. Last but not least, we wish to thank Murray Pearson for his efforts to correct our English.

Part 1

A Qualitative Study of Collective Decision-Making Processes

First, in this part, we will discuss theories which pertain to collective decision-making (Chapter 1). We shall see that so far there exists no unified theory of collective decision-making but only diverse models that mainly deal with the identification of specific aspects of the group decision-making process. We need, therefore, to develop our own framework derived from these theories within which the foreign policy decisions can be studied (Chapter 2). In Chapter 3, the text analysis instrument for the study of the decision-making process is introduced and illustrated by examples. Chapters 4 through 8 present five case studies relating to different decision-making units and nations. These studies serve to illustrate the way in which decision-making processes may differ, depending on the decision-making group involved and the initial level of disagreement.

Chapter 1

Theoretical Frameworks for Group Decision-Making in the Context of National Government

Decision-making in foreign policy is normally conducted by a group of people who evaluate different possible options. The decision-making unit can be an entire cabinet, a specialized group of advisers such as the National Security Council in the United States, or an ad hoc group of ministers and/or advisers.

Reading the minutes of such meetings makes it clear that the decision-making process often begins with some exchange of information about the issue to be discussed. Subsequently, arguments in favor of a particular option by one or several of the participants are presented. This means that at least some participants enter the discussion with some preestablished opinions. In general, the first speaker is an expert in the field who presents the different options and indicates the possible consequences of these actions. The consequences are evaluated and a preference for one of the options is indicated. The structure of such arguments is discussed by Gallhofer and Saris (1996). If the participants in the meeting agree with the arguments of the first speaker, the decision can be made without further discussion. Problems arise when one or more participants suggest different options, or when they have different opinions about the possible consequences of the options, or evaluate them differently, and as a consequence prefer a different alternative. In such instances more than one person presents his argument and a discussion follows.

In this book we want to concentrate mainly on the process which ensues when decision-makers have presented their arguments in favor of different options. We shall address the question of how decision-makers are able to arrive at a collective choice, especially when there are initial differences in preferences. Clearly, it is not very difficult to come to a collective choice if all participants agree with the person who has presented his argument, since in that case a unanimous decision follows. The process is more complicated, however, if different participants have different preferences. The participants then have to engage in further discussions during which individuals have to change and/or modify their evaluations or proposals in order to arrive at a solution which is acceptable to most or all of the participants in the group, depending on the required degree of consensus. This process of changing and/or modifying individual proposals and/or preferences in order to arrive at a common solution can be achieved by verbal interactions whose aim is to influence others (persuasion) and/or by concession exchanges (bargaining).

In this chapter we describe the theories formulated in the literature concerning group decision-making. In Chapter 2, on the basis of the literature we develop the framework within which we wish to study the foreign policy decisions.

Group decision theories can be classified according to the decisional unit and the degree of rationality assumed, as summarized in Table 1.1. The table shows that in group settings a distinction is made between those models which assume that the decision-makers involved have conflicting objectives and those which assume that the decision-makers all have the same objectives. The latter postulate that the government, though composed of several individuals and organizations, behaves as if it were a unitary actor. A distinction is also made between models which assume that decision-makers have the capacity to make optimal choices with respect to their objectives ("objective rationality") and models which assume that the decision-makers are only capable of "bounded rationality"; that

Table 1.1
Classification of Theories of Group Decision-Making

Assumptions about Decisional Unit	Assumptions about Rationality	
	Objective rationality	*Bounded rationality*
Many decision-makers with conflicting objectives	I Social choice theory Game theory	III Multiple paths to choice models: Analytic, cybernetic, cognitive models Groupthink model Bureaucratic politics model Incrementalism Garbage can model Communication models Decision unit models
Many decision-makers with the same objectives	II Decision theoretic / Analytic model	IV Input-process-output approaches

is, they adapt to the characteristics of the situation within the limits of their knowledge and computing capacities (Simon 1957, 1985).

MODELS OF OBJECTIVE RATIONALITY

Social Choice Theory

Social choice theory (Table 1.1, cell I) examines the relation between group choices and individual members' conflicting preferences. It focuses on finding satisfactory methods for determining group preferences on the basis of the individual members' preferences. Condorcet (1979) had already shown that coherent individual preferences do not necessarily lead to a coherent collective choice by majority rule. Sometimes, when three or more individuals order their preferences for three or more alternatives, choosing between pairs, they might choose in such a way that the individually preferred alternatives cannot produce a coherent collective choice.

This phenomenon is called the "paradox of voting" and can be illustrated by the following example borrowed from Riker and Ordeshook (1973). For instance, the first person indicates a preference order (from the best to the least desired alternative) ABC, the second person mentions BCA, and the third person CAB. From these orderings it follows that A is preferred above B by persons 1 and 3, but B is preferred above C by persons 1 and 2, and C is preferred above A by persons 2 and 3. It is clear from this example that no coherent collective choice can be established which takes into account the individual preferences of all three persons.

When Arrow addressed this problem (1951) he established four reasonable conditions of fairness and rationality which should be fulfilled in order to determine a group's preference on the basis of the preferences of its individual members. Watson and Buede (1987, 108) summarize Arrow's conditions as follows:

1. Whatever the preferences of the group members, the method must produce a group preference order for the options being compared.
2. If every member of the group prefers option A to option B, then the group must also prefer A to B.
3. The group choice between two options, A and B, depends only on the preferences of the group members between A and B, and not on their preferences between A and B and any other option.
4. There is no dictator; no individual always gets his way.

Many scientists have tried to find satisfactory procedures for aggregating individual preferences to a group preference, sometimes ignoring Arrow's conditions. In these procedures the evaluations and preferences remain the same. Given this condition, rules are studied that derive a social choice from individual preferences and that give equal weight to all participants. Craven (1992) discusses in detail several efforts in this direction. Since we are more interested in description of the aggregation process in real-life situations, this theory is not suitable for our purposes.

Game Theory

Game theory (Table 1.1, cell I) was conceived by Von Neumann and Morgenstern (1947) for modeling decision-making in situations of conflict, coalition formation, and cooperation among participants. They described a game as an interaction between actors that is structured by a set of rules specifying the possible actions or moves for each participant and a set of outcomes for each possible combination of moves. The theory thus assumes that the decision unit consists of many decision-makers with conflicting objectives, each with the capacity to make optimal choices. Each decision-maker or player depends on the others with respect to the final outcome, which is a consequence of the choices of all players. A decision-maker is assumed capable of assigning his preferences, which are considered as subjective evaluations of the choices; but he is also considered to have knowledge of the preferences and possible moves of the other players and the rules of the game that specify the order and number of permissible moves such as the allowed interpersonal communications and coalitions for each of the decision-makers. Game theory thus attempts to explain, predict, or prescribe how decision-makers choose or should choose in an interdependent setting if they follow a rational logic. In this "process" the preferences remain fixed and only a choice is made by the different actors. This means that no influence of interaction is modeled.

Despite the considerable enthusiasm in the early years of exploration for the potential of game theory for the study of decision-making with multiple actors, apart from certain limited contexts, these hopes have not been realized in empirical research, for which it is ill-equipped. In Watson's and Buede's view (1987) one of the reasons is that in situations with multiple players, such as in the context of group decision-making, the availability of so many strategies and coalition opportunities means that the complexities are such that no unequivocal recommendations can be made as to which particular strategy should be followed.

According to Rapoport (1969), the most fruitful use of game theory is its employment as a conceptual framework to the extent that it reveals the strategic structure of the game. There are numerous examples of such efforts in political science and we quote as examples the efforts made by Brams (1985) to analyze real-life decisions, such as the Cuban missile crisis and the Watergate decisions, and Mor (1993), who analyzed the crisis decision-making between Israel and Egypt in 1967.

Hargreaves Heap and Varoufakis (1995) give an excellent introduction to game theory for social scientists, extending it to all kinds of social interaction and also explaining in a very comprehensive way the latest developments. From the above it is clear that game theory does not satisfy the purposes of our study.

The Analytic Model

Another, quite different model, which assumes optimal choices from decision-makers pursuing all the same objectives, is Allison's (1971) analytic model (Table 1.1, cell II). In this model the decision-making group is considered as a unitary actor which selects the preferred course of action according to the decision theoretic model. This means that the group is capable of surveying all relevant strategies, considering all important consequences, evaluating them in terms of their utilities and probabilities, and combining this information according to the Subjective Expected Utility calculus to reach a conclusion (Allison 1971; Saris and Gallhofer 1975; Gross-Stein and Tanter 1980).

The analytic model also fails as a realistic alternative for studying the decision-making process and choice in a national government, since it requires an excessive capacity for information processing on the part of decision-makers. The analytic model also assumes the absence of disagreement among decision-makers about the factual information, which is very unlikely in group settings where participants adhere to different political factions and belong to different governmental departments (Gallhofer and Saris 1996). As a result of the above-mentioned considerations, several scholars (Allison and Halperin 1972; Janis 1972; Hermann 1978; Hermann, Hermann, and Hagan 1987; Lindblom 1982; Maoz 1990) have tried to develop more realistic models for group decision-making that assume the involvement of many decision-makers with conflicting objectives, who adapt to the characteristics of the situation within the limits of their knowledge and computing capacities (Table 1.1, cell III). These approaches are more suitable for our purposes, and therefore, we will concentrate on them.

MODELS OF BOUNDED RATIONALITY

Multiple Paths to Choice

Maoz (1990), in his "multiple paths to choice" approach to group decision-making (Table 1.1, cell III), postulates that decision-making groups are inter-organizational in the sense that individual participants represent various government agencies responsible for the nation's foreign policy. These individuals join the ultimate decision-making group with preestablished policy preferences which may be the result of discussions in the organizational setting they belong to. He further stresses that the group choice will not necessarily represent the initial distribution of preferences among participants because these initial preferences may change during the process.

The process as he construes it consists of interpersonal interaction through which individual preferences are modified and aggregated by several means. He discerns two kinds of rules: (1) group interaction rules, which consist of persuasive argumentation, coalition formation and various bargaining activities and (2) preference aggregation rules, such as majority rule, the consensus principle, and tie-breaking rules.

He further distinguishes three different process models: the analytic, cybernetic, and cognitive models. Originally these models were developed for individual choice behavior (Steinbrunner 1974), but Gross-Stein and Tanter (1980) and Maoz (1990) also used these names for processes to aggregate individual preferences to a collective choice. Consequently, the names are somewhat awkward, but the meaning is clear. In order to avoid confusion, we continue with the same names although they do not cover the process very well.

According to Maoz (1990), the analytic model describes a process of argumentation (information exchange based on the consideration of the consequences of options) and bargaining on substantive grounds, where the decision taken reflects some kind of weighted aggregation of preferences. The strategy chosen in the analytic model is thus based on a careful consideration of possible consequences. In contrast with the analytic model, the cybernetic model assumes more restricted argumentation and bargaining. Options are reviewed sequentially until one satisfies the group. The chosen option tends to employ only marginal changes. The cybernetic model thus mainly concentrates on the search for acceptable strategies, while neglecting the consideration of possible consequences. Finally, the group process in the cognitive model is characterized by an excessive concurrence-seeking pattern (groupthink). Members who do not start with the same preferences as others rather quickly shift their opinion to coincide with the dominant view that emerges in the group discussion. Group norms or a leader's preferences determine this view.

According to Maoz, elements of all three models may occur during a single decision process, but he further postulates that the initial distribution of preferences also influences the choice of model. A highly divided group with a nonhierarchical structure would be likely to use the analytic model, while moderately divided groups with fairly nonhierarchical structures would prefer the cybernetic one, and highly cohesive hierarchical groups would tend to engage in a cognitive process (Maoz 1990).

The authors of this book, however, disagree with Maoz's assumptions about the employment of the analytic and the cybernetic model. In our opinion, a highly divided group is more likely to engage in a cybernetic process, because the participants do not believe that they can convince the other members of the group with arguments; they prefer to search for a solution acceptable to all participants. On the other hand, if there is initial agreement they can concentrate thoroughly on the consequences of the available options, and therefore, the use of the analytic model is more likely.

The Groupthink Model

The cognitive model clearly includes the groupthink model developed by Janis (1972) and extended by 't Hart (1990). It is a model which offers an explanation of flawed decision-making in high-level decision-making groups that can contribute to policy fiascoes. According to this model, the excessive striving for unanimity among the highly homogeneous participants in a decision-making group can lead them to end the discussion prematurely and to neglect a realistic examination of alternative courses of action. If a strong leader is present, participants mostly accept the leader's preference. It is assumed to be symptomatic of such group choices that the group overestimates itself, succumbing, for instance, to the illusion of invulnerability and the belief in the group's inherent moral correctness.

Because of the homogeneity of the participants, it is expected that the group's behavior will be characterized by a kind of closed-mindedness with regard to the evaluation of the situation and their own actions, reducing the possibilities of appraising the situation realistically. The group's thinking about the other nations involved is likely to be sloganistic and based mainly on the assumption of their inferiority. Another symptom is the pressure toward uniformity, exemplified by direct pressure on dissenters and self-censorship, that is, group members adjusting in advance to what they perceive as the opinion of the leader. The resulting choice may be extremely risky, but is not perceived as such by the decision-makers.

Janis (1972) pointed out that the groupthink model is context-dependent and does not always provide an accurate description of group decision-making processes, but relates mainly to high-stress situations perceived by a very cohesive decision-making group. P. 't Hart's (1990) studies of the groupthink phenomenon provide little evidence for this decisional mode at the level of a national government, since governments appeared to be plagued rather by excessive heterogeneity than by cohesiveness. He also suggested alternative explanatory frameworks, such as the bureaucratic politics model and incrementalism.

The Bureaucratic Politics Model

Maoz's cybernetic model, assuming a restricted process of argumentation and bargaining, contains elements of the bureaucratic politics model, to which a good deal of attention has been paid in the literature (Allison 1971; Allison and Halperin 1972; George 1972; Rosati 1980; Hilsman 1987; Rosenthal, Geveke, and 't Hart 1994). The latter model describes the decision-making process as a struggle between individual government officials to advance the position of their department and enhance their personal position. Researchers who work with this model agree that the bureaucratic process which formulates the decision through bargaining and compromise significantly affects the resulting policies, since no participant is sufficiently powerful to force a solution when there is disagreement. This means, according to the model, that a political decision is not the consequence of a deliberate strategy, "a solution to the problem, but rather results from compromise, conflict and confusion of officials with diverse interests" (Allison 1971, 162). Scholars have pointed out (e.g., Hermann 1978; Rosati 1980) that this model is not applicable to all issues and that when it comes to important decisions it may not provide an accurate description of the decision-making process, being perhaps mainly applicable at the implementation stage.

Incrementalism

The cybernetic model also incorporates elements of Lindblom's incrementalism (Baybrooke and Lindblom 1963; Lindblom 1980, 1982). According to Lindblom, incrementalism is a decision-making process which reduces controversies in policy-making groups. Whenever power is distributed among a variety of decision-making bodies, he argues, one group is rarely able to impose its preferences on another and policies are mostly the outcome of give-and-take. During the decision-making process participants try to control each other by analysis, persuasion, threats, authority, and exchange of benefits.

According to the model, the participants restrict their search for strategies mainly to familiar alternatives which differ only slightly from the status quo. Decision-makers thus focus on incremental changes of the actual situation, which can more easily lead to a compromise solution since the deviation from the status quo is small and can always be adjusted by future steps.

Of the numerous incremental options, only a restricted set of policy alternatives are considered because of the decision-makers' cognitive limitations. Furthermore, for each alternative only a restricted number of consequences are evaluated. Consequences, which are seen as unimportant or which are poorly understood, are largely omitted from consideration. During the decision-making process, objectives are adjusted to the means available, which means that they are derived in large part on the basis of the available options considered. Thus strategy formulation and goal setting interact. Lindblom's participants in the decision-making process are also more preoccupied with ills that need to be remedied than with the positive goals of ideal positions. Decision-making in the light of this theory becomes a sequence of trials and errors and retrials. In this sense it is a step-by-step approach. As a consequence of the process of power struggle, Lindblom assumes that a compromise will be found containing only marginal departures from the status quo strategy. Lindblom suggests such options are a possible way of reducing controversy in policy-making groups since they do not challenge the fundamental consensus on the rules of the game or other basic values, and they can always be adjusted at a later stage.

The Garbage Can Model

Although Lindblom's decision-makers are described as "muddling through," the model developed by Cohen, March, and Olsen (1972) states that decision-making in organizations is even more confused. Here, the authors claim, procedures are taken from a "garbage can." According to these authors, decision-making in organizations results from four variables: problems, solutions, choice opportunities, and people. Through the interaction of solutions looking for problems, problems looking for solutions, decision opportunities and participants looking for work, decisions may result. These variables are selected more or less randomly as though from a garbage can. Incrementalism already stresses that objectives are frequently discovered through available options, but in this model even preferences are unclear and have to be discovered through action. The participants in decision-making also seem to change continuously, which would help to explain why they do not understand the process. The authors of this model, however, stress that it pertains to decentralized organizations such as universities. We therefore think that it is less appropriate for the study of cabinet decision-making.

Communication Models

Communication research raises a different issue (Fisher 1974; Hirokawa and Poole 1986, 1996; Jensen and Chilberg 1991; Ellis and Fisher 1994; Frey 1994). In this perspective, the essence of group decision-making is interaction, where the participants attempt to influence each other in the choice of an alternative. Researchers in this field view the communication process as "a complex interplay of ideas, preferences, and perspectives" over time, during which premises and options are advanced and discredited, goals are proposed and elaborated, "actors enter and withdraw from discussions and decisions are tested, refined, modified and confirmed" (Poole and Doelger 1986, 239). Through this observed pattern of interactions, in which these authors distinguish between procedural interactions aimed at the organization of the group and its functioning, task-oriented interactions providing the substance of decision-making, and relationship-oriented interactions in the social dimension (Jensen and Chilberg 1991), the form and content of decisions are worked out. Unobservable rules and resources like norms underpin the argumentative interactions.

Frequently, communication researchers conceive decisions as a series of phases or stages each corresponding to a particular decision activity or function (Bales and Strodtbeck 1951; Fisher 1974; Poole and Doelger 1986; Poole and Roth 1989a). By identifying interaction categories, they look at the way patterns are produced that relate to phases and to other contextual characteristics such as group composition, norms, and so on. Poole and Doelger (1986) also distinguish several strategies for decision-making which consist of a sequence of steps that are necessary to arrive at a solution—what they call decision logic.

In their political decision logic, Poole and Doelger (1986, 252–253) assume that participants consider decision-making as a process of winning adherents to their preferred alternative. Political acceptability is their primary concern, whereas originality and effectiveness are less important. According to these authors, politicians follow implicitly the following steps: first, they get the preferred solution on the table; second, they build cases against other solutions; third, by persuasion and compromise they attempt to get the group to accept their preferred solution; and finally, they work out the implementation of their solution.

This logic contrasts with the "rational choice" logic where decision-makers aim at making the best possible decision by employing a sequence consisting of problem definition, problem analysis, solution search, solution evaluation, selection, and implementation. Since these researchers focus on the interaction process, they track the convergence on a final choice by studying especially the observable patterns of interactions, the advancing and modifying of preference orders, the bargaining of preference orders, and the strategic tactics that members employ to win adherents for their positions.

Decision Unit Models

As the last theoretical approach in the category of bounded rationality (Table 1.1, cell III), we want to discuss the ideas of Hermann (1978) and Hermann, Hermann, and Hagan (1987), who point out that there is not just one way to make a collective decision. They discuss the differences in the process for different decision units.

Hermann and her associates (1987, 311) suggest that foreign policy decisions are taken by a group of individuals who are placed in some kind of unit or decision structure and who have, when they agree about a solution, "both the ability to commit the resources of the government and the power or authority to prevent other entities within the government from overtly reversing their position." Although the units vary with the nature of the decision or the problem, on the basis of the research literature these authors could identify three major types. One of these units is termed the "predominant leader," the second is called the "single group," and the third is the "multiple autonomous group." On the basis of this typology of units, Hermann and her associates theorize about situations in which the unit directly affects the decision-making process and situations where factors outside the decision unit must be investigated in order to understand the process.

Where the unit is dominated by a leader at the top, they distinguish between cases where this leader is sensitive to others' opinions or to incoming information and cases where he is not. In the case where he is relatively insensitive to others' opinion and to incoming information, the decision-making process is centered around the leader's preferences, which are substantiated by his previously held opinions and beliefs. As soon as he makes his preferences known, advisers with different opinions will cease to express them because of respect or fear of negative consequences for themselves. The decision is thus more or less solely based on the leader's preferences and can be made rather quickly.

However, if such a leader is sensitive to others' opinions and incoming information, the authors postulate that he will seek a consensus with a broad base of support. This consensus will be forged during a process in which he will first attend to disagreement among his advisers and to those who could challenge his authority and thereafter to the opposition outside the government. He will then make his decision on the basis of these opinions.

The decision process in the second unit is again somewhat different. If the single group, considered as a set of interacting individuals who are members of a single body, rapidly reaches consensus, then the opportunity for factors outside the group to affect the decision is very limited, according to Hermann and her associates. The authors describe this process as follows: when members find their own positions shared by others they become more sure of themselves, and as the discussion continues they will only declare support for the preferred course of action. Eventually, the chosen alternative will become more extreme than that originally advocated by single members. This choice process clearly contains elements of the groupthink phenomenon. Other extreme decision shifts, such as group polarization studied in experiments by Moscovici and Doise (1994) and others, can also occur. Hermann, Hermann, and Hagan also postulate that prompt consensus is easier to achieve when the group is small and when power is unequally distributed within the group so that there is a strong but not pre-dominant leader present.

However, if disagreement occurs among the group members, individual members will be open to the influence of forces outside the group. The ensuing decision-making process may then be characterized by bureaucratic politics, especially if there is enough decision time. In the case where the outside political forces are more or less balanced, their efforts will cancel each other out, and under the assumption of the presence of a strong leader or an influential subgroup a way will be sought to resolve the conflict. This can be, according to the authors, a mix of persuasion, logrolling, compromise, and coercion leading to minimal action or compromise. Hermann and her associates suggest that examples of single-group decision-making bodies include the former Politburo of the Communist Party in the Soviet Union, subcabinet groups in parliamentary governments, and the National Security Council of the United States.

The last type of decision unit mentioned by Hermann and her associates, the multiple autonomous group, applies mainly to coalition governments in a parliamentary system. Hermann, Hermann, and Hagan (1987) characterize the multiple autonomous group as comprising two or more groups made up of members of several parties. If none of these groups has a majority in parliament, none of them can commit government resources without the support of some or all of the others, so that one group can block another's initiatives by using a formal veto or by threatening to end the coalition. The authors concentrate mainly on situations in which the groups disagreed about the preferred course of action. They posit that the relationships between the groups determine whether there is a deadlock or not. If the groups share an underlying acceptance of the right of the other group to participate in the power structure, or if they abide by some formal or informal rules of the game, there is a better chance of reaching agreement than when one of the groups denies the other's legitimacy. In cases where the groups dispute each other's legitimacy, their relationship can be described as "zero-sum"; that is, what some participants win the others lose. During the decision-making process they can use veto power or threaten to terminate the coalition so that the decisions tend to be postponed indefinitely because there is no superior authority able to resolve the differences.

So far we have seen that the characteristics of the decision-making unit affect the way the decisions are made. In fact, the rules of the "game" or working rules can change considerably. Besides the effect of the decision-making unit these authors also mention a second influential factor. That is, if groups accept each other's political legitimacy they have a "non-zero-sum" relationship and can reach agreement, since they are willing to interact and bargain. They mention also that norms play a crucial role. These norms of the decision-making unit may concern the use of decision rules such as the consensus principle or the majority rule, or influences of the individual decision-makers in the process, such as persuasion, trade-offs on another issue, and so on. The likely outcome is a compromise between the positions preferred by the various groups.

Input-Process-Output Approaches

The last approaches we want to discuss briefly also concern bounded rationality but involve many decision-makers with the same objectives (Table 1.1, cell IV). They relate to several frameworks pertaining to the nation-state as decision-maker (Snyder, Bruck, and Sapin 1962; Rosenau 1966; Brecher, Steinberg, and Stein 1969; Wilkenfeld, Hopple, Rossa, and Andriole 1980; Callahan, Brady, and Hermann 1982) and describe decision-making in terms of an input-process-output perspective. These schemes focus on the external verbal and nonverbal behavior of national governments as output of decisions. While the process is blackboxed, however, these frameworks are relevant to the study of the decision-making processes because they indicate a variety of factors which can influence decision-makers during the choice process, notably situational and organizational characteristics.

Empirical results within the frame of this input-process-output approach (Holsti 1979; Brecher and Geist 1980) suggest that crisis has an impact on the decision-making process. Because decision time in crisis situations is more limited than in noncrisis situations, the choice process may be changed. For instance, a consensus-seeking group may switch to majority rule in time of crisis in order to arrive sooner at a choice. Another situational characteristic mentioned in this literature is the substantive issue of decision. Decision-makers may disagree on the importance of military, economic, or status matters which may have an influence on the process, especially when substantive issues are related to the organizational role of the decision-makers. Since decision-making groups are frequently composed of members from different organizations, the bureaucratic school assumes that each participant contributes his organizational perspective during the group process.

CONCLUSIONS

This brief survey, without claiming to be exhaustive, shows the great diversity of efforts to explain group decision-making. Each highlights in its own way a different component. Although diverse, together the theories seem to identify the most important aspects of group decision-making.

Models in cells I and II (Table 1.1) are prescriptive and focus on the outcome of decisions given a specific starting point, while the descriptive models in cell III try to link different conceptions of process descriptions with outcomes. The descriptive frameworks in cell IV mainly focus on the outcome of decisions, but also stress the importance of situational and organizational characteristics which could modify decision-making processes. On the basis of these theories, in the next chapter we will develop a unified framework which we will employ in this study as our starting point.

Chapter 2

Theoretical Framework Used in This Book

The previous chapter looked at a number of different theories encountered in the literature. These different theories were presented independently, without any indication as to whether they are contradictory or whether they can be integrated into a single, more complete theory. In this chapter we shall try to integrate some of these models in order to construct a more complete theory for collective decision-making.

THREE NECESSARY STEPS TO ARRIVE AT A GROUP DECISION

In order to arrive at a decision, a group has to go through several necessary phases or steps. The communication literature (Poole and Doelger 1986; Hirokawa and Poole 1986, 1996; Poole and Roth 1989a, 1989b; Jensen and Chilberg 1991; Ellis and Fisher 1994; Poole and Holmes 1995) suggests the following steps:

1. The specification of the problem, the gathering of information, and the general orientation about available solutions
2. The specification by one or more people of arguments in favor of one of the options
3. A process of aggregation of individual preferences into a group preference

These steps are essential to the process of reaching a group choice. The process in which these steps are carried out may differ from situation to situation and from group to group. The steps may also be repeated several times. In all cases, however, a group has to go through these three steps in some way.

Step 1: The Specification of the Problem

There are periods in the group process where participants engage in analyzing the causes of the problem. They also evaluate these causes in terms of agreement or disagreement, suggest the need for more information about the problem, and propose in general terms how to solve it, for example, creating a subcommittee or asking experts for advice. Contributions or acts of this kind serve as preliminary work to finding a solution. Most of these problem-oriented concepts are derived from Poole and Holmes (1995) but have been slightly modified for our purposes.

Step 2: The Specification and Evaluation of Arguments

In this phase, decision-makers develop options, criticize them, and provide an argument in support or rejection of an option. The communication literature speaks about solution-oriented acts. Most of these concepts are derived from Gallhofer and Saris (1996) and Poole and Roth (1989a, 1989b), but they are again modified for our specific purposes.

The formulation of a rather complete argument will be illustrated by an example. For more details we refer to Gallhofer and Saris (1996), where the argumentation of individual decision-makers has been discussed at length. The example given here is the advice of the secretary of defense, Robert McNamara, and the chairman of the Joint Chiefs of Staff, Maxwell Taylor, to President Kennedy on October 2, 1963 (McNamara 1995, 77–79), concerning American engagement in South Vietnam. They argue as follows:

The military campaign has made great progress and continues to progress.

There are serious political tensions in Saigon (and perhaps elsewhere in South Vietnam) where the Diem-Nhu government is becoming increasingly unpopular.

Further repressive actions by Diem and Nhu could change the present favorable military trends. On the other hand, a return to more moderate methods of control and administration, unlikely though it may be, would substantially mitigate the political crisis. It is not clear that pressures exerted by the United States will move Diem and Nhu toward moderation. Indeed, pressures may increase their obduracy. But unless such pressures are exerted, they are almost certain to continue past patterns of behavior.

We should monitor the situation closely to see what steps Diem takes to reduce repressive practices and to improve the effectiveness of the military effort. We should recognize we may have to decide in two to four months to move to more drastic action.

We particularly emphasized we do not believe action to organize a coup should be taken at that time.

Arguments can be analyzed in different ways, but we chose decision theory. Figure 2.1 summarizes this argumentation in a decision tree. The argument reads as follows: If we do not exert pressures on Diem and Nhu (course of action or strategy [S_1]) it is unlikely that they will move toward moderation, which would mitigate the political crisis. It is almost certain that they will continue their repression, which may well change the present favorable military trends. On the other hand, it might not affect the present favorable military trends.

They rejected this strategy because of the low probability of a positive outcome. However, if the United States were to exert pressures on them (S₂), it is possible that they might move toward moderation, which would substantially mitigate the political crisis. However, it is also possible that this tactic will increase their obduracy. They advised choosing this strategy because of the "higher" chance of a positive result. The choice seemed to be the lesser of two evils, since the chance of a positive result was only "possible" compared with the other strategy, higher than "unlikely."

From the above, it is obvious that when presenting an argument, individuals communicate to their colleagues their knowledge about available options or strategies and their consequences. They also attach subjective values to the consequences and estimate subjectively the probabilities of their occurrence, and on the basis of this information they establish their choice. Different individuals

Figure 2.1
Decision Tree Based on the Argument of McNamara and Taylor

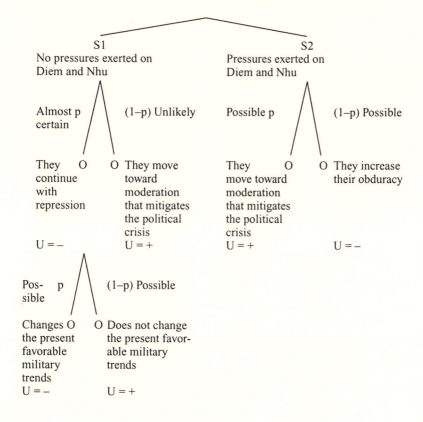

might gather different information and therefore reach a different conclusion.

It will be clear that not all participants in the decision-making process will provide such elaborate argumentation. Some will only give their approval to one of the options, while others will say why they are against one of the options but not indicate which option they prefer, and so on.

During the problem-solving phase, all this information will be exchanged, but after that the diverse individual preferences or choices must be aggregated into a collective choice. This last process is discussed in the next section.

Step 3: Aggregation

This step consists of two components: the interaction process and the application of aggregation rules. We first discuss the aggregation rules and then the interaction process.

Aggregation Rules

Preference aggregation or group decision rules can be hierarchical, majority, or unanimous. The preference aggregation rule most discussed in the literature (Scharpf 1989; Maoz 1990; Moscovici and Doise 1994) is the unanimity or consensus rule, which requires that all participants give their explicit agreement with the decision. In practice, it will mean at least that all members agree that the decision is acceptable. To achieve consensus in a group is rather time-consuming but, nevertheless, it seems to be a practical need in policy groups, even though formally a majority decision would often be sufficient. The reason why politicians attach so much importance to consensus may lie in the fact that in democracies politicians are accountable for their decisions to the electorate and their representatives and therefore prefer to strengthen their position by appearing as a united body to the outside world.

Moscovici and Doise (1994, 2) observe that consensus and compromise are very frequently used together. In fact, a compromise is the middle ground on which initially divergent proposals may converge after a process of mutual concession-making. This outcome is finally acceptable to all participants. Ellis and Fisher (1994, 141) argue that consensus does not necessarily imply a unanimous decision, but a total personal commitment of all group members to carry out the decision, even though they may not agree with it. We, however, will use consensus in the sense of a unanimous decision, which means that all participants agree with the chosen option. If participants only accept an option although they do not agree with it, they are not actually making a unanimous decision but have switched to another mode of decision-making requiring a less restrictive aggregation rule. For example, hierarchical rules may be used.

Hierarchical procedures imply that unequal weight is given to the preferences of different group members. One or a few participants determine the choice of the entire group. For example, specialists or key decision-makers may determine the choice, and the result is then overtly or tacitly accepted by the remaining members. Such a decision can also be determined by the unequally weighted preference of a small group of key ministers. This group may have a majority in the meeting but this does not have to be the case.

Another rule discovered by Steiner and Dorff (1980a, 1980b), which they call "decision by interpretation," posits that one actor, usually the chairman of the meeting, interprets at the end of the meeting what he considers the essence of the discussion, although he does so mainly to represent the arguments of the high-status members and to provide an interpretation that is then tacitly accepted by the other participants.

The well-known majority rules provide equal weight for all participants and give to the numerically larger faction the right to determine the group choice. There are several variants of majority rule. Simple majority or plurality imposes no restriction on the absolute number of proponents for a chosen option; it requires only that this number be larger than the number of supporters for other alternatives. Absolute majority requires that the selected option must be supported by over 50 percent of the participants, while the qualified majority rule prescribes that at least two-thirds or three-quarters of participants must have supported the selected option. A weighted "majority" rule means that some important decision-makers have more influence on the choice and if there is consensus among them the choice is made.

The literature (Maoz 1990; Wilson and Hanna 1990) also mentions tie-break-ing rules that serve to resolve deadlocks when discussions or voting have had no success. But these "rules" are mostly not preestablished in a formal way. A tie-breaking rule reported by Maoz, which has been employed by the Israeli govern-ment, consists of the predetermined decision that the status quo should prevail in situations where the cabinet failed to agree to a new option.

Given the variety of preference aggregation rules mentioned above, it will be obvious that the choice of such a rule can vary from group to group. The construction of any theory of group decision-making will require specification of those characteristics of the decision unit and the decision situation which lead to differences in the selection of a decision rule.

Interaction Process

The communication process which, at some point in time, makes it possible to apply an aggregation rule consists of problem-oriented acts, problem-solving acts, and conflict-oriented acts. Since the first two types of acts have already been mentioned before, we concentrate here on the conflict-oriented acts. Conflict-oriented acts can be acts that increase conflict, such as threats, or conflict-reducing acts, such as requests for unity, compromise, and so on. These concepts are also derived from Poole and Roth (1989a) and again modified for our purposes.

There is an entire repertoire of acts available to manage conflict. "Requests for postponements" frequently suggest that further information should be acquired or that a smaller group meeting is needed where the problem can be discussed off the record and participants eventually engage in coalition formation by bargaining activities, such as offering some participants benefits unrelated to the issue under discussion in return for support for this specific issue (logrolling).

"Requests for a compromise" involve suggestions that the group should either shift from argumentation to the search for an alternative course of action that can be seen as a middle ground between the initial proposals, one that is acceptable to all participants, or shift from an analytic process to a cybernetic one. "Requests for unity," on the other hand, are pressures to conform to the majority or the leader's opinion in order to achieve consensus.

"Requests for accommodation" suggest that further effort to obtain consensus should be abandoned and certain members pressed to accept the view of the other group. The context alone can clarify whether the other group constitutes an unequally weighted minority, or a simple or a qualified majority.

"Requests for a vote" suggest that further discussions are unlikely to bring about a solution and that, therefore, the group decision should be determined by voting. "Requests to leave the decision to another group or person" constitute an even more dramatic change in the procedure. In this case, the group abandons its efforts to arrive at an acceptable solution and delegates the decision-making to another group, subgroup, or person.

Clearly, these communication concepts fit very well with the theory described above. Empirical research should provide further evidence of the sequence of the different contributions in different groups and in different situations. By studying these sequences, one can get an idea of the speed with which the different groups move from one step or phase to the next. Furthermore, we do not exclude the possibility that the group norms also play an important role in this respect.

Precisely which of the above mentioned interactions are used, and how frequently, in specific decision units is not indicated by the communication researchers. To decide this would seem to be the task of systematic empirical analyses.

DIFFERENT DECISION PROCEDURES FOR DIFFERENT GROUPS

As mentioned in Chapter 1, Hermann, Hermann, and Hagan (1987) have provided a classification of decision units for which they specify the different results expected with respect to the group decision-making process. We use the same classification of units to specify differences in the basic process outlined above. We indicate below what differences we expect in the process for different types of decision units. We begin with processes of groups with a predominant leader and homogeneous groups.

Decision-Making Processes in Cases of Little Disagreement

The first type of group is a group with a predominant leader. Hermann and her associates also make a distinction between a predominant leader who is insensitive to suggestions from outside and a predominant leader who is open to the views of a wider group. In both groups we anticipate that the three steps identified earlier will be carried out rapidly. However, we expect two variations on the same theme. The first is that a predominant leader who is insensitive to his environment will himself specify the problem and the options available (step 1) and will present an argument for his choice (step 2). Thereafter, all members of the group will immediately agree with the leader's choice (step 3). In this case the aggregation rule is not clear. We assume that the leader is so powerful that all participants feel obliged to conform to his choice out of fear for their position or because of his natural or ascribed authority.

In the case of a decision unit with a predominant but open leader, the leader allows different participants to define the problem and specify options (step 1) and to give arguments for their preferred option (step 2). This process stops as soon as the leader makes his choice (step 3). The participants might agree with his choice or not but they have to accept the decision because the leader has the power and/or the obligation to make the decision.

The difference between the two processes lies in the number of speakers and the number of arguments given in the first two steps, but the third step is similar. The decision is made by the smallest possible minority, consisting of a predominant leader with the authority and duty to make the decisions. Aggregation seems irrelevant in these cases where the opinion of others is irrelevant.

Hermann and her associates (1987) also distinguish two decision units without a predominant leader. One is a homogeneous group which they call the "single group"; the other is a heterogeneous group called "the multiple autonomous group." They suggest that the participants of the "single group" are often members of the same organization sharing a high degree of unanimity of opinion. As mentioned earlier, Hermann and her associates (1987) give as an example the members of the Politburo of the former Soviet Union or the participants of the National Security Council in the United States. If such a homogeneous group has to make a decision and one of the prominent members proposes an argument in favor of a course of action (steps 1 and 2) that is acceptable to all participants, there is usually no need for further discussion and a consensus decision can be taken immediately (step 3). In such a situation, the participants even risk becoming so overconfident that the option chosen may be more extreme than members of the group would individually have preferred.

However, if there is initial disagreement in such a group about the option to be selected, but a strong informal leader or an influential subgroup is present, then consensus may be reached after these influential people have ventilated their opinion and convinced the remaining participants. Like Hermann and her associates, we also predict such extreme decision shifts as described by Janis (1972) and by Moscovici and Doise (1994). If the disagreements cannot be resolved quickly, then the process will evolve into that of the multiple autonomous group, which we describe next.

Coping with Disagreement

The last type of group to be mentioned, the multiple autonomous group, is assumed to consist of participants of different organizations with different opinions. A typical example of such a unit is a coalition government where none of the parties has a majority in parliament, or a decision group consisting of officials affiliated with different branches of government. In such a group the decision-making process is much more complex and slower than in the other groups outlined above. The first two phases will already take much more time because participants in the group who are affiliated with different parties or organizations will present different preferences and arguments (steps 1 and 2). Given initial disagreement, it is more complicated to aggregate the preferences in order to arrive at a group choice. For this purpose rules are needed.

As mentioned before, one needs not only aggregation rules, but also inter-action rules as communication researchers (Fisher 1974; Hirokawa and Poole 1986; Poole and Roth 1989a) and Maoz (1990) stress. Hermann, Hermann, and Hagan (1987) speak of "norms" or standards of behavior that groups impose upon their members. What is clear is that through a sequence of actions, such a group lacking unanimity has to try to find a solution that will satisfy all partici-pants. In groups which exist over a longer period and which frequently have to make decisions together, it is likely that some patterns of group behavior or norms will be developed that establish how the group process leading to a group decision will be conducted.

These norms can be very different for distinct groups, and we therefore want to look closely at these expected behavior patterns. First of all, we think that in all groups a tendency will exist to try to reach a consensual decision whenever possible. There is also an extensive literature that confirms this idea (Scharpf 1989; Maoz 1990; Moscovici and Doise 1994). Thus, for example, if only a little more time is required to arrive at a consensus, we expect groups to use this time. The reason for this tendency is that, should the choice turn out to be wrong, all participants will be equally wrong. This is undoubtedly a strong argument in favor of consensus. However, the way that groups try to reach that consensus can differ. The amount of time devoted to achieving it can also differ.

There are three alternative procedures for coping with disagreement. One is to try to convince the others of the correctness of one of the arguments (for examples, see Gallhofer and Saris 1996). This method, where participants continue to discuss arguments in favor of or against the different options, is called by Maoz (1990) the analytic model. However, such a process cannot be continued indefinitely, because it is hard to convince people of the correctness of estimated probabilities and utilities of outcomes. An alternative procedure, therefore, is to delay the decision and to search for better information with respect to the point of controversy. Often such an approach means a delay in order to ask experts to join the meeting to provide detailed information about options, consequences, and their probabilities (for examples, see Gross-Stein and Tanter 1980). If one of these two procedures is successful, the group can still make a consensual decision, but if neither approach leads to success in the sense of agreement on the description of the problem or the evaluation of consequences, or if success was not possible because of lack of time, the group has to cope with a situation where no unanimity exists.

In such a situation, other methods can also be employed to solve the problem. The second procedure consists of searching for a compromise, a middle course of action that is acceptable to all members of the group. If one is going to look for an alternative course of action on which all can agree, then one enters a process of bargaining and other conflict-reducing interactions described by communication researchers (Fisher 1974; Poole and Doelger 1986; Poole and Roth 1989a, 1989b; Hirokawa and Poole 1986; Jensen and Chilberg 1991; Ellis and Fisher 1994) and political scientists who adhere to the bureaucratic politics model (Allison and Halperin 1972; Rosati 1980; Hilsman 1987). Maoz has referred to this process as a cybernetic model. At the end of such a process an option will often be formulated which differs only slightly from the status quo. This can be done in such a way that the total action is split into more steps, the first of which would provide an indication of the direction of the next step while the second or subsequent step contains the controversy. In such a case the decision-makers can agree upon the first step and can leave the next steps open for later decisions. Such decision-making was termed incrementalism by Baybrooke and Lindblom (1963) and Lindblom (1980, 1982).

The third method for coming to a group decision is to drop the requirement for consensus. If one drops the requirement for consensus, it is of course much easier to arrive at a group decision, but it requires a shift to another preference aggregation rule or a hierarchical procedure. The studies presented in this volume will show that some decision units shift to another preference aggregation rule in special situations when a quick decision is required.

What course in the decision process is taken—that is, new information is asked for, a new course of action is sought which can be supported by all participants, or an adjustment of the choice rule is made—depends on the norms that exist in the decision unit with regard to group decision-making. This cannot be predicted in general. It may also differ from country to country. Some groups will employ voting to arrive at a group choice, while others will only resort to voting if all other means of winning support for a collective choice produce a deadlock. If groups rely on voting devices they may employ simple voting with each member given an equal weight, or they may weigh the preferences of participants unequally because some participants are more specialized in the field or have more to lose than others if a wrong decision is made.

It will be clear that the decision-making process in the last type of unit, the multiple autonomous group, is extremely complex and most interesting, but it is also clear that one cannot concentrate exclusively on the last type of group and its decision-making. It is thus evident that there are different processes in different groups and that these processes prevent us from formulating a general theory. Nonetheless, in this section we have attempted to connect several theories which apply to different groups in a wider context.

EFFECTS OF SITUATIONAL CHARACTERISTICS

As mentioned in Chapter 1, the decision-making process can differ not only from group to group but also from situation to situation. We must therefore identify what characteristics of a situation affect the decision-making process.

Holsti (1979) and Brecher and Geist (1980) have suggested that when a group is confronted with a crisis situation, for example, when a country's core values are at stake and the decision time is limited, the decision-making processes might be entirely different from those in situations where there is adequate time to consider and reconsider the preferred course of action. It seems plausible that in a situation of very restricted time and serious threat to a country's core values entailing a high likelihood of war (Brecher and Geist 1980, 16), the decision unit will take less time to pass through the whole decision-making process than otherwise. It may also be true that, from the start, a group may concentrate on a majority decision whereas normally the group strives for consensus, as we have suggested above. On the other hand, an argument can also be made that the decision-making process will be more thorough because of the serious threat. One could argue that in such a situation decision-makers do not want to make a mistake which could be disastrous for the country. For the time being, therefore, no prediction can be made as to what direction the change in the approach will take, but a change in the decision-making procedure does not seem unlikely in the case of a crisis situation.

CONCLUSIONS

In this chapter we have tried to place the theories of Chapter 1 in a more general framework. We have also derived the following basic assumptions and testable propositions concerning the process by which a group of decision-makers arrives at a choice.

Basic assumption 1: The process contains mostly three steps:

1. The specification of the problem and the general orientation about available solutions
2. The specification by one or more persons of arguments in favor of one of the options
3. A process of aggregation of individual preferences into a group preference

These three steps need not be carried out in sequence; the first two steps especially can be combined. There may be different people who provide information during steps 1 and 2. In general, however, these two steps will be made before step 3. But when step 3 is unsuccessful, they can also return to the earlier steps in order to proceed again with step 3.

Basic assumption 2: The way in which the three steps are taken depends on the type of decision-making group. A distinction is made between the following types of groups:

1. Groups with a predominant leader who is insensitive to advice from others
2. Groups with a predominant leader who is sensitive to advice
3. Homogeneous or single groups whose members have more or less the same opinions with regard to the topic of the decision
4. Heterogeneous or multiple autonomous groups with participants holding different opinions regarding the topic of decision

We expect the differences in opinion to arise especially in group 4.

Basic assumption 3: The situation the group finds itself in will affect the decision-making process. The characteristic of the situation most expected to influence the decision-making process is whether or not there is a crisis situation. By "crisis" we understand a situation with limited decision time, where a decision is necessary because the problem poses a serious threat to the country's interests and an increased likelihood of war.

On the basis of these distinctions the following propositions are specified.

Proposition 1: In homogeneous groups and groups with a predominant leader, the decision-making process will be much shorter than in heterogeneous groups because of fewer differences of opinion. The process will consist mainly of a presentation of the problem and one or a few arguments, after which the decision can be made. It will be clear that the process can only be as short as this where there are virtually no differences of opinion indicated. Because of this, it may appear that these groups make their decisions solely on the basis of arguments and that other procedures such as compromising or voting become redundant. This is, however, only due to agreement between participants. As soon as this agreement disappears, these groups will behave in the same way as the heterogeneous groups.

Proposition 2: Groups with a predominant leader do not need aggregation rules because the predominant leader makes the decision himself. Aggregation rules are needed in homogeneous and heterogeneous groups.

Proposition 3: In groups with a predominant leader there is no reason for conflict because the advisers do not make the decision. Therefore, conflict-oriented behavior will not occur, or will occur only minimally and normally not in public.

Proposition 4: In homogeneous groups conflicts can occur occasionally, especially when the group has to arrive at a unanimous decision. In such cases a dissenter can cause considerable problems requiring intense efforts at conflict management.

Propositions 1 to 4 will be illustrated on the basis of the qualitative research in the first part of this book. The remaining propositions relate to heterogeneous or multiple autonomous groups and will be tested on the basis of the quantitative study in Part 2 of this volume.

We also distinguish between propositions relating to the process (propositions 5 to 7), propositions concerning the preference aggregation rules (propositions 8 to 11), and propositions concerning the mode of decision-making (proposition 12).

Proposition 5: Decision-makers will spend more time on problem-oriented acts in noncrisis situations because there is more time available for such discussions.

Proposition 6: There will be more conflict-oriented acts when the key decision-makers (i.e., those most involved in the decision) disagree about the course of action to choose. But if decision-makers disagree and if the topic has already been discussed several times, conflict-oriented acts will be employed less frequently because the participants are aware of the presence of conflict and try to control it.

Proposition 7: If disagreement arises in a crisis situation, positive conflict-oriented acts especially will be employed in order to arrive at a decision because of lack of time.

The next propositions concern the use of preference aggregation rules.

Proposition 8: We expect decision-making groups to strive for consensus as the most preferred aggregation rule in political decision-making.

Proposition 9: If no consensus can be achieved, a decision-making group has in principle three options available to solve the problem:

1. To postpone the decision in order to collect further information and/or to have bilateral discussions
2. To shift from argumentation to a procedure where the search concentrates solely on a course of action which is acceptable to all participants
3. To shift to an aggregation procedure which requires not consensus, but a less restrictive aggregation rule

Proposition 10: What solution or combination of solutions is adopted by a group, and how quickly the shift from one procedure to the next is made, depend first of all on the norms of the specific group.

Proposition 11: The aggregation rule employed will be affected not only by the disagreement but also by the situation (whether or not there is a crisis).

From proposition 9.2 our last proposition follows.

Proposition 12: In the case of lack of consensus the decision-making mode will change from an analytic approach to a cybernetic one. In the cybernetic mode more options will be evaluated sequentially without consideration of consequences. These options will usually deviate only slightly from the status quo.

PLAN OF THE BOOK

Now that we have specified the basic assumptions and propositions of this book, the following chapters show how far these propositions are confirmed by the existing evidence. Some parts of the process, like the effect of the group norms, the interactions, the effect of the situation, and the changes in aggregation rules, remain unclear. For these parts of the theory, we must look at the data for indications of how to make the theory more complete. We begin with five different case studies: one for a decision-making group with a predominant leader who is insensitive to his environment, another with a predominant leader who is sensitive to his environment, one for a homogeneous group, and two for a heterogeneous group. These chapters illustrate the differences in procedure that we have anticipated.

Subsequently, in Part 2 we study a heterogeneous group which, with respect to its decision-making process, is the most interesting case. This study is based on a sample of decisions taken by the Dutch government during this century. At the end of the book we come back to the theory and show which of the mentioned propositions are correct and which are incorrect, and we list further propositions that can be added to the theory on the basis of these empirical studies.

Before we introduce the case studies, however, the methodology used is described in the next chapter.

Chapter 3

Methodology

In this chapter we discuss the design of our qualitative studies. The results of these qualitative studies, of the decision-making process in the different types of decision units outlined earlier, are presented in Chapters 4 through 8.

A selection has been made of one decision-making process for each type of unit with the exception of the heterogeneous group, where we studied two decision-making processes. For each decision-making process, minutes of the meetings have been taken from published accounts by historians or political scientists in documentary editions. As an illustration of a decision unit with an insensitive predominant leader, we took meetings of Hitler with his supreme commanders relating to the decision to invade Poland in August 1939 (Chapter 4), a decision which led to World War II. President Kennedy and his advisers during the Cuban missile crisis in October 1962 exemplify a decision unit with a sensitive predominant leader (Chapter 5). An example of a homogeneous decision unit is provided by the Common council of ministers of the Austro-Hungarian monarchy, which had to decide in July 1914 whether or not to declare war on Serbia, a decision which led to World War I (Chapter 6). Finally, an illustration of a multiple autonomous group is given by the Dutch council of ministers, who had to decide in the fall of 1948 whether or not to intervene militarily in Indonesia (Chapters 7 and 8).

It should be clear that no general statements can be derived from these case studies. However, the processes in the different cases were so clear, with the exception of the multiple autonomous group, that we did not see the necessity of conducting more case studies to illustrate the fact that different decision units have different decision processes.

The second part of this book presents a quantitative study, for which a sample has been drawn from a large series of decisions of the Dutch government. In that part we concentrate on the decision-making process in a multiple autonomous group, because this unit is considered the most complex one.

A problem we encountered when developing the methodology was the identification in the texts of the relevant parts that indicate the different concepts or acts introduced in the previous chapter. For this purpose, a text analysis instrument has been developed. Our demand was that this text analysis instrument should be able to detect reliably the following concepts:

1. The problem-oriented interactions (step 1)

2. The formulation of arguments by different speakers in favor of a specific option and the remaining solution-oriented interactions (step 2)

3. The aggregation process of individual preferences to a collective choice within the frame of the conflict-oriented interactions (step 3)

4. Implementation-oriented interactions

5. The formulation of the aggregation rule employed

6. Situational characteristics, especially the perception of crisis and noncrisis, and organizational role characteristics of the participants in the decision-making process

7. The graphical representation of the decision-making process

In this chapter we first describe the method of text analysis for these concepts, and then we discuss the reliability of the measurement of the different concepts.

TEXT ANALYSIS OF THE VARIOUS INTERACTIONS

Problem-Oriented Interactions (Step 1)

In order to carry out the text analysis, we took a paragraph from the minutes of a particular meeting as context unit (Holsti 1969), that is, the largest body of text that has to be searched for the concept. The recording unit (the specific segment of text into which the concept or act is classified; see also Holsti 1969) was variable, consisting of one or more full sentences of the same speaker. These units were actually also used for the text analysis of the other concepts; if no other unit is indicated, then these units apply. The same speaker can produce, during an uninterrupted verbal utterance, several acts according to the function of the contribution, such as providing information, analyzing the problem, and requesting information.

These contributions refer to the first step or phase of the group decision-making process, the specification of the problem and the general orientation about available solutions. In the literature Poole and Holmes's (1995) classification of a problem definition and orientation phase comes the closest to ours. In our coding system the step of problem orientation consists of the following concepts or acts: problem analysis, problem critique, solution analysis, requesting and contributing information, and requesting and contributing clarification. We now proceed to operationalize the different concepts.

Problem Analysis (PA)

This concept refers to statements that relate to the causes of a problem. It is similar to the one Poole and Holmes (1995, 104) are using. Thus, parts of the text that contain an enumeration of causes or motives of the opponents are characteristic for this concept. The following would be an example of problem analysis:

When questioning myself about the Russians' motives to deploy missiles in Cuba, I came to the conclusion that their reasons might have been at least threefold, such as a reciprocation to our missile installations in Turkey, a compensation to their missile gap, and to prevent the overthrow of Castro's regime in Cuba.

Problem Critique (PCR)

This concept is characterized by statements that evaluate problem analysis in terms of agreement or disagreement. Poole and Holmes (1995, 104) also use it with this definition. Hypothetical examples would be:

I sincerely disagree with your analysis about the Russians' motives to deploy missiles in Cuba.

I completely agree with your analysis of the Russians' motives.

Solution Analysis (PSA)

This concept refers to statements about how the group should proceed in general terms in order to find a solution, including criteria and general directions (Poole and Roth 1989a, 334). Such statements, if they occur, are mainly made by the chairman of the meeting in order to facilitate the task where the problem is very complex. It is characteristic of a text segment constituting a problem solution analysis that a prescription is given for the way the group should proceed. Examples of such texts that are indicative of solution analysis would be:

We cannot consult the parliament on this issue but must find a solution here in this council. I would suggest that we first ask our embassy for more information and then start the deliberations here.

We will split this problem into several parts. First we will investigate what the possible actions of our opponents could be. On the basis of these results we will study the ensuing consequences for us and then in order to avoid the worst outcomes we will look at our available means.

Requesting and Contributing Information (PI)

Participants may ask for further information when others analyze the problem or may give the information in response to a request. But they may also report their own perceptions of the problem that are unrelated to its causes. These acts are thus indicated by parts of texts that ask for further information regarding the problem analysis, or that provide this information or report some other aspects unrelated to the causes. Examples would be:

Are you sure that there are no other reasons the Russians might have had to deploy the missiles?

In my opinion no other reasons can be detected.

Yesterday a member of parliament told me that they did not expect this change of mind by our allies.

Requesting and Contributing Clarification (PCL)

The meaning of a communication might be unclear to some participants. Sometimes the communicator may even have been deliberately ambiguous in order to allow multiple interpretations. These concepts then relate to the request of a participant to clarify the message and to its response. Thus, parts of texts containing demands for elucidation of a message and the given explanation indicate these acts. Examples could be:

Could you specify which sources you used to detect the Russians' motives? Do you only rely on the State Department or also on the CIA?

Only the State Department's information was available at that time.

Solution-Oriented Interactions (Step 2)

These interactions refer to the development of options, the agreement or disagreement with one option, the specification of arguments in favor of or against one of the options, and the confirmation of the solution reached, which could be a collective choice or the postponement of a decision.

Option Formulation (SOF)

This concept refers to the development of an option without consideration of the consequences. It is just the suggestion of an available alternative. Poole and Holmes (1995, 104) also use this concept and call it "suggestion of alternatives." Thus, parts of the text which merely state an available alternative without arguing in terms of consequences may be characterized by this concept. An example of option formulation would be:

Wouldn't it be feasible to ask them to remove the missiles and if they reject it to denounce them in the United Nations?

Option Critique (SCR)

In our study, "option critique" relates to statements that support or reject a strategy without explication of consequences. Statements that do discuss consequences are classified as arguments. Poole and Roth (1989a, 334) use "solution critique" in a different context. Thus, parts of text that only reject or support an option without arguing in terms of consequences reflect this concept. Examples of solution critique would be:

I agree completely with the proposal made by the minister of foreign affairs.

I reject this option because I think it is not practicable.

Argumentation (SA)

Since the text analysis of arguments has been discussed in depth by Gallhofer and Saris (1996), the discussion in this chapter will be brief. For more details of this instrument we refer to the volume cited. Chapter 2 illustrated as an example of an argumentation the advice of the secretary of defense, Robert McNamara, and the chairman of the Joint Chiefs of Staff, Maxwell Taylor, to President Kennedy on October 2, 1963 (McNamara 1995, 77–79) about American engagement in South Vietnam. On the basis of this text, the argumentation was represented in a decision tree (Figure 2.1).

This decision tree consisted of a chronological sequence of the alternative actions or options (A) available to the decision-maker, the possible actions of other nations (AO), where appropriate, and the possible outcomes or consequences for the decision-maker's nation (O). On the basis of the subjective probabilities (P) and the subjective values or utilities (U) of these outcomes, which are also included in the tree, the decision-maker comes to a conclusion to support or reject a specific strategy (S). The latter in its simplest form can consist of only one alternative or option (A), or of a series of options to be adopted under certain conditions. McNamara and Taylor discussed two strategies for which they considered consequences: S_1, do not exert pressure on the Diem-Nhu regime and S_2, exert pressure on the Diem-Nhu regime (see also Figure 2.1). On the basis of the consequences and their utilities and probabilities of occurrence they chose S_2. It is clear, then, that participants may set out an entire argument, which means that they consider at least two strategies on the basis of consequences and indicate the preferred one.

But it is also possible that they only evaluate one strategy on the basis of consequences, either the supported or the rejected option. This can be called a partial argumentation. They can also restrict themselves just to the rejection or support of an option without indicating consequences. This was the case in McNamara's and Taylor's advice with the option "to organize a coup." We call this latter act an option critique (SCR).

Requesting and Contributing Information (SI)

During the solution-oriented phase, participants may also ask and provide information to the group regarding the solution. They may, for instance, hand out to their colleagues notes from persons outside the decision-making group who had considered available solutions. Thus, it is characteristic of a text containing an informative contribution in the solution-oriented phase that it asks for information about available options or responds to it, or that it reports reactions of others to available solutions, or that it hands out notes or discusses the content of notes from persons outside the decision group, relating in some way to the substance of the decision. Examples would be:

Could the minister of foreign affairs tell us about the results of his meeting with his French colleague?

During the last meeting with our allies I sounded them out about a possible military intervention and I got the feeling that they were very reluctant.

The leader of the Social Democrats informed me recently that he hoped that the cabinet would make a decision with respect to this issue quickly.

I received yesterday a note from a famous economist dealing with our problem and would like to pass it on to you to share this information.

Request for Clarification and Contributing Clarification (SCL)

As in the problem-oriented phase, the meaning of a communication may also be unclear when the participants discuss solutions. These concepts relate then to the request of a participant to clarify the message and to its response. They can refer to a variety of solution-oriented interactions. Parts of texts that contain demands for elucidation of a message or give this elucidation are characterized by these concepts. Examples could be:

What do you mean exactly by the reluctance of our allies in the event of our eventual military intervention? Would they protest against it in the United Nations or would they apply sanctions against us?

I must admit, I am also not sure what they would do.

Could you specify who is this unknown source?

Unfortunately not, because I promised to keep the source secret.

Solution Confirmation (SCF)

This interaction refers to requests for a choice to be confirmed (see also Poole and Roth 1989a, 334). This is mostly provided by the chairman of the meeting at the end of the session and contains frequently a summary of the course of action which has emerged as the chosen one. This course of action, in fact, can also be a postponement to another meeting. During the solution confirmation the speaker may also mention the preference aggregation rule used. Thus, parts of text which summarize the preferred course of action (preferred at least by a majority of participants) and which ask for its final confirmation embody this concept. Examples could be:

Before closing the meeting let me summarize the conclusion. We unanimously agreed that we should restore diplomatic relations with the Soviet Union. Is there anybody who wishes to add anything to this?

As I understood the discussion, the majority prefers to postpone a decision until we have heard the militaries. If I am mistaken, please speak up!

Conflict-Oriented Interactions (Step 3)

Conflict-oriented interactions relate to the aggregation process of preferences (step 3). If there is disagreement about the choice of option a conflict among the participants may arise, but since their task consists of making a collective decision, there are several interactions directed toward changes in the procedures in order to keep the group functioning. To this class of interactions belong negative acts like threats; neutral acts like requests for postponement, requests for a vote, or requests to leave the decision to another person; and positive acts like requests for unity, requests for a compromise, requests for accommodation, and conciliatory statements. Most of these concepts were also mentioned by Poole and Roth (1989a, 334–335) but used in a rather different way.

Threat (CT)

This concept refers to severe disagreement or opposition associated with the substance of the decision. It is expressed when opposing sides have formed and a participant threatens to resign or to provoke a cabinet crisis in regard to himself or the entire faction he represents in the decision-making unit. It is frequently used to put pressure on another faction to accommodate. Ellis and Fisher (1994, 217) also speak about substantive conflict.

However, emotional clashes might also occur between participants about procedures in which participants threaten to disrupt the decision-making process or accuse colleagues personally of inappropriate measures and suchlike. Ellis and Fisher (1994, 217) speak in this case of "affective conflict." Parts of texts that reflect this concept deal with severe pressures to disrupt the decision-making process on the basis of substantive or emotional grounds. Examples of this concept would be:

If you try to push this option through, I will resist it with all means available to me.

If we cannot find an acceptable solution quickly, we will have to submit our resignation to the Queen.

The council should know about the tricks my colleague played when formulating the instructions for the governor.

Request for Postponement (CP)

This contribution suggests, particularly, that where there is disagreement about preferences, further information should be acquired to resolve the disagreement or to make a break in order to call in an expert for clarification. But it can also suggest that a smaller group meeting or bilateral discussions off the record are required, in order to arrive at a solution by bargaining. It is thus characteristic of a text which constitutes a request for postponement that the chairman or another member asks explicitly to suspend the meeting and, eventually, indicates the reason. Examples could be:

Let the problem sink in for a while and discuss it at the next meeting.

I suggest postponing the discussion until we can hear the military experts.

Request for a Vote (CV)

This contribution implies that further discussion would appear unable to bring about a solution, at least not within an acceptable time span, and that, therefore, the group decision should be determined by voting. Parts of the text where the chairman or another participant explicitly asks for a vote and specifies the alternatives on which the vote should be cast reflect this concept. An example would be:

I would like to call for a ballot on the two last proposals.

Request to Leave the Decision to Another Group or Person (CO)

This contribution constitutes a quite dramatic shift in procedure. Since the group has been unable to resolve the internal disagreement with respect to preferences, they delegate the decision-making to another unit or person. Statements in texts that reflect this concept must contain an explicit request to ask another person or group to make the decision, together with a summary of reasons. The following example might illustrate this request:

I would suggest that the minutes of our meetings be given to the Queen so that she is fully informed and that we ask her to make the decision herself this time.

Request for Unity (CU)

This interaction consists of pressures to conform to the preference of the majority, to some specific faction, or to the leader. The purpose of the request is to achieve consensus in situations of disagreement. A part of the text which refers to this concept must contain an explicit statement by one of the participants which solicits homogeneity and further indicates the reason for it. The following examples illustrate this concept:

I call upon the other participants to maintain unity in these difficult circumstances.

The cabinet should be united in front of the national and international arena and therefore I urge our colleague of social affairs to express his agreement with the view of his colleagues.

Request for a Compromise (CC)

This concept refers to the shift from argumentation to the search for an alternative course of action as a middle ground between the initial proposals, where each side is required to make concessions. Texts that reflect this concept represent a participant explicitly asking his colleagues to compromise in some way in order to reach a solution or telling that he himself would be ready to do so. Examples of this would be:

Since it is very important that the cabinet stays on, I call upon both factions to give some ground.

I strongly believe that my colleague will allow some minor changes in his proposal, which will then be acceptable to all of us.

In order to find a solution everybody has to give in a bit. I am ready to do so.

Request for Accommodation (CA)

This request suggests that the group should abandon the effort at consensus and try to convince some members to accept the decision of the majority or even a minority with more influence. Parts of the text which contain this concept must consist of statements by one of the participants either urging others who disagree with the majority to acquiesce or, of his own accord, announcing his acquiescence. For example:

I call upon my colleagues to accept the decision of the majority.

I would regret it if some members were not to acquiesce in the decision made by a large majority yesterday.

Although I do not share your opinion, I should acquiesce.

Management of Group Tension (CM)

This concept covers the mediation of disagreement by, for instance, stressing some commonalities in the opinions as well as differences, showing respect to a group member who has been treated disrespectfully by another participant, sending confirming messages to acknowledge the right of everyone to have an opinion, and so on. Thus, parts of text which embody this concept must contain some explicit efforts at mediation in the form of conciliatory statements. The following examples illustrate this concept:

Although there are some differences in opinion, I got the impression that nevertheless we also share some common elements in our approach.

I would suggest that everyone has the right to speak up, even when he differs in opinion with the majority. Perhaps the majority can get some fruitful suggestions from minority members that have never occurred to them before.

Implementation-Oriented Interactions

When a group of politicians has reached a decision it frequently occurs that they then engage in discussion of the way to implement it. Implementation itself, however, is mostly delegated to other officials. The concepts we use are implementation proposals, exhortation to solidarity, and assurance of solidarity. Requests for information and clarification can, of course, also occur in an implementation phase. We did not encounter these concepts in communication research and, therefore, we think that they might be specific for political and organizational decisions.

Implementation Proposals (IP)

When a collective decision is reached by a group, the leader of the group frequently begins formulating proposals or orders for its implementation that others, not necessarily present in the group, are supposed to carry out. Thus, parts of texts that relate to proposals, instructions, or orders to carry out a decision are indicative of this concept. Examples would be:

In order to initiate action we first need a propaganda campaign, claiming provocation of war, that will be carried out by the ministry of propaganda.

We have to start immediately with military preparations. That means that we first increase the reconnaissance flights and put the airforce on alert.

Exhortation to Solidarity (IE)

An authoritarian leader or dictator who is quite insensitive to the opinion of his advisers and who uses them more as an audience when discussing a decision might exhort them to carry out his decision with firmness. Thus, parts of texts where participants are summoned by the leader to implement a decision with a high resolution reflect this concept. An example could be:

You have to carry out this action with an iron resolution and to retreat from nothing; only then can we win.

Assurance of Solidarity (IA)

This concept refers to the participants' response to the leader's exhortation and contains the guarantee to implement his decision with great efforts. An example could be:

We solemnly swear to vow loyalty to our leader and to carry out our duty with great firmness.

Text Analysis of a Meeting's Result

There are also other codes derived from the text. On the basis of solution confirmation (SC) where the leader or chairman of the meeting summarizes whether a decision was taken or whether it was adjourned to another session, one can observe the result of the meeting. The following categories were used for the classification:

1. Decision taken (DT)
2. Decision postponed (DP)

It will be obvious that the measurement of this variable is straightforward.

Text Analysis of the Aggregation Rule

The chosen strategy is mostly known on the basis of solution confirmation (SCF). The question of whether the choice is based on unanimity or on some kind of majority, or eventually by interpretation of the chairman (the aggregation rule discovered by Steiner and Dorff, 1980a, 1980b), can also be determined.

We mentioned earlier that chairmen of meetings frequently cite the group choice rule explicitly in their solution confirmation so that the choice rule used can be established *directly* on the basis of this concept. Examples would be:

We have unanimously agreed that

With great majority the members expressed their preference for

Summarizing the discussion, the conclusion should be that we establish diplomatic relations with Iran and if we do not get the weapons deal then we break off the relations again by creating some incident. (No explicit objections, no explicit agreements)

The first example clearly refers to a unanimous decision; the second example refers to a majority decision; and the third example could refer to a decision by interpretation, that is, a decision that is ultimately agreed upon by tacit unanimity.

In order to verify the correctness of the indicated decision rule, the researcher has to establish for the selected option (1) the number of participants who ultimately agreed with it explicitly, either by argumentation or by solution critique in terms of support, (2) the number of participants who ultimately objected to it either by argumentation or solution critique, and (3) the number of participants who did not speak up, which means that they tacitly agreed with the ultimate decision. If this coincides with the cited preference aggregation rule, then the choice rule mentioned in solution confirmation is correct. If not, the choice rule *indirectly* established by counting the ultimate agreements is the correct one.

If a decision by interpretation should occur, then the selected alternative in the solution confirmation cannot have been agreed upon by all or by a majority of the participants before the solution confirmation, on the basis of the count of ultimate agreements. It might have been preferred by a minority. Usually, however, it can be seen as a new course of action taking some middle course between the different participants' views, one that is developed during solution confirmation by the chairman (see also Steiner and Dorff 1980a, 1980b), which is then unanimously, tacitly, agreed upon by the participants.

TEXT ANALYSIS OF ORGANIZATIONAL AND SITUATIONAL VARIABLES

Organizational Variables

The organizational characteristics refer to the departmental affiliation of the decision-maker, his party affiliation, and his organizational role or function. The following categories are used for the classification of departmental affiliation of the decision-maker:

1. Foreign affairs official
2. Finance or economics official
3. Overseas territories official
4. Defense official
5. Official from another department

The measurement of this variable was straightforward. Given the name of the decision-maker, his affiliation can be established on the basis of the attendance list at the beginning of the minutes.

Party affiliation can also be measured quite straightforwardly. This variable was only used for the Dutch studies because of the nature of the coalition government. It is not appropriate to the German, Austrian, and American case studies. The following four categories are used:

1. Labor
2. Confessional
3. Liberal
4. Independent

The third variable measured relates to the organizational role or function of the decision-maker. Three categories are discerned:

1. Key minister
2. Minister
3. Adviser

The remaining ministers were classified in the second category. The "adviser" category comprises officials from several departments or even experts from outside the government who are asked to give their views.

The notion of "key minister" needs some clarification. It covers those ministers who play a crucial role in the decision-making unit. The qualitative studies all relate to crisis situations, that is, situations of threat to basic values, with limited decision time and an increased likelihood of war (Brecher 1977, 44–45). In these situations the issue area of decision is "military-security" (Brecher, Steinberg, and Stein 1969), which means that the military ministers hold a key position. However, depending on the type of government, different decision-makers are classified in this category.

In the American case study (Chapter 5), the president nominated an advisory committee, of which we considered the secretaries of state, of the treasury, and of defense, the attorney general, and the assistant to the president for national security affairs as key advisers, while the others were considered as mere advisers.

In the Austro-Hungarian monarchy (Chapter 6), the Common minister of foreign affairs, who also functioned as chairman of the meeting; the Common minister of war; and the Common minister of finance were considered as key ministers because of their central role in government. The Hungarian and the Austrian prime ministers were also classified as key ministers since they represented the two parts of the monarchy.

In the case of the Dutch government (Chapters 7 and 8 and the quantitative studies in Part 2), the prime minister, the deputy prime minister, and the minister of finance are considered important in all kinds of decisions, because of their central role in government. Dutch governments are mostly coalition governments and the prime minister and deputy prime minister are the leaders of their party in the cabinet. The minister of finance provides the financial means for all endeavors and can therefore be considered as an important decision-maker. With respect to other ministers, their importance depends on the issue area of decision. Since all decisions studied relate to foreign policy, the minister of foreign affairs also always has a key position. If the issue is security-military, the ministers of defense and maritime affairs are in a key position, and if it also relates to the colonies the minister of overseas territories is also involved. From this it follows that arguments relating to economic-developmental issues bring the minister of economic affairs into a key position.

The Situational Characteristic of Crisis

For the term *perception of crisis* we decided to use Brecher's definition (Brecher 1977, 44–45; Brecher and Geist 1980, 16), which states that if a decision-maker perceives the situation as threatening to the core values of his country, with a limited decision time available and an increased probability of war, then he perceives the situation as one of crisis. If any of these components is absent then the situation is not perceived as critical. Another salient crisis definition is Hermann's (Hermann 1972, 187), which characterizes a crisis situation as one which threatens high-priority goals of the decision-making unit, with only a short decision time available, and which takes the members of the decision-making unit by surprise. However, we found Brecher's definition more suitable because, in our opinion, neither surprise nor short decision time is a basic characteristic of crisis, while an increased probability of war does seem to be typical of crisis.

In order to assess whether the group perceived the situation as a crisis or not, one must aggregate the perceptions of crisis of individual participants. However,

findings from research (Maoz 1990, 74–75) suggest that group-shared perceptions of crisis are not a simple sum of individual crisis perceptions; rather,
they depend on the role certain participants fulfill in the group. This means that
when most of the key decision-makers individually perceive the situation as
threatening to the core values of the country, with limited time for decision-
making and an increased likelihood of war, their views will contribute more
heavily to a group-shared perception of crisis than the views of some less
important members who consider the situation as a crisis. We therefore classify a
situation as critical if most of the key decision-makers individually perceive the
presence of the three components that Brecher suggests. In the following, we will
operationalize the three components at the individual level.

Following Brecher, we operationalize a decision-maker's perception of a threat
to basic values with respect to the military-security issue in three ways:

1. If a key decision-maker indicated during his argumentation that the interests of his
   nation were threatened with respect to the military-security issue, then this concept
   characteristic was present. The survival of the population, independence as an
   international actor, maintenance of territorial integrity, and the autonomy of the
   political system were suggested as "basic values" (see also Brecher 1977, 66–67).

The following statements are examples of the presence or absence of perceptions
of threat:

In conclusion I would like to state that the German occupation of Antwerp does not at all
threaten our status of neutrality. (No perception of threat)

We now run the risk that under the auspices of the Security Council the United States will
take over Indonesia. (Perception of threat)

Sometimes, however, decision-makers did not mention these perceptions explicitly, so that they had to be measured indirectly on the basis of the argumentation
tree. This was done as follows:

2. If a key decision-maker indicated, on the basis of his argument, that if the status quo
   strategy were pursued only negative outcomes would result or that the probability of
   negative outcomes was very high, then he perceived the situation as threatening to the
   interests of his nation.
3. If the same key decision-maker produced several arguments relating to the same
   decision situation and if he had mentioned the first time that there were threats to the
   interests of his nation while omitting it in the following arguments because it seemed
   self-evident, then the situation was coded as perception of threat.

The second component of Brecher's crisis definition relates to the perception
of limited time. This was measured in the following way:

1. Each paragraph (context unit) in the minutes of a meeting was searched for one or more sentences (recording unit) which contained statements of a key decision-maker indicating some time limit for the decision. This indication could be quite vague, such as "we cannot delay our answer indefinitely," or with a more precise indication of a time limit, which needs not necessarily be short, such as "we still have some weeks to work out a solution but then we have to react."

Sometimes, however, there were no direct indications of time limits made in the document at all, in which case we proceeded as follows:

2. The time intervals between the arguments of several key decision-makers relating to the specific decision were established, and if they occurred within a limited period, such as two or three months, and a final decision was made at the end of this period, then we considered these situations as perceptions of limited time.
3. If the same key decision-maker produced several arguments relating to the same decision situation and if he had mentioned the first time that there was a time limit while omitting this in the following arguments because it seemed self-evident, then the situation was coded as perception of a time limit.

If there was no time limit detected at all, the situation was classified as "absence of a time limit."

The third characteristic which relates to crisis situations according to Brecher is the perception of increased likelihood of war. This is measured in the following way:

1. Each paragraph of the minutes of a meeting was searched for a key decision-maker's statements consisting of one or more sentences (recording unit) which would indicate that he considered war more likely than formerly.

The following are examples of such statements:

The German invasion of Antwerp increases the chances that we will have to enter the war.

I foresee that we will have to resort to military measures during the next weeks.

In addition, a second coding rule has been devised for cases where a key decision-maker did not mention again the likelihood of war in a later argument with respect to the same subject:

2. If the same key decision-maker produced several arguments relating to the same decision situation and he had mentioned the first time that there was an increased likelihood of war while omitting it in the following arguments because it seemed self-evident, then the situation was coded as perception of increased likelihood of war.

PROCESS CODING

When the documents were coded, each minute of a meeting was split up into a sequence of subsequent acts or contributions to the discussion; we also registered on the coding form the function and party affiliation of the decision-maker and his specific contribution to the discussion.

Interaction or communication patterns can be derived from this. Figure 3.1 illustrates a possible interaction pattern. The figure displays in the first column the acts headed by the main categories, that is, problem-, solution-, decision-, conflict-, and implementation-oriented. If no specific acts within a main category occur during the process, only the main category is shown for the sake of brevity, such as in this case with conflict-oriented acts. A phase can consist of one specific act or a sequence of uninterrupted acts of the same kind.

Figure 3.1 shows that the process began with a solution-oriented phase with argumentation (1). Then a participant gave an option critique (2), followed again by an argumentation (3). Thereafter, a participant gave a problem analysis (4)

Figure 3.1
Representation of an Interaction Pattern

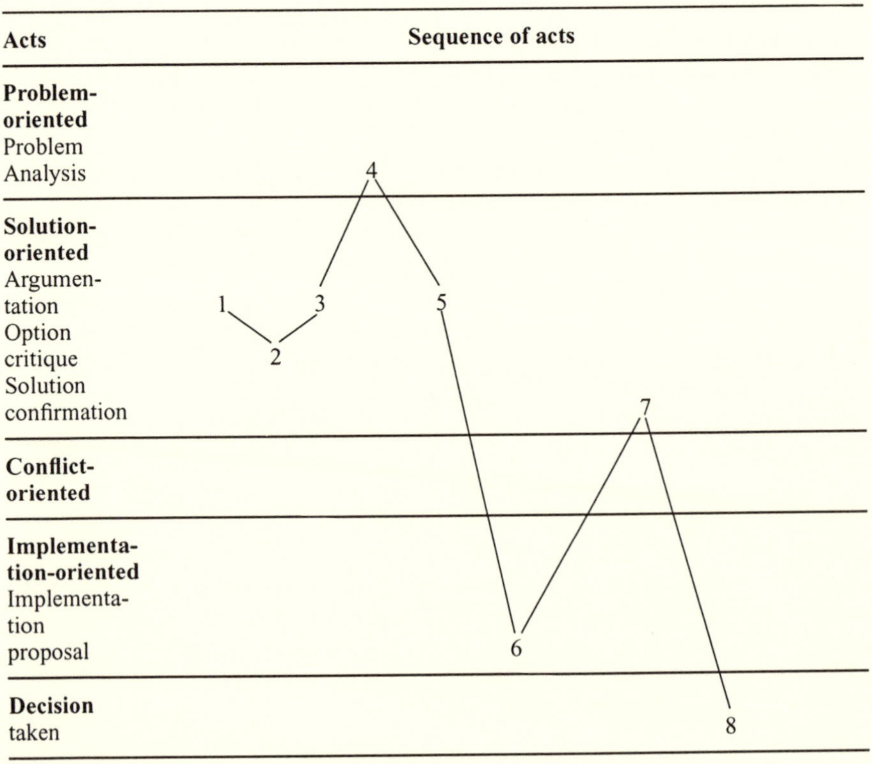

and thus switched to a problem-oriented phase. Participants again returned to argumentation (5). Subsequently, somebody made an implementation proposal (6), interrupting again the solution-oriented phase. Finally, the solution was confirmed (7) and the decision was taken (8). This process thus consisted of a solution-oriented phase (S) consisting of a sequence of three acts of the same kind (acts 1 to 3), which was interrupted by a problem-oriented phase (P) containing only one act (4); thereafter, the solution-oriented phase continued (S) with one act (5) but was then interrupted by an implementation-oriented act (I) (one act: 6); the process finished with a solution-oriented phase (S) (one act: 7) and a decision (D) (one act: 8). This sequence in Figure 3.1 may be summarized as follows: SPSISD. In Part 2 of this volume we make use of these summaries in order to study the process patterns.

ASSESSMENT OF THE CODING RELIABILITIES

We had to assess two kinds of coding reliabilities: the reliability of the construction of argumentation trees and the reliabilities of the classification of the other interaction concepts and the organizational and situational variables. The principle was always the same. Since the process coding is as good as the coding of the different parts, the coding reliability of the process coding was not assessed separately.

Two coders first performed the coding (construction of argumentation trees and classification of concepts) individually. They then compared results. If there were differences they tried to reach a common solution which could be used for further analysis.

For the assessment of the intercoder reliability of the construction of argumentation trees an ad hoc measure, constructed for this purpose, was used as the measure of agreement. It assumes values ranging from 0 to 1. Table 3.1 summarizes the results of the intercoder reliability and shows that the mean agreement for the construction of argumentation trees was .88, which is highly satisfactory. Taking into account that group codings rather than individual codings are used for the analysis, to correct for errors one may assume that the agreement is almost perfect. The reader interested in more technical details of the assessment of coding reliability of decision trees is referred to Gallhofer and Saris (1996).

For the assessment of the intercoder reliability of the other interaction concepts and the organizational and situational variables, we used Scott's π, an agreement measure which takes on the value of zero if the level of agreement equals chance expectancy. If perfect, it is one and if the agreement is less than can be expected by chance, its value becomes negative. Table 3.1 also summarizes the results of these coding efforts and shows that in general, the scores of Scott's π are quite high. Almost all scores are above .80, but depending on the difficulty of the concept, they vary slightly. Given that the coders corrected each other, the joint coding has an even higher reliability, shown by Gallhofer and Saris (1996).

Table 3.1

Intercoder Reliability for the Various Coding Efforts

Concepts	Agreement measure*	Number of cases
Problem-oriented interactions		
Problem analysis	.89	79
Problem critique	.98	65
Solution analysis	.79	45
Information	.97	34
Clarification	.99	21
Solution-oriented interactions		
Option formulation	.97	286
Option critique	.86	234
Argumentation	.91	98
Information	.95	195
Clarification	.93	91
Solution confirmation	.82	62
Conflict-oriented interactions		
Threat	1.00	78
Request for postponement	.98	81
Request for a vote	1.00	11
Request for unity	.83	34
Request for a compromise	.92	21
Request for accommodation	.84	69
Management of group tension	1.00	35
Request to leave the decision to another person	1.00	2
Implementation-oriented interactions		
Implementation proposal	.94	39
Exhortation to solidarity	.98	4
Assurance of solidarity	1.00	3
Result of the meeting	1.00	65
Aggregation rule	.97	59
Organizational variables		
Departmental affiliation	.99	124
Function	.98	124
Party affiliation	1.00	124
Situational variable		
Crisis	.96	59

* The agreement measure of argumentation is a tree structure measure, while the agreement measure of the other concepts is Scott's π.

CONCLUSIONS

In this methodological chapter we have discussed how problem-, solution-, conflict-, and implementation-oriented interactions, which describe the decision-making process, can be detected from the minutes of meetings. First, we explained how to derive substantive arguments for or against different strategies on the basis of consequences. Here we made use of decision theoretic concepts and represented the arguments with decision trees. Subsequently, the function and text analysis of other interaction concepts were introduced. We have also shown that the coding of both arguments and other contributions can be conducted with very high reliability by pairs of coders. Consequently, the process coding is reliable.

In the subsequent chapters, this approach will be applied to the case studies relating to different decision units in order to investigate whether or not these decision-making processes accord with the propositions established in Chapter 2.

Chapter 4

Germany's Decision to Initiate World War II

This chapter presents a qualitative analysis of the decision-making process in a unit where the predominant leader is quite insensitive to suggestions from those around him. As an example, we have taken Hitler's decision to invade Poland in August 1939 in a noncrisis situation, a decision which initiated World War II.

In Chapter 2 we postulated that in such a unit the predominant leader will himself analyze the problem (step 1), specify the options available and present an argument for his choice (step 2), after which all members of the group will fall in with the leader's choice (step 3) and the result will be a decision by some kind of consensus. We have assumed that the leader is so powerful that all participants feel obliged to conform to his choice out of fear for their position or because of his natural or ascribed authority. But before we present the decision-making process, a brief introduction to the political background would seem in order.

POLITICAL BACKGROUND

When Hitler wrote *Mein Kampf* in the 1920s, he had already set out his foreign policy program. It consisted among other things of revising the Treaty of Versailles concluded after World War I, incorporating Austria, and transforming Czechoslovakia and Poland into satellite states for achieving more German Lebensraum. When he came to power in the 1930s, he first began by pursuing the rearmament of Germany, against the provisions of the Treaty of Versailles and notwithstanding the protests of France, Britain, Italy, and the League of Nations, from which he withdrew Germany in 1933.

In 1936 Hitler launched a four-year plan to prepare Germany for war. In the same year he concluded a pact with Mussolini, whom he admired as his equal; the so-called Rome-Berlin axis, of which Japan became the third member in 1938. When, in November 1937, Hitler disclosed to the leaders of the armed forces some of his plans for achieving German Lebensraum, he failed to convince his audience and consequently replaced the leaders of the army, abolished the position of minister of war, and made himself commander-in-chief of the armed forces. By these means he avoided any further objections to the implementation of his decisions. In the spring of 1938 he annexed Austria with no protest from other European powers. This obviously encouraged him further to take over Czechoslovakia in the spring of 1939.

The next country from which he required territory was Poland. When the Poles refused his request to give way on Danzig, the British and French even felt obliged in March 1939 to guarantee Poland its independence. Despite this move by the Western countries, Hitler had by then formed the opinion that they were too weak to stand by this guarantee. He also felt strengthened by his pact with Stalin, which was about to be concluded at the end of August 1939. The latter also had an interest in carving up Poland, while for Hitler this treaty assured him that he could concentrate on the west rather than open two fronts in the event that war did break out. Within this political context he decided that the time had come to invade Poland.

MEETINGS OF AUGUST 22, 1939

On August 22 Hitler convened his supreme commanders to a meeting in his residence at the Obersalzberg. He opened the meeting by explaining the causes of the problem (Figure 4.1 summarizes the acts). Although he had planned first to fight the Western powers, he had changed his plans because of the Polish attempt to gain access to the sea and an impending threat of war on two fronts. The moment seemed propitious for Germany to resolve the problem in the east at once. The leaders of the Western nations were so weak that no serious reactions could be anticipated from them, whereas he himself, his ally Mussolini, and Spain's Franco, who had guaranteed him an amicable neutrality should conflict break out, were strong leaders. Since he continuously ran the risk of being assassinated by some criminal, it was now the right moment to resolve the Polish problem (act 1). In his opinion, the decision-making was straightforward for Germany since it had nothing to lose and much to win (act 2).

Thereafter the führer introduced the two available strategies. Should Germany do nothing (S_1), the country could only survive economically for a few more years. Since this outcome was negative he rejected this alternative and supported the option of invading Poland (S_2) (acts 3, 4, and 5). Before looking at the consequences of the invasion strategy, he outlined once more to the participants his ideas regarding the causes of the problem. In his opinion, Germany's relation with Poland had become untenable, especially after the British and French offer to guarantee its independence. However, the risks were very high for Britain and France (act 6).

He then continued with his consideration of the consequences of both strategies, again rejecting the first strategy on the basis of the certainty that it would sooner or later lead to the destruction of Germany. With regard to the invasion of Poland (S₂), he thought that Britain and France would probably not meet their commitments to Poland, and Germany would then be able to destroy the latter and secure its own economic future (act 7).

He then considered previous risky situations, such as the invasion of Czechoslovakia, when Britain and France could also have entered the war, and informed his audience that his risktaking was always based on his conviction that he would succeed (act 8). After lecturing his commanders that this action should be carried out with an iron determination (act 9), he turned to the possible consequences of an invasion. He considered a British and French attack on the Maginot line or a British and French attack on Italy or a violation of the Belgian and Swiss borders

Figure 4.1
August 22, 1939, Morning Meeting of Hitler with His Supreme Commanders

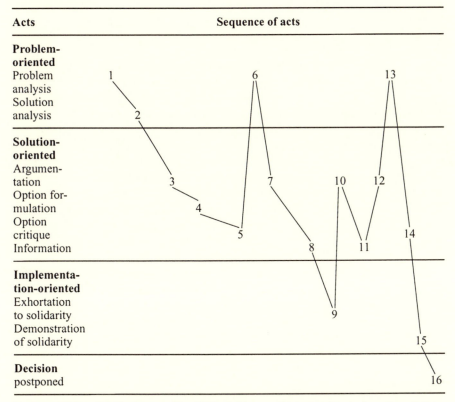

Source: Hitler, Adolf, August 22, 1939, Address, *Akten zur Deutschen Auswärtigen Politik, 1918–1945*, Series D (1937–1945), vol. 7 (Baden-Baden: Imprimerie Nationale, 1956), no. 192.

by the Western powers as inconceivable because they were not yet militarily prepared. They needed several more years to build up their military strength (act 10).

He then informed the participants of the progress of his nonaggression pact with Stalin, which would be signed in a few days and would undermine the hope of the Western powers and Poland that Russia might prevent an invasion (act 11). He continued by considering some of the consequences of this strategy. One possibility was that the Western powers might impose a blockade, but according to him such a blockade would be ineffective since the east could furnish the necessary cereals and raw material (act 12).

Concluding this session, he remarked that Germany had already destroyed the British political hegemony, that the pact with Stalin had made an enormous impact on Poland, and that the way was now open for the military (act 13).

Apart from the minister of aviation, who was also the supreme commander of the air force, all the other participants remained silent. The former supported with enthusiasm the invasion of Poland (S_2), thanked the führer for his explanations, and assured him that the army was ready to do its duty (acts 14 and 15). Thereafter they took a break (act 16).

Figure 4.2
August 22, 1939, Afternoon Meeting of Hitler with His Supreme Commanders

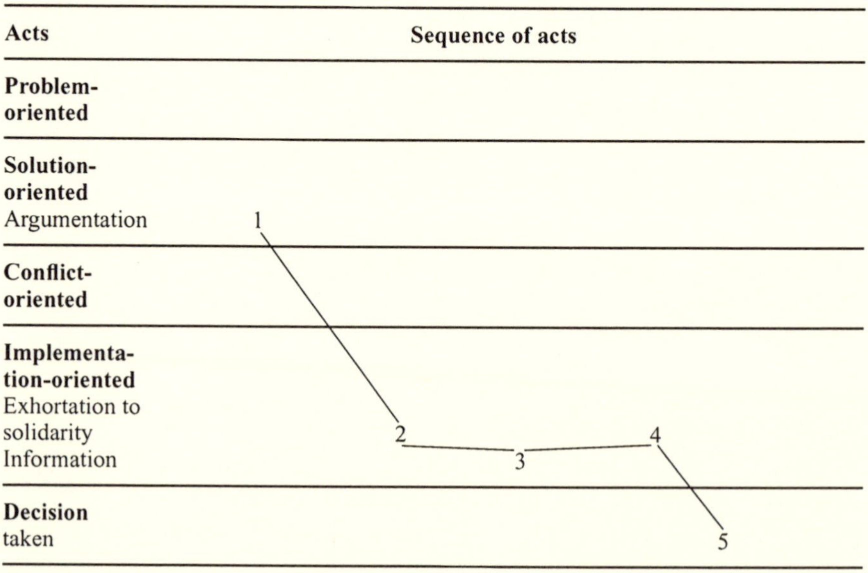

Source: Hitler, Adolf, August 22, 1939, Address, *Akten zur Deutschen Auswärtigen Politik, 1918–1945*, Series D (1937–1945), vol. 7 (Baden-Baden: Imprimerie Nationale, 1956), no. 193.

When the meeting resumed (Figure 4.2 summarizes the process), Hitler continued by enumerating some of the possible consequences of an invasion (S_2). He stated that an economic embargo by the Western powers was more likely than a blockade, although the chance was quite small. If there were an embargo it would lead to breaking off diplomatic relations, but the German economic resources would have been secured. Another possibility, although extremely unlikely, was that breaking off diplomatic relations would lead to war with the Western powers (act 1).

He then exhorted solidarity among the participants, asking them to keep an iron resolution to retreat from nothing, and asserted that Germany could win any war if it stayed firm and united, because qualitatively it had better people than the other nations (act 2).

Finally, he informed them that he would take care of a propaganda campaign claiming provocation of war and he promised that the initiation orders would come soon (act 3). They should act ruthlessly in order to secure the existence of Germany and its eighty million people. Stating his conviction that the army could do the job, he closed the meeting and the decision was taken (acts 4 and 5).

CONCLUSIONS

In this chapter we have presented an illustration of a decision-making process with an insensitive predominant leader in a noncrisis situation. The description of the two meetings showed that everything was conducted exclusively by the leader. He analyzed the problem (step 1), developed available options, presented the argument for the choice (step 2), contributed information, and tried to promote solidarity among the participants to carry out his strategy properly (step 3). The meetings thus consisted of a very long monologue, in which the leader tried to pursue an analytic type of decision-making, discussing the consequences of the available options. Only at the end of the first meeting did the minister of aviation, who was also the supreme commander of the air force, say anything, supporting the preferred option of the leader and promising in the name of the other participants that the army would do its duty. The result was thus a decision of some tacit consensus where nobody dared to take any other position out of fear of his position and/or the ascribed authority of the leader.

In this context, it should be noted that it was not true that everyone agreed with Hitler, even though they did not show their opposition. One member who was also present at these meetings, and who made minutes of a dinner meeting the same day, noted that there were some participants who had objections but did not dare to speak up (*Akten zur Deutschen Auswärtigen Politik*, 1956, 7: 172, n. 1).

When examining the sequence of the process (Figures 4.1 and 4.2), we see that Hitler began with problem analysis (acts 1 and 2); engaged in formulating and discussing solutions (acts 3 to 5), inserting again a problem analysis (act 6); and thereafter continued with the solution (acts 7, 8, 10, 11, 12), a phase only briefly interrupted by a remark relating to implementation (act 11) since he already had made his decision. The session finished with an implementation-oriented remark from a member of the audience. The second session started again with a solution-oriented phase (act 1) and finished with implementation-oriented statements (acts 2, 3, and 4). This process could thus be characterized roughly by three phases, namely, problem analysis, solution development, and implementation. Although the phases are not in complete linear sequence (Hitler sometimes cycles back from the solution stage to the problem stage and from the implementation to the solution phase), this process approaches the classical three-stage model advanced by Bales and Strodtbeck (1951). In the quantitative part we study these process patterns in more detail.

It is very typical here that only the leader speaks and no information is exchanged. This means that the predominant leader has made his decision and he is reporting this to the people who have to execute it. Consequently, there are no conflict-oriented acts present. This is not a real group decision-making process. It is not even a group discussion. We thus saw that the decision-making process was very short (proposition 1, Chapter 2). There was also no aggregation rule needed for the group choice (proposition 2, Chapter 2) and conflict-oriented acts were absent (proposition 3, Chapter 2).

The next chapter presents a decision-making process with a predominant leader who was sensitive to his environment, where we will see a quite different decision-making process.

Chapter 5

The World at the Brink of a Nuclear War: The U.S. Decision to Avoid a Nuclear War, October 1962

We present in this chapter a qualitative analysis of the decision-making process in a unit where the predominant leader is quite sensitive to suggestions from those around him. As an example, we have taken the decision-making process of the United States concerning the initiation of a naval blockade during the Cuban missile crisis in October 1962.

It is generally recognized in the literature (Maidment and McGrew 1992) that the American president is highly autonomous in the conduct of foreign relations. It is in fact up to him to decide who participates in the preparations of the decision. President Kennedy as a leader was sensitive to suggestions and invited an entire group of people to take part in the preparatory meetings. In Chapter 2 we postulated that in such a unit the leader allows different advisers to define the problem (step 1), then to specify options and present arguments for their preferred option (step 2), and that this process stops as soon as the leader makes his choice (step 3). Since the leader allows different opinions to be ventilated, the resulting choice will be some kind of consensus reached by at least a subgroup of advisers that the leader judges to make sense.

In the following, we briefly introduce the political background and then describe the decision-making process.

POLITICAL BACKGROUND

On October 16, 1962, President Kennedy called together a group of his closest high-level advisers to discuss the Central Intelligence Agency's discovery of Soviet missile installations under construction on the island of Cuba. The relations between the United States and the Soviet Union with respect to Cuba had been strained for some time. The attempt to install nuclear weapons in Cuba can therefore be seen as the culmination of a deterioration in relations between these nations (for an extended political analysis, see Chang and Kornbluh 1992; Blight, Allyn, and Welch 1993; and Hilsman 1996).

The motive of the Soviets to deploy nuclear weapons ninety miles offshore from the United States seemed to be at least threefold. One of the reasons was the presence of U.S. nuclear installations and military bases close to and even along Soviet borders. In 1959 the United States had deployed nuclear missiles, the so-called Jupiter missiles, in the NATO countries of Italy and Turkey. These rockets became operational in April 1962. The Soviets thus wanted to reciprocate the threat. Another reason was a desire to compensate for the Russian missile gap in longer-range systems and to restore the balance of deterrence by transferring medium-range missiles to Cuba.

A third reason was the constant threat from the United States to overthrow Castro's regime in Cuba. Before the advent of Castro the pro-American military government of Cuba had largely enjoyed American support. When Castro came to power in 1959 by a national revolution, Washington withdrew its military assistance to Cuba, and by 1960 the planning of operations to overthrow this regime had been initiated by the CIA. Notwithstanding the disaster of the U.S.-sponsored invasion attempt by Cuban exiles in April 1961 at the Bay of Pigs, the U.S. government continued to authorize a covert program to oust Castro. The latter had meanwhile become a major ally of the Soviet Union in the Western Hemisphere and thus intensified the challenge to U.S. security.

On the other hand, the American covert operations, the military maneuvers, a full economic embargo of Cuba, and a diplomatic initiative by the United States to expel Cuba from the Organization of American States (OAS) all increased the fear of both Soviets and Cubans that an American invasion of the island was imminent. In order to take precautions against such an invasion, Soviet and Cuban officials secretly negotiated the deployment of nuclear missiles, as well as other military equipment and a large contingent of conventionally armed Soviet troops. Throughout the summer of 1962 the Soviet transfer of troops and equipment was monitored with great concern by the CIA. But only on October 15 could the CIA identify with certainty the construction of Soviet missile installations.

There were a number of meetings held by presidential advisory groups from October 16 to October 28, when the crisis ended with the announcement by Chairman Khrushchev to withdraw the missiles. In the following, we study the group decision-making process in detail on the basis of transcripts of meetings relating to the decision to initiate a naval blockade. The transcripts of meetings are taken from Chang and Kornbluh's edition (1992), which is generally recognized as sufficiently complete and reliable.

DECISION PHASE 1; OCTOBER 16 TO OCTOBER 18, 1962

October 16, 1962, Morning Meeting

On the evening of October 15 an official of the Central Intelligence Agency informed the president's special adviser on national security, McGeorge Bundy, of evidence about the presence of offensive missiles in Cuba. The next morning Bundy informed President Kennedy of the photographic evidence. The president immediately called for a meeting, indicating the advisers he wanted to be present. This group of advisers, which was later called the Executive Committee of the National Security Council (Excom), consisted of about seventeen high-level specialists such as the secretary of state, Dean Rusk; his deputy, George Ball; the assistant secretary for Latin American affairs, Edwin Martin; the secretary of defense, Robert McNamara; his deputy, Roswell Gilpatric; the assistant secretary of defense, Paul Nitze; the secretary of the treasury, Douglas Dillon; the chairman of the Joint Chiefs of Staff, Maxwell D. Taylor; advisers on Russian affairs, Charles Bohlen and Llewellyn Thompson; the attorney general, Robert Kennedy; the vice president, Lyndon B. Johnson; the ambassador to the United Nations, Adlai Stevenson; the director of central intelligence, John McCone; the national security adviser, McGeorge Bundy; and the presidential counsel, Theodore Sorensen.

According to Robert Kennedy (1969, 116–120), the president wanted the advice not only of his cabinet officers but also of those who were connected with the situation. He also encouraged the presentation of different opinions, in order to hear the arguments for the possible consequences of several courses of action, to hear those arguments challenged, and to make his decision on the basis of the best possible information, although he realized that no course of action would ever be completely satisfactory.

Figure 5.1 summarizes schematically the decision-making process during this first meeting of October 16 at 11:50 A.M. The president presided over the meeting. At the opening of the meeting, Lundal, the director of the national photographic information center, provided information about the photographs, stating that they had discovered a medium-range ballistic missile launch site and two military encampments in west central Cuba (act 1). The president then inquired precisely where it was and how they knew that these were medium ballistic missiles (act 2). Lundal gave him the details (act 3). The president's next questions related to the missiles' readiness to fire (act 4). Graybeal, the chief of the guided missile division of the CIA, first answered that they had no knowledge on this (act 5), but after some clarification by the president and some additional questions by McNamara, Graybeal could provide the president with the information that the missiles were not yet ready to fire with nuclear warheads, since the sites had no fence and there was some evidence that the warheads were not yet present (acts 6 to 13). Then Taylor, the chairman of the Joint Chiefs of Staff, asked the crucial question whether the missiles could be fired from this field very

Figure 5.1
October 16, 1962, 11:50 A.M. to 12:57 P.M., Off-the-Record Meeting on Cuba

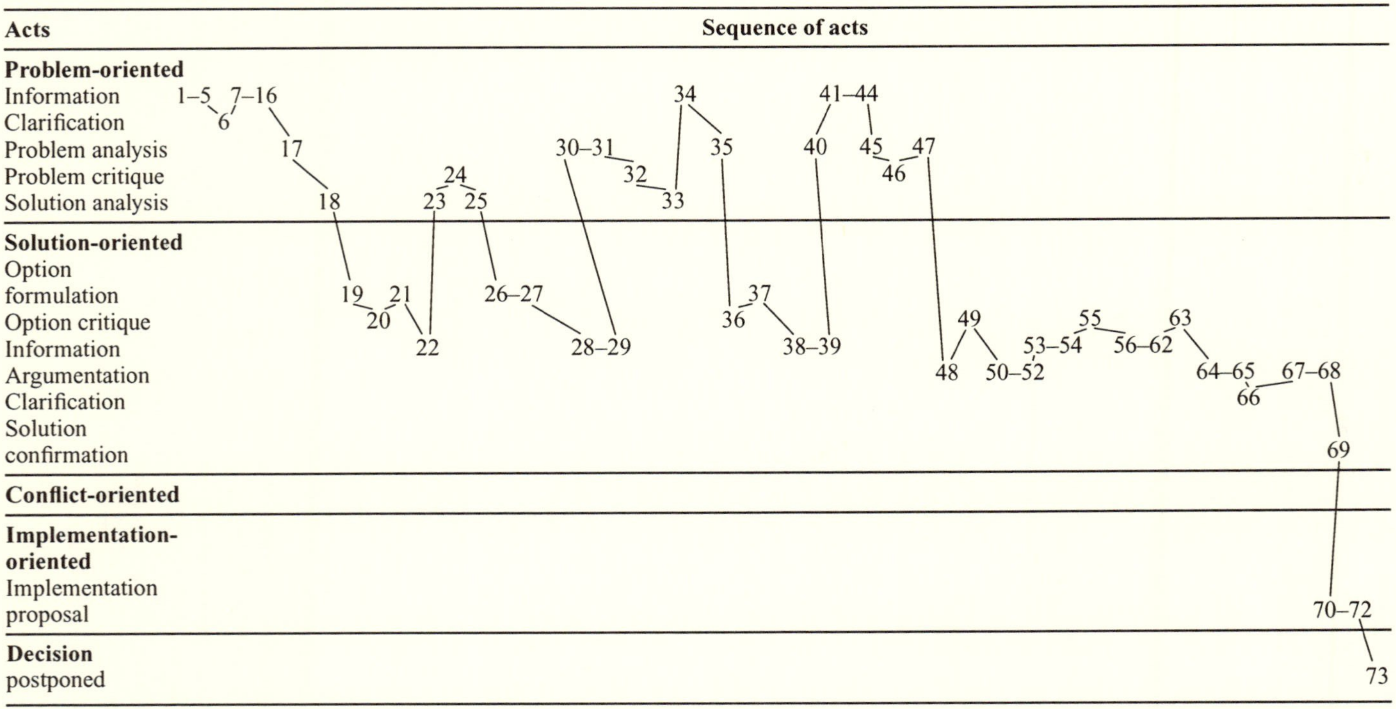

Acts

Sequence of acts

Problem-oriented
Information 1–5, 7–16
6
Clarification 17
Problem analysis 18
Problem critique
Solution analysis

Solution-oriented
Option formulation 19, 21
20
Option critique 22
Information 23, 24, 25
Argumentation 26–27
Clarification 28–29
Solution 30–31, 32, 33
confirmation 34, 35, 36, 37
40, 38–39
41–44, 45, 47, 46
49, 48, 53–54, 55, 50–52, 56–62, 63, 64–65, 67–68, 66, 69

Conflict-oriented

Implementation-oriented
Implementation proposal 70–72

Decision
postponed 73

Source: Transcript of the second Executive Committee meeting, Oct. 16, 1962, 11:50 A.M. to 12:57 P.M., in L. Chang and P. Kornbluh, eds., *The Cuban Missile Crisis, 1962*, doc. no. 15, pp. 85–96 (New York: Free Press, 1992).

quickly (act 14). Graybeal answered that if the equipment was ready it would only be a question of hours. But they had no information about that (act 15).

The president then asked Secretary Rusk his opinion (act 16). The secretary began analyzing the problem by stating that this serious development was unexpected since the Russians had always denied their intent to establish bases on their own (act 17). He then analyzed the situation in general terms. He argued that a solution should be sought by setting in motion a chain of events which would eliminate these bases (act 18), thereafter specifying some available strategies. Considering first the option of the status quo, that is, to do nothing (S_1), he rejected this immediately as unfeasible (acts 19 and 20).

Another available option specified was a quick air strike to eliminate the bases (S_2), while a third option he developed was to warn Khrushchev and Castro about the seriousness of the situation, to alert NATO, and to let the OAS take action against the threats to peace in their hemisphere and require inspection teams on the site (S_3). This could be coupled with an interruption of all air traffic from the free-world countries to Cuba and open surveillance of Cuba, which could be announced publicly with the other developments at some point in time. The only problem with this strategy was that there might not be enough time available (act 21). Secretary Rusk also suggested consulting General Eisenhower about this matter (act 22). Again in general terms, Rusk then analyzed the kind of solution which should be found and indicated that it should give the possibility for all parties involved to deescalate before the situation got out of hand (act 23).

Subsequently, Secretary McNamara took the floor. He agreed with his colleague's analysis and continued by outlining two propositions that should be accepted as foundations for their further thinking (acts 24 and 25). The first was that an air strike should take place before the missiles became operational, because once the missiles were operational an air strike would provoke their launching and lead to complete chaos. McNamara's second proposition was that an air strike ought to be directed not only against the missile sites but also against the airfields and hidden aircraft and all potential nuclear storage sites in order to reduce the possibility of retaliation. The secretary then specified the military action they were capable of carrying out: air strikes on missile sites, airfields, and storage sites within a few days, associated with a degree of mobilization within the limits of the authority granted by Congress, and thereafter an invasion by air and sea (S_4) (act 26).

He then gave the floor to General Taylor, who further elaborated a strategy of large-scale air strikes (S_5). In the general's view there should be three steps: the first would be to prepare completely and to obtain additional photographs in order to be more precise about the position of the targets; the second phase would consist of a concurrent air strike on missile sites, airfields, and storage sites, together with a naval blockade and reinforcement of Guantanamo and evacuation of its dependents; the third step would then be the decision of whether or not to invade, which would present the most difficult military problem (act 27). The general also informed the participants that they would never have the perfect timing required to eliminate every missile before it became operational (act 28).

Secretary Rusk then informed the president that the Soviet foreign minister, Gromyko, had asked to see him on Thursday, October 18, and that he might bring a message on the missile issue (act 29). Referring to General Taylor's outline, Rusk then asserted that in his opinion the critical question was not whether to hit a particular missile before it could be launched in order to prevent a general nuclear war, but whether the Soviets wished to launch them (act 30). Secretary McNamara suggested that it would be best to assume that the Soviets were willing to launch them (act 31). Secretary Rusk immediately agreed with his colleague (act 32). The former then specified that an air strike (S_4) could only be carried out under the condition that no launchable warheads were present (act 33).

At this point the president asked the participants what the Soviets' reasons might be for bringing the missiles to Cuba (act 34). General Taylor mentioned as one of the reasons the compensation for their rather defective Intercontinental ballistic missile (ICBM) system (act 35). The president replied that he did not see how he could prevent other missiles being brought in by submarine and referred to the blockade that Taylor had suggested implementing concurrently with the large-scale air strikes (S_5), which would not work in this case (act 36). Secretary McNamara then suggested that one way to prevent the missiles arriving would be to warn the Soviets that they would be taken out if they came in and to continue open surveillance (act 37). Bundy, the president's special adviser on national security, then asked McNamara why an air strike should be extended to the whole air complex (act 38). The secretary of defense replied that the airplanes might also be carrying nuclear warheads (act 39).

Subsequently, Secretary Rusk continued to present the president with reasons why the Soviets had brought missiles into Cuba (act 40). In his opinion, the Russians lived under the fear of American medium-range missiles nearby, such as those in Turkey, and they wanted to reciprocate by instilling a similar fear in the Americans. The president then asked for information about the number of weapons in Turkey (act 41). Taylor, Bundy, and Rusk subsequently provided the information (acts 42 to 44) that there were approximately fifteen Jupiter missiles with delivery vehicles which could be moved through the air. Rusk then continued by enumerating other possible reasons for the Soviets' action (act 45). Because of America's nuclear superiority the deployment of Soviet missiles in Cuba could be considered as an effort to establish a balance. This reason had actually already been given by General Taylor. But the Soviets might also wish to use Cuba as a bargaining counter against West Berlin, the Western enclave in Communist East Germany. Another possibility might be that if they provoked an American action against Cuba, this would give them an umbrella excuse to take action in Berlin, such as denying access to Western militaries and civilians.

Bundy then mentioned that the Soviets must have made this deployment decision in early summer and that the implementation had begun in August. He referred to a Soviet press statement of October 12, which experts attributed to

Chairman Khrushchev, which spoke of harmless military equipment being sent to Cuba for purely defensive purposes. Bundy further agreed with Secretary Rusk that the Soviets felt that Cuba was comparable to Italy or Turkey and he added that they also believed that missiles were stationed in Japan (acts 46 and 47).

When Secretary Dillon entered the discussion, he rejected the non-military option of warning the Russians and Castro, sounding public opinion, involving OAS, and telling NATO (S_3), since the chance of a Russian retaliation would then be higher than if they were to eliminate the bases by means of a quick air strike (S_2), which he supported (act 48). Bundy also stated that he was inclined to support the quick air strike (S_2) and to reject S_3 because it would be difficult to organize OAS and NATO and would lead to a division in the alliance; he pointed out that Europeans were generally accustomed to living under the threat of Soviet missiles, and the Germans would think that the United States was jeopardizing Berlin through their concern with Cuba (acts 49 and 50). Secretary Rusk then argued against the quick air strike (S_2), arguing that even though the Russians might withdraw after the attack, the United States would nevertheless have exposed all the allies and themselves to great dangers without consultation and warning (act 51). President Kennedy then remarked that warning (S_3) was not possible because it meant warning everybody, in which case the surprise element would be lost (act 52).

He subsequently asked how effective it might be to try to take out the missiles (act 53). General Taylor informed the president that it could never be 100 percent; they could hope to take out a vast majority with the first air strike but that continuous air strikes would be necessary, implying that S_2 was not appropriate, but rather S_4 or S_5 (acts 54 and 55). Next the president asked how long the planning of air strikes could be kept secret within the administration (act 56). Bundy and Taylor informed the president of how many people and what kind of officials would be involved in the planning and McNamara estimated that they could keep it from the public for about one week (acts 57, 58, and 59).

Thereafter President Kennedy asked the opinion of his vice president (act 60). Vice President Johnson agreed with Secretary McNamara's estimate that it would be possible to keep the issue secret for one week (act 61). After stating that he wished to hear the commanders' view of the military alternatives, he said that he supported a military action to eliminate the bases (S_2) and specified his argument against S_3, claiming that the OAS and the NATO allies were too weak to be of much help (acts 62, 63, and 64). Although he realized that no consultation meant a breach of faith, he found that the issue did not lend itself to much discussion (act 65).

President Kennedy then tried to clarify to the vice president that, in his view, three different military operations had come up during the discussion: one was an air strike solely against the three bases (S_2); the second was a broader air strike on the airfields and the Soviet surface-to-air missile (SAM) sites and on anything else connected with missiles (part of S_4); the third was a combination of the first and the second with the simultaneous launch of a blockade (part of S_5). A fourth question was the degree of consultation which should be done (part of S_3) (act 66).

The president was then interrupted by the attorney general, who added the clarification that an invasion was discussed as the fifth step (act 67). Robert Kennedy then rejected the extended air strike on everything connected with missiles (part of S_4) because the strike would kill a large number of people, the United States would incur worldwide condemnation for it, and it would ultimately not lead to any solution because the Russians could again bring in missiles with the United States threatening to do the same in Iran or Turkey (act 68).

President Kennedy then summarized the results that, in his opinion, had emerged from this meeting (act 69). Since he felt that there was not much time left for decision-making, they had to begin immediately with military preparations. The first thing was to increase the number of reconnaissance flights (act 70). The air strike on the missile bases should be prepared because they would certainly carry it out (act 71). They should also prepare for a general air strike, although he was not yet ready to decide whether it would be carried out (act 72). Before closing the meeting he proposed meeting again in the early evening to discuss the various proposals (act 73).

Summary

This chapter already shows a very different decision-making process if one compares it with the previous chapter. The leader listens to his advisers, the members exchange considerable information, they go back and forth through the different phases, and in the end they concentrate on solution-oriented behavior. Conflict-oriented acts did not arise in this meeting. At the end of the session, the leader makes a preliminary decision but announces further discussion of the options in the next session.

October 16, Evening Meeting of the Advisory Group

After the first meeting of the advisory group, staff at the Pentagon immediately went to work to plan the military alternatives, while State Department staff explored the possibilities of support by the Latin American and European allies (Larson 1986, Appendix H, 253). At 6:30 P.M. the advisory committee reconvened for further deliberations. Figure 5.2 summarizes the interactions during this meeting.

President Kennedy opened the meeting by asking for more information on additional photographs (act 1). The deputy director of the CIA, Carter, informed the president that they estimated that between sixteen and twenty-four medium-range missiles were present which could be operational within two weeks (act 2). Secretary Rusk asked Carter whether or not the missiles were real. The latter confirmed that they were positive and that they were no decoys (acts 3 and 4).

Figure 5.2
October 16, 1962, 6:30 P.M. to 7:55 P.M., Off-the-Record Meeting on Cuba

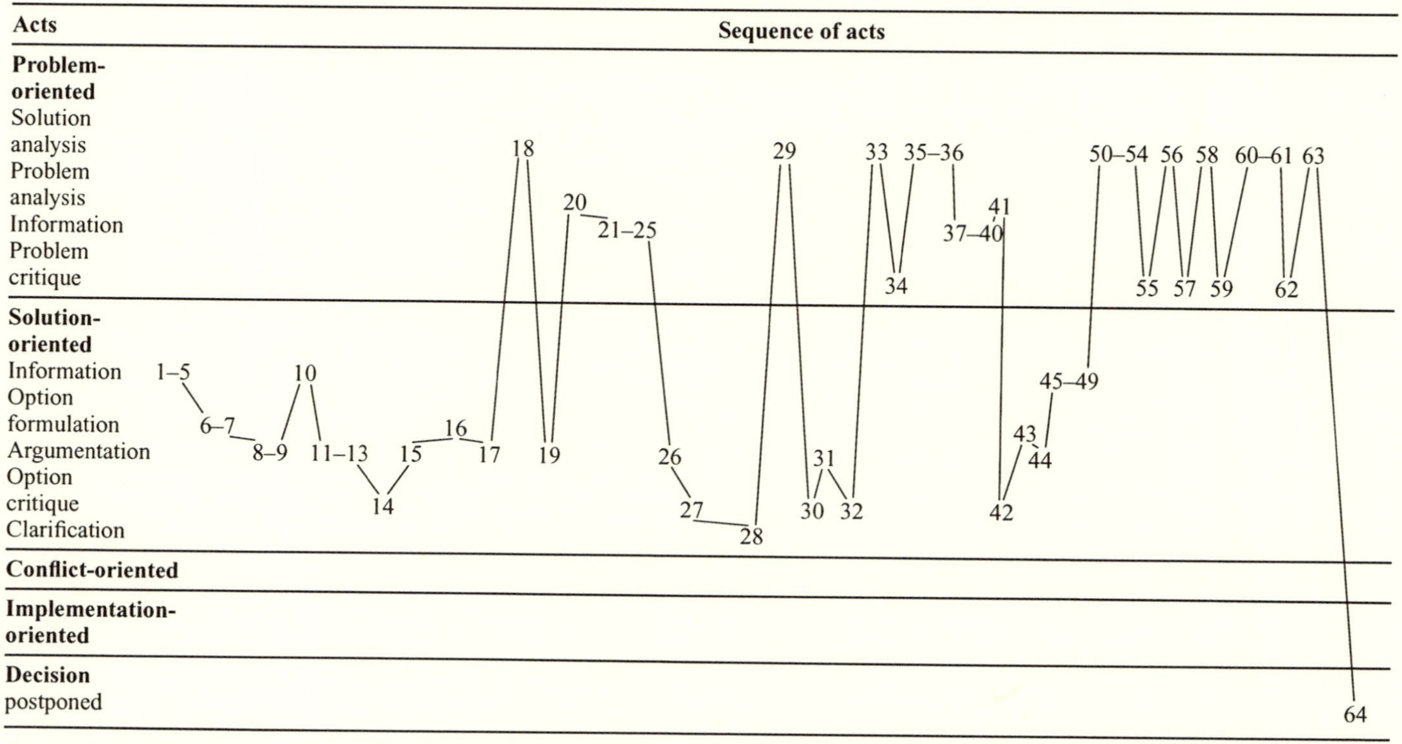
Acts
Sequence of acts
Problem-oriented
Solution analysis
Problem analysis
Information
Problem critique
Solution-oriented
Information
Option formulation
Argumentation
Option critique
Clarification
Conflict-oriented
Implementation-oriented
Decision postponed
1–5
6–7
8–9
10
11–13
14
15
16
17
18
19
20
21–25
26
27
28
29
30
31
32
33
34
35–36
37–40
41
42
43
44
45–49
50–54
55
56
57
58
59
60–61
62
63
64

Source: Transcript of the second Executive Committee meeting, Oct. 16, 1962, 6:30 P.M. to 7:55 P.M., in L. Chang and P. Kornbluh, eds., *The Cuban Missile Crisis, 1962*, doc. no. 16, pp. 97–113 (New York: Free Press, 1992).

Secretary Rusk then informed the participants that he had held that afternoon a State Department meeting where they had discussed a message to Castro (S_3) (acts 5 and 6). Assistant Secretary of State Martin gave further details about the message considered. In short, the message stated that the United States had been informed of the Soviet missile sites in Cuba and that this put Castro in great jeopardy, either through an impending American attack on Cuba or of being bargained away eventually by the Soviets in exchange for concessions against Berlin or other places. If he were to take action to get the Soviets out of the sites, the Americans would refrain from acting and from informing other nations (act 7). Secretary Rusk set out an argument which rejected this strategy (S_3). In his opinion, it might induce Castro to bring up anti-aircraft weapons around the missile sites, which would make an air strike more difficult (act 8). But he also rejected an air strike without warning (S_2) because it might bring about the Communist overthrow of some other Latin American governments, and since the Soviets would certainly take action elsewhere, it might expose the NATO allies to great danger. This might consequently isolate America and lead to the collapse of the alliance (act 9).

President Kennedy then asked about the military consequences of an air strike on the missile sites (S_2) (act 10). Secretary McNamara answered that they would get the launchers and General Taylor added that there was unanimity among the commanders of the Joint Chiefs that they never could be absolutely sure of destroying everything (acts 11 and 12). The general thereafter rejected warning Cuba and then carrying out a quick air strike on the missile sites alone (S_3). He argued that the warning could invite reprisal attacks and mean the loss of the first-strike surprise attack (act 13). He recommended that the reconnaissance flights should first be continued in order to get more insight into the target system and that large-scale air strikes be initiated (S_5), an argument which was in agreement with his recommendation of the morning meeting (act 14).

Thereupon Secretary McNamara specified the arguments for the courses of action his group at the Pentagon had considered that afternoon. Either a quick air strike on the missile bases (S_2) or a quick air strike with prior warning to Castro (S_3) would almost certainly lead to a Soviet response. These strategies were therefore rejected by his group. Warning Khrushchev and Castro, getting public opinion, asking OAS for action, and discussing the issue with NATO (S_4), the strategy introduced by Secretary Rusk in the first meeting, was also rejected by his group because it could very likely lead to unsatisfactory results and almost preclude subsequent military action.

The alternative of large-scale air strikes (S_5) recommended by General Taylor was also rejected by McNamara's group because of the near certainty of a Soviet response. Another military alternative they considered was a quick air strike on the missile bases and a naval blockade (S_6). They rejected it because it would also almost certainly lead to a Soviet response (act 15). The alternative the group supported was the imposition of a naval blockade against offensive weapons entering Cuba, the continuation of open surveillance, and an ultimatum to Khrushchev (S_7) (acts 16 and 17). However, McNamara did not specify consequences.

Secretary Rusk then took the floor and analyzed how they should proceed to find a solution. In his opinion, every action affected all kinds of policies and therefore they should consider what, if any, political preparations should be made (act 18). President Kennedy rejected any kind of political preparation (S_3, S_4) since they would lose the advantages of a surprise attack, although it would put the burden on the Soviets (act 19). Thereafter Secretary Rusk told the president that in his opinion the Russians were not prepared to use nuclear weapons (act 20). President Kennedy did not react to the secretary's statement but informed his audience that he had already previously considered the possibility that the Soviets would bring medium-range ballistic missiles to Cuba (act 21). Bundy then asked about the impact of these weapons on the strategic balance (act 22). Secretary McNamara answered that the chiefs of staff considered it a substantive change whereas he himself did not (act 23). General Taylor then remarked that the weapons could become a very important adjunct to the Soviet strike capability (act 24). In obvious reply to McNamara's statement that he himself did not consider it a substantive change of the strategic balance, the president stated that it might not make any difference whether one got blown up by an intercontinental ballistic missile flying from the Soviet Union or one that was ninety miles away, but the point was that the Soviets violated the agreement not to go ahead (act 25). He then rejected the option of doing nothing (S_1) because it would increase the risk that the Soviets would deploy more weapons and would start to coerce them in Berlin (act 26). He supported the alternative of a quick air strike with a prior warning (S_3) (act 27).

The undersecretary of state, Ball, seemed to be quite astonished and asked the president for clarification (act 28). But Secretary McNamara took the floor and said that it should first be decided whether or not to strike and in the event of an air strike no announcement should be made (act 29). This induced President Kennedy to support again the option of a quick air strike (S_2), which would be much more explicable and politically satisfactory than the large-scale air strikes (S_5) (act 30). Bundy, the president's special adviser, immediately rejected the quick air strike (S_2) because it was then possible that the Soviet bombers would come into action, which would provoke a general war (act 31). President Kennedy then proposed to consider S_5, the large-scale air strikes (act 32).

Since the discussion became quite disorganized, Secretary McNamara proposed how to proceed to find a solution. In his opinion two things were important. One was to develop a specific strike plan limited to the missile and storage sites and to estimate the number of sorties. The second thing was that they had to consider the consequences of the different courses of action, which had been neglected until then. He proposed that the State and Defense Departments could do that later in the evening (act 33). Robert Kennedy agreed with McNamara and proposed to consider the consequences for both the United States and Cuba at a longer time perspective (acts 34 and 35). McNamara added that the alternative courses of action with consequences should be put on paper and if State and

Defense did not agree on them, both views should be put on paper (act 36).

President Kennedy then asked information from an expert on Russia about the advantage of deploying these missiles in Cuba and mentioned at the same time that it would be as dangerous as if the United States would suddenly deploy missiles in Turkey (act 37). Bundy answered that they had already done that and Johnson, a deputy undersecretary of state, informed the president that they had done that, too, in the United Kingdom (act 38). The president's reply was that these deployments related to another period (act 39). Deputy Undersecretary of State Johnson then asked again about the Soviets' reasons for the deployment and Ball mentioned that they were in his opinion twofold, namely, to balance their deficiencies in intercontinental ballistic missiles and to use them as a trading ploy for some arrangement in Berlin (acts 40 and 41). Johnson then suggested considering these missiles as Cuban ones and knocking them out (S_2) (act 42).

This brought the attorney general to the idea of initiating the air strike from Guantanamo (variant of S_2) (act 43). General Taylor immediately rejected an air strike from Guantanamo because that would probably invite an attack on their base and they would have to defend it (act 44). The president then informed those present that if they were to decide in two or three days on military action (S_2 or S_5), they also would need information about Guantanamo (act 45). General Taylor immediately replied that this schedule was too short, because they would need more intelligence reports for the decision (act 46). The president then countered that they were under a time pressure to initiate some kind of action and asked McNamara about new events (act 47). The secretary informed the president that nothing new had occurred, that the military planning was being carried out with no risk of leaks, and that the group had to consider fully the alternatives (act 48).

The president then asked the audience to reflect on what Gromyko should be told when he came to visit him on Thursday, October 18, but the group did not enter into discussion of this topic (act 49).

McNamara and Bundy, mainly, then discussed how they should approach the analysis of the alternatives. Bundy proposed that they should consider the different military options and the option of doing nothing and that they should take notes (act 50). McNamara stressed that there should be many gradations of military options (act 51). Bundy then offered to take notes himself and said the others should also do so individually (act 52). McNamara then stressed that some alternatives that had not been fully discussed during the meeting should therefore be studied thoroughly (act 53). One of these options was the political approach (S_4), which in his opinion had some chance of success (act 54). Bundy agreed with McNamara and suggested analyzing it "in terms of the plusses and minuses of non-success because there is such a thing as making this thing pay off in ways that are of some significance, even though we don't act" (acts 55 and 56). McNamara completely agreed with Bundy and referred to the alternative of open surveillance and a naval blockade to prevent any further offensive weapons (S_7), which should be studied (acts 57 and 58). Ball found this an acceptable alternative and stressed that it should be examined to see whether it meant a greater involvement than the other military actions (acts 59 and 60).

McNamara then continued analyzing how the military actions should be examined in terms of their consequences and indicated that they should be divided into subcategories by intensity and probable subsequent effect on the world. He expected a tentative draft the next morning for further discussion (act 61). When the deputy secretary of defense asked whether they should also look at vulnerable areas in the world besides Berlin, McNamara agreed and proposed that precautionary measures be developed (acts 62 and 63). It seems that the meeting was then adjourned (act 64). The president then left Washington for a Democratic campaign in Connecticut the next day, October 17.

Summary

In this session there is again considerable exchange of ideas. But this time the meeting begins with solution-oriented activities since the problem is clear and known by all members. Thereafter, when the participants fail to arrive at a clear solution, they go back to problem-oriented activities. The speed with which the leader tries to force a decision is also very remarkable. Kennedy had also already tried to do this in the previous meeting. Others, especially Secretary of Defense McNamara, however, prevent this by suggesting a longer decision-making process in order to find a satisfactory solution.

Meetings of October 17 and 18

During the night of October 16 and all day October 17 the members of the advisory group met in informal discussion (Larson 1986, 254) where no minutes were recorded. Sorensen, the president's special counsel, made on October 17 a summary of agreed-upon facts, possible courses of action, and unanswered questions (Chang and Kornbluh 1992, 114–115). The four courses of action considered coincided in the main with those discussed at the second meeting of October 16 and were only slightly modified and refined. The participants had considered again the following strategies:

S2: A surprise attack accompanied by messages of a limited nature (mentioned on October 16)

S4: Warning, sounding public opinion, OAS action, telling NATO, followed by a military strike if they could get no satisfaction (mentioned on October 16 with the explicit extension of an eventual military strike)

S7: Political action, pressure, warning, followed by a total naval blockade under the authority of the Rio Pact (also mentioned on October 16)

S8: A full-scale invasion to remove Castro (this alternative was not discussed at the meeting of October 16)

The disagreements among the participants at the meetings centered mainly on which of the alternatives would draw a heavier response from the Soviets.

Adlai Stevenson, the American ambassador to the United Nations, had advised the president in a letter on October 17 (Chang and Kornbluh 1992, no. 19, pp. 119–120) to deliver messages to Castro and Khrushchev demanding restoration of the status quo ante and to negotiate thereafter about missile bases in the context of a disarmament treaty. The ambassador argued that in this way the chances of Soviet reprisals elsewhere would be reduced; a surprise attack on Cuba, on the other hand, would certainly lead to Soviet reprisals elsewhere, to divisions among U.S. allies, and possibly to a nuclear war. Stevenson's preferred course of action was quite novel, but no other adviser had considered it.

Secretary Dillon also made a note on October 17 (Chang and Kornbluh 1992, no. 18, pp. 116–118) in which he argued in favor of a stronger action, namely, a naval blockade with the exercise of pressure, followed by a military strike if the weapons were not removed. He was certain that this course of action would lead to the missiles' removal anyway, either by the deployers themselves or by the United States. He rejected a surprise attack because it would lead to difficulties with public opinion, even though the missiles would be removed. He did not favor implementing a naval blockade alone, because it would lead to endless negotiations and they would in the long run lose Latin America to communism, and in other Third World countries there would be similar reactions, because the United States had failed to resist communism. The last alternative that he considered was doing nothing, which he rejected because it would lead to similar results in Latin America and in the Third World.

On October 18 the deliberations of the advisers continued throughout the entire day and evening (Larson 1986, 256), but unfortunately no minutes are available of these discussions. However, Undersecretary of State Ball set down his position in writing (Chang and Kornbluh 1992, no. 20, pp. 121–122). The undersecretary of state rejected large-scale air attacks on Cuba because they would destroy the U.S. moral position and alienate her allies and friends. He supported the naval blockade. Although he was certain that it would not prevent missiles from becoming operational, it would be accepted as legal by friends and allies, possibly also by the Soviets, which would isolate the Cubans and topple the Castro regime. However, it was also possible that the Soviets would not accept it and would take reprisals elsewhere.

An intelligence report brought alarming news that the missiles in Cuba could be ready to launch in eighteen hours.

That afternoon, the president met the Soviet foreign minister, Gromyko. The missile issue was, however, not discussed, because no decision had been made about the action to take and the president also feared that the Soviets could take some evasive initiative after a warning (Larson 1986, 257; Kennedy 1969, 39).

The Joint Chiefs of Staff had unanimously recommended to the president an air strike on the missiles and other key installations.

In the evening, nine members of the planning group met with the president.

According to the recollections of some participants (Larson 1986, 257; Kennedy 1969, 43), most members supported the blockade at the beginning of this meeting. However, during the discussions the consensus broke down: "minds and opinions began to change again, not only on small points. For some it was from one extreme to another. Supporting an air attack at the beginning of the meeting and by the time we left the White House, supporting no action at all" (Kennedy 1969, 43). Given this fact, the planners had to continue their deliberations into the following days.

Summary of Decision Phase 1

In order to deal with the threat posed by the missiles in Cuba, during the morning meeting on October 16 the members of the group first asked for information from experts, specifically for more details about the missiles and especially the time frame of their readiness to fire (see Figure 5.1). They also spent much time repeatedly exchanging information and on problem analysis in order to diagnose the situation, but they also began developing some alternatives. These ranged from the status quo, that is, doing nothing (S_1), via the purely diplomatic actions of different warnings (S_3), to three military variants of increasing degree of force, that is, a quick air strike on the missile sites (S_2), a full-scale air strike on the entire missile complex and an invasion (S_4), and a full-scale air strike on the entire missile complex together with a naval blockade and an invasion (S_5). The status quo alternative was immediately rejected. The secretaries of state and defense, two key advisers, mainly developed the courses of action and specified how they should resolve this problem in general terms.

Evaluation of options then began. Some options were simply rejected or supported, while others were considered on the basis of consequences. These contributions also mainly came from key advisers such as Secretary Rusk; Secretary Dillon; the president's national security adviser, Bundy; the attorney general, and Vice President Johnson. The consideration of available options was frequently interrupted when the leader felt he needed more information about the actual situation. The president was especially interested in the Soviets' motives for deploying the missiles, which was crucial in anticipating their future reactions to the various courses of action.

At the end of this session, the president summarized what were in his opinion the military alternatives. He thought the problem should be resolved by military means. Because of time pressure he already had given instructions for preparation for the quick air strike to eliminate the bases (S_2) and a large-scale air strike followed by an invasion (S_4), and for their eventual implementation, although the latter was rejected by the attorney general on the basis of its consequences. The president further directed that discussions of the available options should continue in the evening session.

During the second meeting, on the evening of October 16, part of the discussion centered around information gathering (see Figure 5.2). When the president opened the meeting he asked immediately for additional information about the missiles in Cuba. The development of available courses of action had continued, for in the afternoon planning groups had been convened at the State Department and the Pentagon for this purpose. The courses of action raised again included doing nothing (S_1); purely diplomatic actions in the form of various warnings (S_4); and also some additional variants of a limited surprise attack on the missile sites (S_2, S_3, S_6), a full-scale air strike without invasion and blockade (S_5), and open surveillance with a blockade and an ultimatum to Khrushchev (S_7). This session thus shows an increase in the activities around argumentation and solution critique.

Secretaries Rusk and McNamara presented arguments concerning the courses of action considered in their respective groups during the afternoon. Secretary Rusk supported none of these courses of action, while McNamara supported open surveillance and a blockade with an ultimatum to Khrushchev (S_7), without indicating the consequences. Argumentation was frequently interrupted by attempts to show how they should find a solution and by additional information gathered about the Soviets' purposes behind the deployment and the effectiveness of U.S. air strikes.

During the discussion it became clear that no consensus would be achieved as to which alternative should be chosen. General Taylor supported the full-scale air attack (S_5), Secretary McNamara supported the blockade option (S_7), and secretary Rusk rejected all alternatives. President Kennedy had first rejected the quick air strike with a prior warning (S_3), but subsequently in the course of the discussion he came to support it. Having been dissuaded by his advisers, he then reverted to support for a quick air strike without warning (S_2). But this decision of the leader was not immediately accepted by the group.

In this confusion, Secretary McNamara took over the leadership and indicated how the group should proceed to find a solution. He was obviously worried about the group's rather disorganized decision process and urged the members to engage in a more analytic type of decision-making by further elaborating the alternatives with more gradations of military options and by paying special attention to the consequences. This was accepted by the participants.

Since this had all been conducted in informal discussions, the special counsel to the president made a summary of the refined strategies with possible consequences and disagreements about them. According to this summary, the disagreements among participants grew mainly out of deciding under which strategy the Soviet response would be heavier.

When the advisers met the president on October 18, a majority of the participants seemed to support the blockade option while the military advisers and others supported the large-scale air attack. During the discussion, however, opinions began to shift again because, according to Robert Kennedy (1969, 44), "there was no obvious or simple solution. A certainty of viewpoint was not possible. For every position there were inherent weaknesses; and those opposed would point them out, often with devastating effects." In this state of affairs, the president ordered the group to reconvene for the next two days in order to study further details.

DECISION PHASE 2; OCTOBER 19 TO OCTOBER 21, 1962

Meeting of October 19

On October 19, the president was again absent from Washington campaigning, so the planners continued their deliberations without him. Figure 5.3 summarizes the October 19 meeting. The State Department's legal adviser took the minutes of this meeting and Secretary Rusk appears to have chaired it.

At the beginning CIA officials informed the meeting of the most recent intelligence estimates (act 1). Thereafter Secretary Rusk asked information about the legal framework surrounding possible military measures (act 2). The previous day, Robert Kennedy had already given instructions to establish the legal basis for a blockade option. The deputy attorney general, Katzenbach, informed the group that a declaration of war was not needed (act 3). Meeker, the State Department's legal adviser, agreed with Katzenbach but added that a defensive quarantine, as legal advisers preferred to call the blockade, would involve a use of force which had to be considered in relation to the United Nations Charter. For obvious reasons no resolution from the Security Council could be obtained, and therefore, he suggested asking for a resolution from the OAS under the Rio Pact, which did not allow the deployment of offensive weapons in the hemisphere (act 4). He then asked for information on obtaining the necessary two-thirds of votes (act 5). Assistant Secretary of State Martin assured him that they could obtain this within twenty-four hours (act 6). The attorney general then asked whether the president could be sure of the outcome before seeking concurrence, because if he failed, it would put him in an undesirable position (act 7). Martin assured him that a last-minute approach to the heads of state would in any case produce the necessary votes (act 8).

The group then resumed its deliberations about courses of action. An unidentified participant stated that in his opinion yesterday's tentative conclusion was to institute the blockade (S_4) (act 9). General Taylor immediately replied that he did not agree and that the Joint Chiefs of Staff reserved their position (act 10). Bundy then rejected the blockade option (S_4) by arguing that it did not remove the missiles, the effects of it would be felt too slowly, and it would lead to pressures from the United Nations for a negotiated settlement. He supported the air strike on the missiles and key installations (S_3) because it would quickly take out the bases, had the advantage of surprise, and would confront the world with a fait accompli (act 11).

Secretary Rusk then asked Acheson, a former secretary of state, who had been brought in for consultation, for his view (act 12). Acheson also supported the air strike (S_4) because it removed the missiles (act 13). He also informed the meeting that he shared Katzenbach's legal position of self-defense and was

Figure 5.3
October 19, 1962, 11.00 A.M., Meeting of the Executive Committee

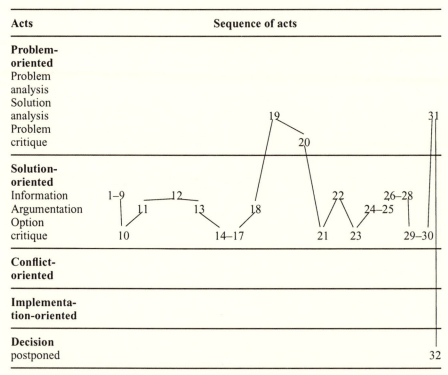

Acts	Sequence of acts
Problem-oriented Problem analysis Solution analysis Problem critique	
Solution-oriented Information Argumentation Option critique	
Conflict-oriented	
Implementation-oriented	
Decision postponed	32

Source: Minutes of the Executive Committee meeting, Oct. 19, 1962, taken by State Department Legal Adviser, Leonard Meeker, in L. Chang and P. Kornbluh, eds., *The Cuban Missile Crisis, 1962,* doc. no. 21, pp. 123–127 (New York: Free Press, 1992).

against involvement of the OAS (act 14). Secretary Dillon also supported the air strike course of action (S_3), as did McCone, head of the CIA, and General Taylor (acts 15, 16 and 17). The latter rejected the blockade (S_4) because it excluded the possibility of an air strike (act 18). He also stated that the decision ought to be made now for the air strike since it would only remain feasible some few days more, after which the missiles would be operational (act 19). Secretary McNamara assured the general that he would give the orders for the necessary dispositions in the event the president decided to do it (act 20). The secretary rejected the air strike (S_3) and confirmed his support for the blockade (S_4) (act 21). Undersecretary of State Ball informed the group that he was wavering between S_3 and S_4. The previous day he had supported S_4 (act 22).

Thereafter the attorney general stated that in his opinion there were three main alternatives. One was doing nothing (S_1), which was unthinkable (act 23). Another one, the air strikes (S_3), he argued would lead to the killing of thousands of

Cubans and many Russians too. It would be a sneak attack, a kind of Pearl Harbor, which was not in the tradition of the United States. The blockade (S_4) left the possibility that the Soviets would pull back from their overextended position, and therefore, he supported it (act 24). The president's national security adviser, Bundy, rejected the blockade option (S_4) since it would not eliminate the missiles and supported the air strike alternative (S_3) because it would do so (act 25). The State Department's legal adviser, Meeker asked the group whom they would expect to govern Cuba after the air strike (act 26). Undersecretary Martin suggested that Castro might be toppled after the air strikes, while other participants remarked that the United States would then have to invade Cuba (acts 27 and 28). Again, other participants indicated that they only wished to eliminate the bases (S_2), which brought Secretary McNamara to reply that this alternative would be militarily unattractive (acts 29 and 30).

Since these discussions obviously did not promote the planning task of the group, Secretary Rusk then analyzed how the group should further perform its task. Since the group did not have to make the decision—rather, the president together with his constitutional advisers did—Rusk suggested that the participants split up into two working groups. One would work out thoroughly the blockade alternative and the other the air strike option and thereafter they would reconvene. Johnson, Gilpatrick, Martin, Nitze, and Meeker worked on the blockade option, while Bundy, Dillon, Acheson, and Taylor concentrated on the air strike alternative (act 31).

When they reconvened at 4 P.M. they first discussed the blockade alternative, making some amendments, and then proceeded in the same way with the air strike option (acts 1 and 2). Figure 5.4 summarizes the acts. Since the minutes of the second part of this meeting (Chang and Kornbluh 1992, 126–127) are less detailed, the substantive group discussion about the two courses of action could, unfortunately, not be studied. The minutes, however, clearly indicate that key advisers, such as Rusk, McNamara, and Robert Kennedy, still favored the blockade option (S_4) (acts 3, 4, and 5). According to the minutes, Secretary Rusk stated that "the United States needed to move in such a way that a planned action would be followed by a pause, in which the great powers could step back from the brink and have time to consider and work out a solution, rather than to be drawn inexorably from one action to another and escalate into general nuclear war" (act 6). Secretary McNamara and the attorney general agreed that the blockade would be the first step but that other subsequent steps such as an air strike were not precluded if the first step did not produce results (acts 7 and 8). In his memoirs (Papp 1990, 234) Secretary Rusk mentioned that the president's national security adviser, Bundy, also finally came around to supporting the blockade option.

Figure 5.4
October 19, 1962, 4:00 P.M., Meeting of the Executive Committee

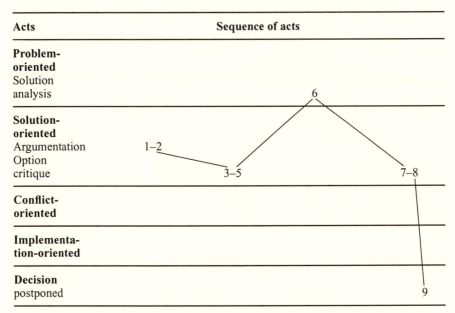

Acts	Sequence of acts
Problem-oriented Solution analysis	
Solution-oriented Argumentation Option critique	
Conflict-oriented	
Implementa-tion-oriented	
Decision postponed	

Source: Minutes of the Executive Committee meeting, Oct. 19, 1962, taken by State
Department Legal Adviser Leonard Meeker, in L. Chang and P. Kornbluh, eds., *The
Cuban Missile Crisis, 1962,* doc. no. 21, pp. 123–127 (New York: Free Press).

The President's Decision, October 20 and 21

On October 20 the planning group met again in the morning. Sorensen had
prepared a draft speech for the president in order to inform the public about the
situation. This speech was amended and approved during the morning session.
Secretary McNamara then gave orders for the preparation of the air strike and the
blockade in order to leave the decision open to the president.

At 2:30 the meeting between the entire group of planners and the president
took place. According to his memoirs (Papp 1990, 234), Secretary Rusk was
asked to begin with his recommendation. He had written a note considering the
consequences, read it to the audience, and then offered it to the president. But the
president refused it and indicated that "he did not want anything in writing from
this meeting." Schlesinger (1967, 738) reports that Kennedy's reason was "that
he did not want people, if things went wrong, claiming that their plans would
have worked." Next Secretary McNamara presented his arguments for the
blockade and others for the military option (Kennedy 1969, 48). Schlesinger
(1967) also reports that a straw vote indicated that eleven participants were for
the blockade and six, military advisers supported by some civilians, were for the
air strike.

Although there exist no minutes of this meeting, the arguments of proponents and opponents of the blockade and air strike presented to the president must have been similar to those summarized in Table 5.1. The arguments of proponents of the blockade and opponents of the air strike are derived from a summary of consequences made by Sorensen (Chang and Kornbluh 1992, October 20, no. 23, p. 133), and the arguments of opponents of the blockade and proponents of the air strike are derived from a CIA report on this matter (Chang and Kornbluh 1992, October 20, no. 24, pp. 134–143).

Proponents of the blockade option thought that this alternative was the least likely to lead to a nuclear war. Further, it was possible that the Soviets would remove the missiles, but it was also possible that they would not. In this case an air attack was not precluded and at least the United States would not then destroy its moral position throughout the world. Opponents of the blockade were certain that the buildup would continue. In their opinion, it was highly likely that the Soviets would compel the United States to desist, that the allies would disagree with the United States, that the Cuban regime would not be brought down, and that the Soviets would threaten with retaliations in Berlin such as harassments, interruptions of access to the city, or even a blockade. A less likely outcome would be that the Soviets would compel them to desist, the allies would disagree with them, the Cuban regime would not be brought down, but no retaliation would occur in Berlin or elsewhere. The last possibility, although it was very unlikely, was that the Soviets would use force.

The supporters of the air strike (Table 5.1) were certain that by this means the missiles could be eliminated and that U.S. forces could then quickly invade Cuba, which would most likely not lead to a nuclear war and probably not to Soviet retaliations elsewhere; it was even more likely that there would be no retaliations at all. The opponents of this strategy, on the contrary, foresaw that it would destroy the moral position of the United States throughout the world and that the subsequent invasion might lead to a nuclear war or at least to retaliations elsewhere in the world.

At the end of this meeting the president instructed Sorensen to redraft the blockade speech, although he indicated that he would make his final decision about the course of action to be implemented after speaking to the air force officials the next morning.

The next day the president met with the air force officials. The attorney general, General Taylor, the director of the CIA, and the secretary of defense were also present. The latter made notes of this meeting which provide an accurate picture of the discussion (Chang and Kornbluh 1992, no. 25, pp. 144–145). Figure 5.5 summarizes the decision-making process of this meeting. The secretary of defense informed the president of preparations for the invasion of Cuba after the air attacks and the most recent intelligence estimate of the amount and location of missiles deployed in Cuba (act 1). The director of the CIA, McCone, added that on the basis of the trips of a specific Soviet vessel, they estimated that eighty missiles were on the island, although they had only located

Table 5.1
Major Arguments of Proponents and Opponents of the Two Available Courses of Action

Outcomes considered by	Courses of action	
	A naval blockade	**A major air strike**
Proponents	• Least likely: a nuclear war • Possible: Soviets remove the missiles • Possible: Soviets do not remove the missiles and we have to initiate a major air strike. In this case the U.S. moral position is ensured.	• Almost excluded: a nuclear war • Certain: weapons eliminated Less likely: Soviets retaliate in Berlin or elsewhere • More likely: no Soviet retaliations
Opponents	• Certain: buildup continues • Very likely: Soviets compel U.S. to desist, adverse reactions from allies, Cuban regime not brought down, Soviets threaten retaliations in Berlin or elsewhere • Less likely: Soviets compel U.S. to desist, adverse reactions from allies, no Soviet threats of retaliations elsewhere • Very unlikely: Soviets use force	• Certain: would be considered as a U.S.-initiated Pearl Harbor attack and would lead to an invasion • Possible: a nuclear war • Possible: no nuclear war, but other responses in kind

thirty (act 2). Thereafter General Sweeney outlined the kind of air attacks they would need to destroy the known missiles, which indeed constituted a major air attack on missile sites, storage sites, and aircraft with a subsequent invasion (act 3). General Sweeney then spoke about the expected result of the air attacks and mentioned that it was unlikely that they could destroy all the known missiles; they could destroy probably 90 percent or less of those known (act 4).

The president then directed that an air strike be prepared in order to be able to carry it out the next or the following day (act 5). He also acknowledged that the secretary of defense was opposed to such an attack while General Sweeney supported it (act 6). He then asked the opinions of the attorney general and the director of the CIA (act 7). The attorney general again strongly opposed an air

Figure 5.5
October 21, 1962, 11:30 A.M., Meeting with the President

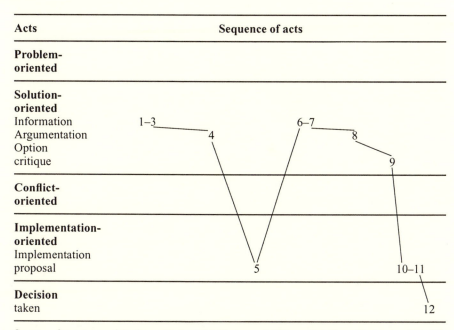

Acts	Sequence of acts
Problem-oriented	
Solution-oriented Information Argumentation Option critique	
Conflict-oriented	
Implementation-oriented Implementation proposal	
Decision taken	

Source: Secretary of Defense Robert McNamara, Military Briefing, Notes on Oct. 21, 1962 meeting with the president, in L. Chang and P. Kornbluh, eds., *The Cuban Missile Crisis, 1962,* doc. no. 25, pp.144–145 (New York: Free Press, 1992).

attack and repeated that it would be a Pearl Harbor kind of attack with unpredictable Soviet responses, one of which could possibly be a general nuclear war (act 8). McCone agreed with Robert Kennedy but emphasized that they should be prepared anyway for a major air attack with an invasion (acts 9 and 10). The president then ordered the initiation of a blockade (act 11). According to Robert Kennedy (1969, 48), General Sweeney's information that even a major air attack could not destroy all the nuclear weapons in Cuba finally settled the president's doubt that an air attack could eventually remove them, while a blockade at least reduced drastically the chances of a nuclear war.

Summary of Decision Phase 2

In this phase the alternatives were more or less narrowed down to two options, that is, the large-scale air strike (S_3), where the subsequent invasion was not explicitly mentioned in the minutes, and the blockade together with OAS action (S_4). First, participants exchanged detailed information about the legal frameworks surrounding both options (Figure 5.3). Then they engaged partially in argumentation and in supporting or rejecting specific options. The solution-oriented acts dominated this phase, which is quite normal in view of the task of the advisers. Although there was a difference in opinion among them, no conflict-oriented phase occurred, probably because their task was not to make the decision but to furnish available solutions.

Finally the president's key advisers all came to support the blockade, while other advisers, mostly those in the military, were in favor of a large-scale air attack with an invasion. It is typical of this type of decision unit that the key advisers did not seek a compromise with the military advisers. This must again be due to the fact that decision-making was not their task. The president thus had to choose in an analytical way between two options which were presented together with arguments.

CONCLUSIONS

This decision process clearly shows that the ultimate decision-maker was the president. From the above, it is obvious that the president was sensitive to his environment. Although expressing several times his own choice (at the end of the first session and during the second and last session), he finally complied with the suggestions of his key advisers to allow the study of alternatives to continue and he chose the strategy recommended by the majority of his key advisers.

An examination of the sequence of the interaction processes during the meetings shows that the first four sessions alternated between solution- and problem-oriented stages, where the number of solution-oriented interactions overruled slightly the problem-oriented ones. The last session centered on the solution and ended with an implementation phase. These interaction processes appear quite logical given the task of the advisers.

The advisory group in this decision unit had as its task to prepare available courses of action with consequences for the president. When disagreement occurred among the participants about which course of action should be preferred and the decision-making process threatened to become a cybernetic one with members neglecting the consideration of consequences because they disagreed about them, the leaders of the group (such as the secretary of defense and the secretary of state) again directed the process in the direction of an analytic type by instructing proponents of a specific course of action to work it out in more detail and then let it be criticized by its opponents in order to refine it. The advisers thus provided the president with two fully worked-out alternatives.

A majority of advisers, among them his key advisers, had indicated their preference for the blockade option. On the basis of this information the president made his choice and finally chose a relatively cautious, incremental alternative which could be adjusted at a later date if necessary. No preference aggregation rule was therefore needed (proposition 2, Chapter 2). Given the task of the advisory group in this decision-making unit, conflict-oriented phases were completely absent (proposition 3, Chapter 2). They neither had to make compromises nor did they have to engage in conflict management.

Our findings from this study corroborate results from earlier systematic empirical research on this topic (Anderson 1983, 1987; Purkitt 1992) that summarized the decision-making process as a satisfying one, that is, the advisers focused on understanding the nature of the immediate task and tried to find an appropriate answer to the issue. However, we do not agree with Purkitt (1992, 221) that this decision-making process did not differ from more routine decision-making, unless systematic empirical research can demonstrate that.

The reader will be aware that we did not study all decisions involved in the Cuban missile crisis since the first part seemed adequate to illustrate the decision-making in this specific unit.

Chapter 6

The Austro-Hungarian Cabinet Decision to Initiate World War I

In this chapter we will present a qualitative analysis of the decision-making process where a homogeneous or single group is the ultimate decision unit. As an example, we have taken the Austro-Hungarian cabinet's crisis decision to declare war on Serbia in August 1914 because of the latter's involvement in the assassination of the Austro-Hungarian heir to the throne.

Before we study the group decision-making process of members of the Common Austro-Hungarian council of ministers, some words about this institution would seem to be in order. In 1867 Hungary had obtained a parity position in the internal and external affairs of the dual monarchy that led to the foundation of a Common council of ministers. The chairman of this institution was the Common foreign minister, who was formally responsible to the Common parliament and to the Austrian emperor and Hungarian king. The latter acted as head of state. Other Common ministers were the ministers of war and finance. Although the Common minister of foreign affairs was very powerful, for decisions he needed the consent of at least one of the prime ministers, the Austrian or the Hungarian, who therefore were also members of the Common cabinet (see also Komjáthy 1966; Sked 1992). Historians (e.g., Komjáthy 1966, 50–59) mention that the members of this group had mainly identical interests concerning foreign affairs because they all belonged to the ruling establishment of the dual monarchy. This means that this group qualifies as homogeneous but hierarchical since the Common foreign minister was the leader and the two prime ministers, who might eventually have special loyalties to the parts of the empire they represented, carried more weight in the decision-making process than the remaining Common ministers.

In Chapter 2 we postulated that if such a homogeneous group has to make a decision and one of the prominent members proposes an argument in favor of a course of action (step 2) which is acceptable to all participants, there is no need for further discussion and a consensus can be taken immediately (step 3). However, if there is initial disagreement about the option to be selected, but a strong informal leader or an influential subgroup is present, then consensus may be reached after applying a mixture of persuasion, compromise, and coercion. When the latter occurs the process becomes similar to that of the multiple autonomous group.

But before we study this group process, the political situation in which the decisions took place will be briefly summarized.

POLITICAL BACKGROUND

Since the second half of the nineteenth century the foreign policy of the Austro-Hungarian monarchy had been aimed at reducing the threat of Balkan nationalism and Russian-inspired Pan-Slavism in this region in order to protect the Habsburg territories of Croatia-Slavonia and Dalmatia. In 1878 the great powers had even agreed that Austria-Hungary occupy the territories of Bosnia-Herzegovina, which were annexed in 1908. In the view of Austria-Hungary, this was necessary to protect its territories in this region from attacks by Serbs or Pan-Slavs supported by Russians. After 1903 the Serbs changed their policy of good relations with Austria for an anti-Austrian policy with the aim of constructing a southern Slavic state under the leadership of Serbia with the consent of Russia; however, the Serbs had no agreement with Russia for military assistance in the event of a war with the dual monarchy.

When the Austro-Hungarian heir to the throne and his wife were assassinated in the Bosnian capital of Sarajevo on June 28, 1914, by Bosnian students who had apparently been supported by Serbia, the dual monarchy felt threatened in its great-power status in the Balkans and in its prestige for the future. Since neither the finances nor the army of the monarchy was capable of enduring a long war with Serbia, the monarchy first discussed the matter with Germany, its ally. Germany quickly offered its military support and encouraged Austria-Hungary to declare war on Serbia. Nevertheless, the responsible decision-makers still hesitated, with a month elapsing between the assassination and the declaration of war, since they anticipated difficulties if the hostilities spread: a war with Serbia could easily involve Russia, and Russia's ally France could also take sides. On the other hand, what would happen with the monarchy's other allies, Italy and Rumania, who were not considered very reliable?

DECISION PHASE 1; JUNE 28 TO JULY 7, 1914

One of the first steps the Common minister of foreign affairs undertook after the assassination of the heir to the throne was to secure Germany's military support in the event of war with Serbia, which was assumed to have supported this crime. The Germans indeed proved reliable allies, for as early as July 6 the minister of foreign affairs got their assurance of military support; they even encouraged him to declare war immediately on Serbia (Geiss 1963, no. 27, p. 93).

July 7, Morning Meeting

On July 7, therefore, a first meeting of the Common council of ministers was convened to discuss the further details. All relevant specialists were present: the Common minister of foreign affairs as chairman, both the Hungarian and the Austrian prime ministers, the Common minister of finance, and the Common minister of war. The group, consisting of five decision-makers, was thus quite small. Figure 6.1 summarizes the group process of this meeting.

Opening the meeting, the chairman reported having received the unconditional military support of Germany in the event of war (act 1). In his opinion, two strategies were available to them, for which he considered the likely consequences. If they should do nothing in response to the assassination (S_1), the states in the Balkans would certainly interpret this as a sign of weakness in the monarchy and join with Russia against Austria-Hungary. Since this outcome was negative he rejected this strategy. But if they were to declare war immediately on Serbia (S_2), it would be possible with the support of Germany to reverse the negative development in the Balkans by restoring the monarchy's prestige. On the basis of the perceived favorable outcome, he opted for this strategy (act 2).

Then the Hungarian prime minister took the floor and stated that the results of the investigations in Bosnia brought them closer to war with Serbia (act 3). However, he rejected an immediate declaration of war (S_2) because, in his opinion, it was more likely that the Balkan states would become their enemies and they would then need to fight indefinitely against Russia. He developed another strategy (S_3), however, which he supported on the basis of the consequences he foresaw. He argued that they could deliver an ultimatum to Serbia, with heavy but feasible demands and only in the event of nonacceptance initiate war without the aim to destroy Serbia entirely. It was then quite likely that Serbia would accept their demands, which would lead to the restoration of the monarchy's prestige in the Balkans and to the humiliation of Serbia (act 4). He also communicated to the participants that, in his opinion, Germany had not the right to decide whether and when the monarchy should initiate war with Serbia, and he discussed further the political situation in the Balkans (act 5). If the monarchy initiated war on Serbia it also would have to defend its Hungarian borders with troops since Rumania could use this situation to annex parts of Hungary. But if they should succeed with the ultimatum (S_3), Germany could continue with its alliance plans with Bulgaria and Turkey, which might also induce Rumania to become again a member of the triple entente and to forgo its annexation plans. He also expected that in the long run, Germany would have more troops to deploy against Russia because France would be less dangerous as a result of a severe decline in birth rates. He therefore again supported S_3 (act 6).

In reaction to the Hungarian prime minister, the Common minister of foreign affairs then gave the participants his opinion of past diplomatic successes with Serbia and stated that they were only of brief duration, after which the negative propaganda against the monarchy was resumed (act 7). He also denied the danger from Rumania for the monarchy, presenting specific evidence, and rejected the idea that Germany would later have more troops available against Russia since the Russian troops would always be more numerous than the German troops (act 8). He then rejected the Hungarian prime minister's preferred strategy (S_3) by arguing that their relations with Serbia would become even tenser. He again supported S_2, the immediate declaration of war, because in his opinion and contrary to the Hungarian prime minister's opinion, the probability was quite low that the Balkan states would become their enemies (act 9).

The Austrian prime minister then took the floor and reminded his colleagues that they had first intended in this session to discuss what measures should be taken in Bosnia because of the assassination and the Serbian propaganda against the monarchy. But since the governor of Bosnia had reported that no internal measures would be effective if they did not take immediate measures against Serbia, the topic of discussion was changed (act 10). He then proposed in general terms how they should proceed. In his opinion, they should investigate whether a military initiative could solve the problem and if this were found to be so, they should keep in mind that the necessary German support was offered now but that there could be no guarantee that Germany would provide it at a later date (act 11). He continued his argument as follows.

If they were to do nothing (S_1), they would certainly lose their provinces in the Balkans. On the basis of the consequences he foresaw, he rejected this strategy. If they delivered an ultimatum to Serbia with heavy but feasible demands, and initiated war only in the event of nonacceptance (S_3), he was certain that an eventual diplomatic success would not improve the monarchy's position in the Balkans. On the basis of the evaluation of this consequence he rejected the alternative put forward by his Hungarian colleague (act 12). He then stated that he himself could support an immediate declaration of war (S_2) but since his Hungarian colleague was against it, he suggested a compromise solution (S_4) which he then elaborated (acts 13 and 14). If they were to deliver an ultimatum to Serbia with demands that were not feasible and then initiated war (S_4), he was certain that with German support they would restore law and order in the Balkans (act 15). In his view, the restoration of law and order could only be achieved by war, and they could only wage war with the military support of Germany, which was now urging them to go to war, but which might deny military support at a later date (act 16). He then asked his colleagues to accept this compromise solution (act 17), but none of the participants responded to this proposal.

The Common minister of finance then entered the debate and began to discuss a completely new strategy, namely, to reorganize Bosnia thoroughly from the interior (S_5) (act 18). He rejected this strategy as not viable because of the Serbian population in Bosnia, which could not possibly be divided into loyalists and Serbian nationalists; therefore, no measures could be taken (act 19). He also

Figure 6.1
July 7, Morning Meeting of the Common Council of Ministers

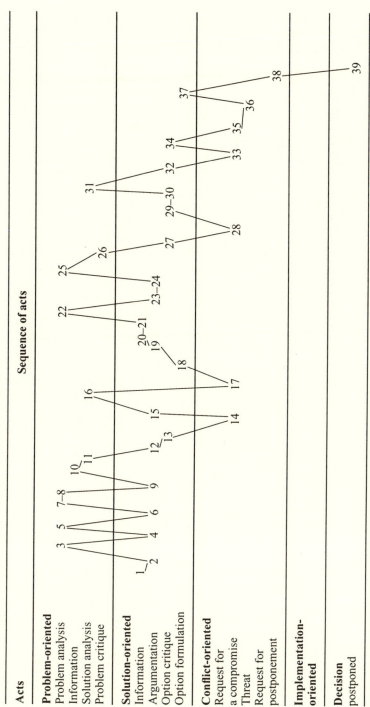

Source: Minutes of a meeting of the Common Council of Ministers of the Austro-Hungarian monarchy, July 7, 1914, in M. Komjáthy, ed., *Protokolle des Gemeinsamen Ministerrates der Österreichisch-Ungarischen Monarchie (1914–1918)*, no. 1, pp. 141–148 (Budapest: Akadémiai Kiadó, 1966).

rejected the ultimatum with heavy but feasible demands (S_3), which was preferred by the Hungarian prime minister, since a diplomatic success would not improve the monarchy's position in the Balkans (act 20). In his opinion, the only viable option was to declare war immediately (S_2) because Serbs were only susceptible to force (act 21).

The Hungarian prime minister again entered the discussion and told his colleagues that in his opinion the civil administration in Bosnia was very disorderly because the police did not arrest potential criminals who were present on the streets when the assassination occurred. He now voiced his support for S_5—to reorganize the administration in Bosnia—as a viable solution, since it would improve the monarchy's position in Bosnia (acts 22 and 23).

Subsequently, the Common minister of war gave his view. He rejected S_3, using the same argument that most of his colleagues had previously put forward, namely, that a diplomatic success had no value for the monarchy. To do nothing (S_1) would be considered as a sign of weakness, and the agitation against the monarchy would increase. He then gave his support for S_2, the immediate declaration of war. Russian troops were not currently at the ready because of the harvest, so that immediate action would bring military advantage (act 24).

Till now all of the ministers apart from the Hungarian prime minister had given their support for S_2, the strategy proposed by the chairman, the Common minister of foreign affairs. All ministers had also explained their choice by giving full arguments.

The participants then began a discussion of their war aims and agreed with the Hungarian prime minister (last part of S_3) that the aim would not be to destroy Serbia entirely, but only to diminish it, since Russia would not tolerate a destruction of this country (acts 25 and 26). Thereafter they unanimously supported delivering an ultimatum to Serbia with nonfeasible demands and initiating war with Serbia without the aim of destroying it (S_4), the slightly modified compromise option the Austrian prime minister had earlier proposed (act 27). The Hungarian prime minister then took this opportunity to call again for compromise with his preferred option (S_3) by mentioning the danger of a European war, which would be the consequence of the immediate declaration of war on Serbia (S_4). He claimed that applying S_3 might postpone the war to a later date when the political constellation of the Balkans might be more favorable to the monarchy (acts 28 and 29).

The Common minister of foreign affairs, however, again rejected S_3, repeating the argument that no diplomatic success would improve the monarchy's position in the Balkans and beyond that, they had to act now, since the vital interests of the monarchy were threatened (acts 30 and 31). He then voiced his support for S_4, to deliver an ultimatum to Serbia with nonfeasible demands and then to initiate war, the compromise alternative earlier introduced by the Austrian prime minister (act 32). He also asked his colleagues to support this option, which apart from the Hungarian prime minister, they did (acts 33 and 34).

This attempt to make a concession to the Hungarian prime minister thus failed again. The latter then announced that he too wished to make a concession and developed another compromise option, S_6, for which he asked support, and he threatened that if his point of view were not taken into account, conflict would ensue (acts 35 and 36). This option consisted of delivering an ultimatum to Serbia which had nonfeasible demands, but which was formulated in such a way that the intention would not be clear, and then to initiate war without the aim of the entire destruction of Serbia (act 37).

Having heard this proposal, the ministers decided to postpone further deliberations till after the lunch break (acts 38 and 39). This postponement may also be considered as tension management in response to the threats of conflict by the Hungarian prime minister.

It is interesting to note that when the compromise alternatives were introduced at the end of the session, the argumentation phase was finished; that is, the analytic approach was replaced by a cybernetic one (Maoz 1990). Neither the Common minister of foreign affairs nor the Hungarian prime minister considered consequences for the compromise alternatives S_4 and S_6, which might reflect their different views on the likely outcomes. In this way they allowed the opponent mentally to fill in whatever consequences he wished in order to reduce conflict.

However, it may also be inferred that the compromise option S_4 might lead to the same results as S_2, according to the Common minister of foreign affairs, namely, to war with the support of Germany and to the reversal of the negative development in the Balkans. The Hungarian prime minister, on the other hand, may have thought that S_4 would lead with certainty to a European war (see his evaluation of S_3) and may therefore have put forward the other compromise proposal, S_6. S_6 differs only slightly from S_4 with respect to the formulation of the nonfeasible demands and the explicit statement not to destroy Serbia entirely, which was already implicitly agreed upon during the discussion by his colleagues. It may be inferred that by this option he thought to localize the war.

We also see that this principally homogeneous group strives for consensus. The opposition of the Hungarian prime minister was therefore a problem. It seems that this striving for consensus is so strong a norm that the Hungarian prime minister can even use it as a threat to force the others to accept his proposal. Given these problems, a postponement of the decision was necessary.

July 7, Afternoon Meeting

When the meeting resumed in the afternoon (Figure 6.2), the chief of the general staff and the deputy of the commander of the navy were also present to provide information about military matters. The calling in of military expertise can also be considered as an attempt to resolve the conflict between the Hungarian prime minister and the remaining ministers. The Common minister of war asked the military advisers if it would be possible to mobilize first only against Serbia and later, if necessary, against Russia too. He also asked them if they could concentrate troops on the border with Rumania in order to discourage this country from annexing parts of the monarchy; and finally where they should initiate war with Russia, if necessary (act 1). The chief of the general staff then provided the necessary information and thereafter the participants discussed the potential courses of a European war, the details of which were not reported in the minutes because of their highly secretive nature (acts 2 and 3). A brainstorming session then ensued about possible demands on Serbia (act 4).

After this discussion the Hungarian prime minister again repeated his preference for S_3 to avoid a war and appealed in vain to his colleagues to accommodate his view (acts 5 and 6). Closing the session, the Common minister of foreign affairs stated that although there was still a difference in the views between the majority of the ministers, who supported S_4, and the Hungarian prime minister, who preferred S_3, their views had come closer during the discussion because it was agreed that his strategy would also probably lead to war (acts 7 and 8). This noting of similarities in opposing positions was again obviously an attempt to manage the tensions.

The Common minister of foreign affairs then mentioned that he would report to the emperor the view of the majority. At the request of the Hungarian prime minister a note containing the view of the latter would also be brought to the attention of the emperor (acts 9, 10, 11, and 12).

Summary of Decision Phase 1

We have seen that in this homogeneous group there was one dissenter, namely, the Hungarian prime minister. It seemed that the chairman tried to solve the conflict by introducing new information about the military situation and the possible consequences of some courses of action. However, this move did not work because the opposing minister stuck to his position, and conflict management was needed. A last effort was made by the chairman with his suggestion that they had become closer since they all expected war.

DECISION PHASE 2; JULY 14 TO JULY 19, 1914

On July 9 the Common minister of foreign affairs reported the majority advice of the council of ministers to the emperor, who agreed with it (Geiss 1963, no. 66, pp. 144–145). The emperor was also informed in a note of the view of the Hungarian prime minister, but did not share his opinion. Meanwhile, the formulation of the demands in the ultimatum to Serbia had to be completed. The minister of foreign affairs therefore put much effort into persuading the Hungarian prime minister to adopt the view of the majority. Legally a unanimous decision was not necessary, but in practice it would be difficult to go to war when the head of government of the other part of the monarchy disagreed with this decision. There were several meetings between the minister of foreign affairs, the Austrian prime minister, and the Hungarian prime minister, but no minutes were kept.

Figure 6.2
July 7, Afternoon Meeting of the Common Council of Ministers

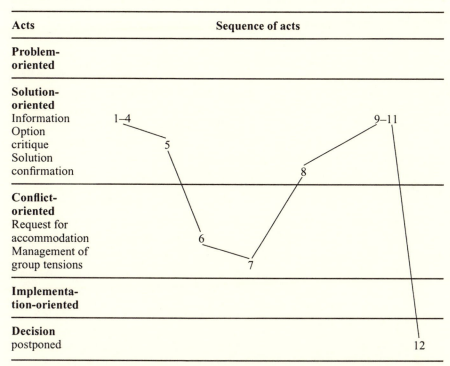

Source: Minutes of a meeting of the Common Council of Ministers of the Austro-Hungarian monarchy, July 7, 1914, in M. Komjáthy, ed., *Protokolle des Gemeinsamen Ministerrates der Österreichisch-Ungarischen Monarchie (1914–1918)*, no. 1, pp. 148–150 (Budapest: Akadémiai Kiadó, 1966).

On July 14 the minister of foreign affairs could report to the emperor that the Hungarian prime minister now agreed to their point of view (Geiss 1963, no. 86, pp. 160–161) under the condition that the cabinet unanimously agree not to incorporate Serbian territory into the monarchy, apart from some minor border corrections. This choice was very close to the compromise the Hungarian prime minister had proposed at the end of the morning meeting on July 7 (Figure 6.1, S_6) which at that time had not been discussed further.

The same day the Hungarian prime minister met the German ambassador (Geiss 1963, no. 91, pp. 164–165) and stated that he was now convinced that war was necessary. On July 19 the definitive version of the ultimatum would be formulated. It would be phrased in such a way that its unconditional acceptance was impossible, and Austria-Hungary would submit it to Serbia after the departure of the French president from St. Petersburg so that the Russians could not immediately discuss possible reactions with their ally.

July 19, Meeting of the Common Council of Ministers

At the beginning of this meeting (Figure 6.3) the Common minister of foreign affairs presented the definitive text of the ultimatum to Serbia, which was accepted by the ministers (acts 1 and 2). It contained very harsh demands: the renouncing by the Serbian government of the Pan-Slavic movement, a purge of elements hostile to the Austro-Hungarian monarchy in the army, the civil service, and the press, and the dissolution of anti-Austrian secret organizations. It also demanded that officials of the Austro-Hungarian monarchy should take part in the investigations of the assassination.

The Common minister of foreign affairs then announced that because of German pressure to begin war as quickly as possible, the ultimatum should be handed to the Serbs very soon, on July 23 at 5 P.M., with a deadline for the answer of forty-eight hours (act 3). These points were also accepted by the participants of the meeting (act 4). Subsequently the Hungarian prime minister communicated to his colleagues that in the event of a premature leak of the ultimatum in Hungary, he would have to give a statement to the parliament, which was accepted by the council (acts 5 and 6).

Then the general chief of staff, who was also present at the meeting, gave information about military matters (act 7). Following that the Hungarian prime minister requested the other members to declare unanimously that the aim of the war was not the incorporation of parts of Serbia into the monarchy, the condition on which his consent to delivering an ultimatum with nonfeasible demands and initiating war (S_7) (acts 8 and 9) depended. The Common minister of foreign affairs replied with support for this condition, but with some reserve, explaining that in the given situation, if they won the war it would not be useful to incorporate Serbian territory but rather to distribute parts of the territory to neighboring countries such as Bulgaria, Greece, and Albania. But if the situation changed and Russia had, for instance, succeeded in Bulgaria in replacing the government friendly to the monarchy with a hostile one, incorporation of Serbian territory into the monarchy might be deemed necessary (act 10).

The Hungarian prime minister was obviously not satisfied with this reply. He again asked his colleagues to stick together and even threatened conflict if they could not agree with this condition (acts 11 and 12). He further argued that this strategy (S_7) was reasonable, and that the aim not to annex Serbia should be announced publicly at the initiation of war because it would improve the monarchy's international position. If they delivered the ultimatum and initiated war without such a statement (S_4), it would not only be nationally unacceptable in Hungary, but it would also worsen the monarchy's international position. Russia, in particular, could enter the war for this (act 13).

The Common minister of foreign affairs then replied that he already intended to make this declaration (act 14). The Austrian prime minister then gave his consent, mentioning that in any case it allowed the present Serbian dynasty to be replaced later by another, and so did the remaining ministers (acts 15 and 16). At

Figure 6.3
July 19, Meeting of the Common Council of Ministers

Acts	Sequence of acts
Problem-oriented	

Solution-oriented
Solution confirmation
Information
Option formulation
Option critique
Argumentation

Conflict-oriented
Request for unity
Threat

Implementation-oriented
Implementation proposal

Decision taken

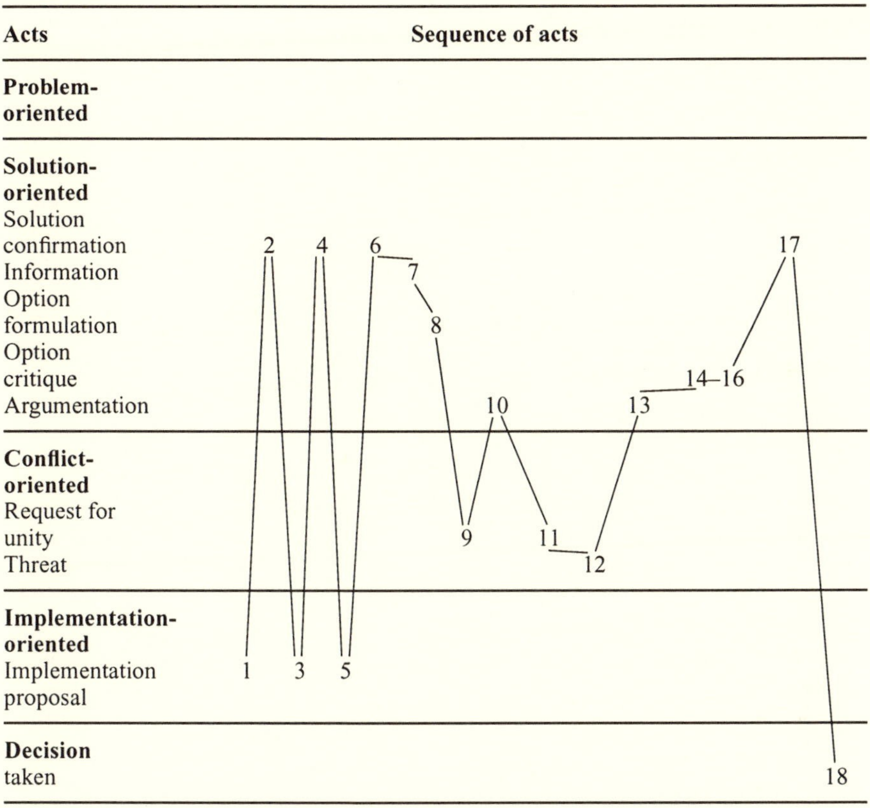

Source: Minutes of a meeting of the Common Council of Ministers of the Austro-Hungarian monarchy, July 19, 1914, in M. Komjáthy, ed., *Protokolle des Gemeinsamen Ministerrates der Österreichisch-Ungarischen Monarchie (1914–1918)*, no. 2, pp. 150–154 (Budapest: Akadémiai Kiadó, 1966).

the end of the meeting the Common minister of foreign affairs summarized that they had reached a unanimous agreement (act 17).

The result of this meeting on July 19 was that the Austro-Hungarian cabinet had unanimously decided to deliver an ultimatum to Serbia with nonfeasible demands, in order to initiate war without the aim of incorporating Serbia into the monarchy. As it turned out, the decision was fatal, leading to a world war, which the decision-makers had not anticipated in previous meetings, apart from the Hungarian prime minister (act 18).

Subsequent events followed each other very rapidly (see Bihl 1989). On July 23 the ultimatum was handed to the Serbian government. The Austro-Hungarian ambassador in Belgrade had instructions to demand "pure and simple" acceptance in order to secure war (Geiss 1963, no. 156, p. 237). On July 24 Britain proposed a European mediation effort between Austria-Hungary and Russia which was rejected by the Germans on July 28. On July 27, after the Serbian answer, diplomatic relations between Austria-Hungary and Serbia were broken off and the declaration of war followed on July 28. Britain again tried in vain to mediate on July 29 and proposed that Austria-Hungary should halt hostile activities after the occupation of Belgrade and that its differences with Russia should be solved at the negotiating table. Thereafter, mobilizations and declarations of war followed each other.

Summary of Decision Phase 2

Because the chairman had worked out a compromise with the sole dissenter in a private meeting, the last official cabinet meeting focused on the confirmation of some details such as the presentation and acceptance of the text and procedures concerning the ultimatum. The beginning of the meeting went quite smoothly, with everybody consenting to the ultimatum. But then the Hungarian prime minister demanded that, in exchange for his consent to the earlier matters, the other members should clearly give their consent to his demand to announce that the war aim was not to annex Serbia. While other members maintained silence, the Common minister of foreign affairs spoke up and gave his consent with some reservation, reviewing some possible political constellations in the future. Since this provoked the anger of the Hungarian prime minister, who threatened to withdraw his earlier consent on the other matters, the Common minister of foreign affairs quickly complied with his demand, probably out of fear of disrupting the achieved consensus. We see again how strong in this so-called homogeneous group is the implicit norm with respect to consensus, although legally a majority decision would be sufficient. The strength of this norm seems to be a source of conflict-oriented behavior which we have not seen in the other decision units previously described.

CONCLUSIONS

This case study shows how a small group of specialists in a crisis situation arrived at a strategic decision. They first tried to convince each other by argument, after which they moved from the analytic to the cybernetic approach, that is, looking for compromises without detailed discussion of the consequences. When this approach also failed to lead to the required consensus, the leader of the group postponed the decision and tried to convince the sole dissenter in separate meetings, leading to an acceptable compromise. However, the dissenter, a high-status member, although he had consented to a compromise option, challenged the achieved consensus again in the last session, by altering this option and asking for explicit unanimous agreement. It is clear that he did this on substantive grounds in order to minimize the chances of a European war.

Although the decision process can be classified in the beginning as being of an analytic type, the consideration of consequences was not too thorough. The choice was primarily based on a consideration of the most likely short-term outcome: a localized war to restore law and order in the Balkans. This restoration could not have been achieved by doing nothing or by reorganizing the area. However, the less likely consequence of a European war was not considered in any depth. Furthermore, no contingency planning was made since they seemed to believe in the strength and wisdom of their German ally. It seems that this "homogeneous" small group avoided this debate, although the issue of a large-scale war was introduced by the Hungarian prime minister. Possibly they felt too confident with the support of Germany.

A new phenomenon in this case study is the occurrence of conflict. In the case of a predominant leader like Hitler, conflict could not occur without serious consequences for the persons involved. They therefore refrained. In the case of the predominant but open leader Kennedy, the group preparing the meetings had no basis for conflict because its task was not to arrive at a common conclusion. They only had to prepare reasonable alternatives with consequences for the predominant leader, who would make the decision.

Finally, the homogeneous small group can come quickly to a decision or can have longer debates, even with conflict, as shown in this chapter, because of the requirement for consensus (see proposition 4, Chapter 2).

The next chapter deals with the decision-making process in a multiple autonomous unit, a coalition cabinet, where we will see that the efforts to build consensus were much greater.

Chapter 7

The Dutch Cabinet Decision to Take Military Action in Indonesia, Autumn 1948: Consensual Decision-Making in a Heterogeneous Group

In this chapter, the decision-making process in a multiple autonomous unit, a coalition cabinet, will be studied. The case study concerns the second Dutch military intervention in Indonesia in 1948 and illustrates crisis decision-making in the Dutch cabinet. The Dutch cabinet consisted mainly of a coalition between the Labor and Confessional parties, plus one Liberal minister and two Independents. The prime minister was a member of Labor and the vice prime minister a member of the Roman Catholic party. It is thus an example of a multiple autonomous group where no party has a majority either in the cabinet or in parliament so that parties depend on each other in decision-making. Since the participants will frequently disagree about preferences, decision-making in such a group will take much longer to achieve a consensus. They will also adopt several procedures to cope with disagreement, such as postponing the decision in order to collect further information, or holding discussions in smaller groups, or shifting from argumentation to a search for a course of action acceptable to all of them. The latter might be a compromise and/or a course of action which deviates only marginally from the status quo. But before we study this group process, the political situation in which the decisions took place will be briefly summarized.

POLITICAL BACKGROUND

During World War II, the Dutch East Indies (subsequently Indonesia) were occupied by Japan. After Japan's capitulation to the Allies in 1945, Indonesian nationalist leaders proclaimed the independence of the Republic of Indonesia. Their government exercised its authority primarily on the most densely populated and most economically developed islands of Java and Sumatra. When the Dutch returned they regained control mainly of the outlying islands apart from Java and Sumatra. They soon developed a plan to reorganize the archipelago on a federal basis comprising four equally autonomous areas, that is, Java, Sumatra, Borneo, and the Great East (including the remaining islands) which would become sovereign after an interim period in which the Dutch would exercise power, and form the United States of Indonesia. The latter would, after obtaining sovereignty, be linked with the kingdom of the Netherlands by a union headed by the queen, which would look after joint interests such as foreign relations and defense.

This program of principles constituted the main body of the Linggadjati agreement between the Netherlands and the republic signed in March 1947. However, subsequent talks on the implementation of the program made no progress and between May and July 1947 the negotiations reached a deadlock. Each side had attempted to put its primary objective forward: the Dutch wanted to create a federal state which would diminish the position and role of the republic, while the republic was aiming at the hegemony of the Indonesian archipelago.

On July 20, 1947, the Dutch took military measures against the republic, the so-called "first police action," in order to create conditions of law and order that would permit the implementation of the Linggadjati program. Since the military action did not lead, as expected, to quick cooperation between the Indonesians and the Dutch, the Dutch authorities seriously considered occupying the republican capital of Jocjacarta, in order to destroy the republic as a political entity. The intervention of the United Nations Security Council in August 1947, however, averted the destruction of the republic.

Subsequently, a Good Offices Committee (GOC) was set up by the Security Council to assist both parties in working out a peaceful settlement to the dispute. The committee consisted of American, Australian, and Belgian delegates. The period from September 1947 to mid-December 1948 was characterized by various efforts at negotiation between the republic and the Dutch, mainly under the auspices of the GOC. However, Dutch-republican relations deteriorated to the point where even the truce agreement was not observed.

In August 1948, a change of cabinet took place in the Netherlands. Although the Labor party provided the prime minister, who was seen as a dove in the Indonesian question, the Confessional parties, especially the Roman Catholics, represented in the cabinet were determined to pursue a hard line in the matter. They also provided the minister of overseas territories and the high representative of the crown in Indonesia. The cabinet decisions studied in this chapter will therefore frequently be characterized by strong disagreement among the decision-makers about the course of action to adopt. The cabinet was often divided into two factions along party lines.

DECISION PHASE 1; OCTOBER 1948

On October 26, 1948, the council of ministers convened in order to decide what to do in Indonesia. The Dutch authorities in Indonesia had advised them to send an ultimatum to the U.S. delegation of the Security Council's Good Offices Committee (GOC) and, if agreement was not reached quickly, to take military action. In the opinion of the Dutch authorities, the chance of reaching an agreement was practically nil, but they thought the chance was fairly high that a quick military success might be achieved, which would break the morale of the republic and limit material losses and international sanctions, while the Dutch themselves would not lose Indonesia.

When this message was received at the department of foreign affairs in The Hague, a plan was made to allow the impending military action to go ahead, preceded by a last negotiation effort on the most controversial issues. The chances of reaching an agreement were also considered very low at the department of foreign affairs, but it was thought that such negotiations were likely to limit any international sanctions. The ministry of foreign affairs was extremely concerned about the Dutch international position; they feared an intervention by the U.N. Security Council, as had happened after the first military action.

Rushing off to a meeting in Paris with the Western European countries, whom he informed about the situation in Indonesia and sounded out for their reactions to potential military action, the minister of foreign affairs had instructed two officials from his department to discuss this advice with the prime minister and to indicate that he himself would be willing to begin the informal negotiations. The prime minister, a member of the Labor party, in turn discussed the matter in a meeting with the ministers of overseas territories and defense, who were both key ministers and members of Confessional parties and who were known as defenders of a harder line, in what was clearly an attempt to mitigate cabinet disagreement.

When the cabinet meeting started on the evening of October 26, all ministers were present except the minister of maritime affairs. The group thus consisted of fourteen ministers. Figure 7.1 summarizes the group process. The minister of foreign affairs first informed the cabinet of the reactions of his Western European colleagues to the possibility of military action in Indonesia. While the French seemed to be sympathetic, the British only indicated that they had similar problems in that part of the world. His overall impression was that there was some understanding of the Dutch position (act 1). He then discussed the two strategies which had been put forward: (1) to send an ultimatum to the American delegation of the GOC and to begin military action if the republic did not agree (S_1) and (2) to negotiate with the republic about the most controversial issues and initiate military action if no agreement was reached (S_2). The minister gave his reasons for his choice for informal negotiations with the republic (S_2), on the basis of the likely consequences. He rejected S_1 because of the serious international and national repercussions that could be anticipated. If they began with negotiations he thought that it would be possible to reach an agreement, and only if the negotiations, were unsuccessful and they had to initiate military action could they expect serious international and national repercussions (act 2).

The prime minister immediately supported the suggested strategy (S_2) and even indicated that if they did have to resort to military measures, in his opinion the international sanctions would be less severe than the minister of foreign

Figure 7.1
Meeting of October 26, 1948

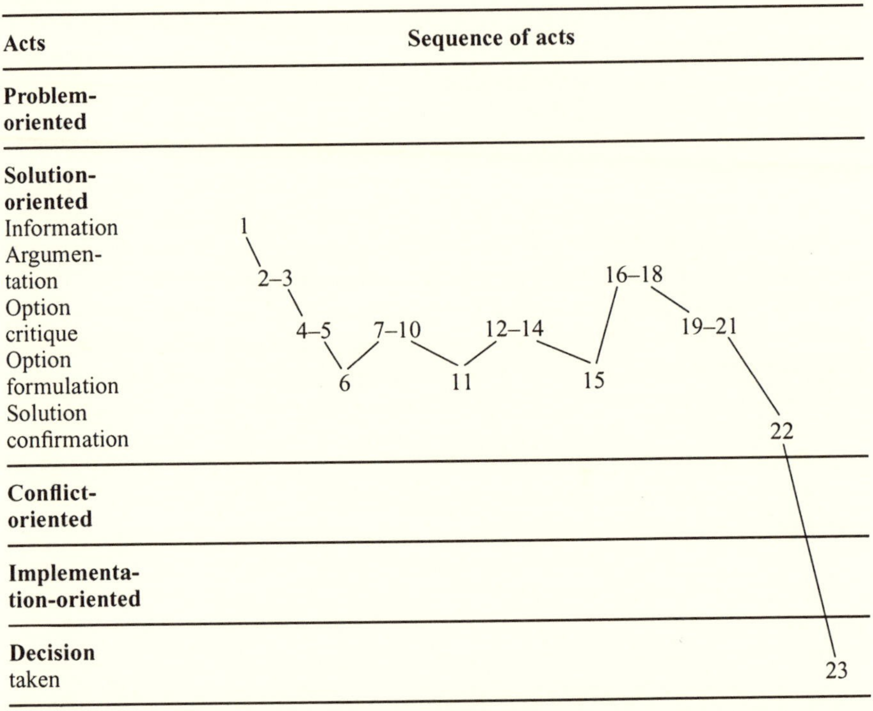

Acts	Sequence of acts
Problem- **oriented**	
Solution- **oriented** Information Argumen- tation Option critique Option formulation Solution confirmation	
Conflict- **oriented**	
Implementa- **tion-oriented**	
Decision taken	23

Source: Minutes of a meeting of the Council of Ministers, Oct. 26, 1948, in P. J. Droog-
lever and M. J. van Schouten, eds., *Officiële bescheiden betreffende de Nederlands
Indonesische betrekkingen, 1945–1950*, vol. 15, no. 259, pp. 517–525 (The Hague:
Nijhoff, 1989).

affairs depicted (act 3). The minister of the interior, a member of a Confessional
party, and a minister without portfolio, an Independent, also supported S_2 (acts 4
and 5).

Then the minister of finance, a member of the Labor party and a key minister,
introduced some further suggestions with respect to the negotiations. He proposed that they should negotiate in two steps: first ask for some assurances about
the observation of the truce, with some verbally agreed upon deadline, and if this
was obtained, start the political negotiations; otherwise, initiate military action
(S_3) (act 6). It seems that he introduced this intermediate strategy when he saw
that only one member of the Confessionals (the minister of the interior)
supported S_2.

The minister of economics, a member of the Confessionals, immediately
supported this compromise (act 7). Thereafter three non-key ministers (social
affairs, agriculture, and reconstruction) agreed with S_3 (acts 8 to 10). The deputy

prime minister, a key minister and member of the Confessionals, then gave his support to S_3, stressing that the deadline should be very short (only one week for the truce implementation) in order to avoid overlong delays in implementing military action, which would be undesirable from a military point of view (acts 11 and 12). Then two other non-key ministers and members of the Confessionals (justice and education) gave their support to the amended version of S_3 (acts 13 and 14).

The minister of defense, a key minister in this case, stressed the necessity of a short deadline. He also put forward his argument for setting a deadline. If no deadline were set, the negotiations could drag on with little chance of success and with a very high chance of losing the support of the federals, which would force the Dutch to evacuate from Indonesia since they would no longer have the means to carry out military action. For these reasons, he qualified his support for negotiations by saying they had to have a deadline of fourteen days (acts 15 and 16). The minister of overseas territories finally supported the negotiation strategy of the minister of finance (S_3), arguing, however, that he did not expect it to be successful (act 17). Subsequently the minister of foreign affairs also gave his support for the amended version of S_3 and in reply to his colleague of overseas territories he argued that in his opinion the chance of an agreement was not so small (act 18).

Once all the key ministers had explicitly given their consent to S_3, the remaining non-key ministers who had not spoken also agreed with S_3 (acts 19 to 21), and the prime minister summarized the decision that they had unanimously agreed upon: to negotiate in two steps, to try first to get an oral deadline for the truce within two weeks and if this worked to continue with the negotiations; otherwise to initiate military action (acts 22 and 23).

Summary of Decision Phase 1

The prime minister succeeded in mitigating initial disagreement by first discussing the matter in a small group. In the meeting itself, agreement was reached by discussion and by slightly adjusting the original proposal so that everyone was willing to support it.

The third alternative is in fact merely an elaboration of the second. It makes concessions to the Confessionals by setting a time limit on the negotiations because they did not want overlong negotiations, possibly without result. The minister of finance introduced this alternative when he saw that, of the Confessionals, only the minister of the interior explicitly supported the negotiation alternative (S_2). The consequences of the chosen strategy were considered by the minister of foreign affairs. During the discussion, some key ministers made minor corrections to the probabilities of outcomes. The ministers of defense and overseas territories estimated the chance of reaching an agreement by negotiation as close to zero, although the minister of foreign affairs indicated at the end of the session that the chance was not that small. The prime minister evaluated the outcome of international and national repercussions as less severe than did the minister of foreign affairs. The decision process in this phase, based on the search for a generally acceptable compromise, can therefore be described as approximating Maoz's (1990) cybernetic model.

DECISION PHASE 2; NOVEMBER 15 TO NOVEMBER 20, 1948

Between November 3 and 9, 1948, the minister of foreign affairs and a second Dutch negotiator held meetings with members of the republican government. On November 10, they received a memorandum from the republicans, in which the republicans put forward their views and made some concessions with respect to the observation of the truce, but stated that it would be impossible to dismantle the republican army; apparently they had no control over several guerrilla factions. The high representative of the crown and the negotiators communicated separately two lines of advice to the cabinet about what should be done next. The minister of foreign affairs went back to the Netherlands in order to report personally to the cabinet about his negotiations with the republic and to take part in the further decisions of the cabinet. Since this decision phase consisted of several meetings, for the sake of clarity the different sessions will be discussed separately.

November 15, First Session (Afternoon)

When the complete cabinet convened on the afternoon of November 15, 1948, for its first meeting (Figure 7.2), they were faced with two divergent kinds of advice. The high representative of the crown advised them to inform the GOC that the negotiations had failed, since the truce violations were continuing, and to begin military action (S_1). Only with this strategy did he see the possibility of reaching a genuinely satisfactory solution. The minister of foreign affairs, in contrast, advised continuing the negotiations, by trying to reach a less demanding agreement before December 1, and to initiate military action only if this effort failed (S_2). He thought it likely that a compromise agreement could be reached with the republic in which not all details were settled.

When the prime minister opened the meeting he immediately indicated that there were two factions in the cabinet, one supporting the high representative of the crown's advice (the ministers of the Confessional parties supported S_1) and the other (the Labor ministers) supporting S_2, the advice of the minister of foreign affairs (act 1). This insight must have been gained from preliminary informal meetings not reported in the minutes.

The minister of foreign affairs referred to his report and stressed that a decision had to be made soon, as they were under pressure from the military, who considered December 1 as the deadline for action (act 2). Then the minister of overseas territories took the floor and urged the participants in the meeting to seek a compromise solution (act 3). However, as the republic had given no sign

Figure 7.2
November 15, First Session (Afternoon)

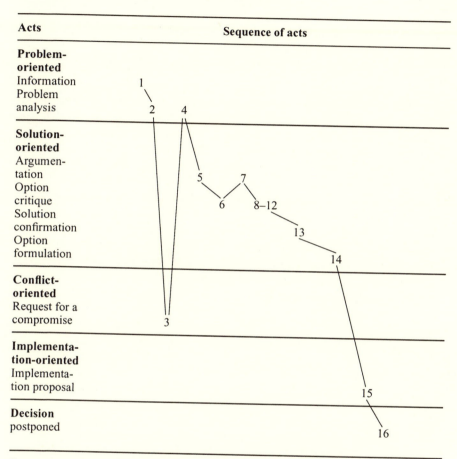

Acts	Sequence of acts

Problem-oriented
Information
Problem
analysis

Solution-oriented
Argumen-
tation
Option
critique
Solution
confirmation
Option
formulation

Conflict-oriented
Request for a
compromise

Implementa-tion-oriented
Implementa-
tion proposal

Decision
postponed

Source: Minutes of a meeting of the Council of Ministers, Nov. 15, 1948, in P. J. Droog-
lever and M. J. van Schouten, eds., *Officiële bescheiden betreffende de Nederlands
Indonesische betrekkingen, 1945–1950*, vol. 15, no. 328, pp. 662–667, (The Hague:
Nijhoff, 1989).

that it was about to reduce the number of violations of the truce (they had even
increased) despite this being the very first point of the negotiations, he would be
willing to ask again for some clarification, preferably via some military advisers
in Indonesia. If the answer were satisfactory, they could continue with negotiations; otherwise, they would go ahead with military action (S_3) (acts 4 and 5).
The second negotiator immediately supported this compromise (act 6).

The prime minister then discussed the two approaches. If they informed the
GOC that the negotiations had failed and started military action (S_1), he

anticipated serious repercussions both in Indonesia and in the international arena. But if they continued with the negotiations as the minister of foreign affairs had suggested (S_2), the chance was high, in his opinion, that an agreement could be reached. He therefore supported this strategy. Referring to the compromise solution put forward by the minister of overseas territories (S_3), he indicated that he did not agree with the proposed delegation since the military might proceed in an ultimatum-like way which would completely spoil the negotiators' efforts. He clearly preferred a more diplomatic approach (act 7).

The ministers of finance and agriculture and the minister of the interior indicated that they would support the compromise (S_3) (acts 8 to 10). The minister of defense, however, rejected the compromise strategy (S_3) and supported the high representative of the crown's advice (S_1) (act 11). Then the minister of social affairs, a member of the Labor party, gave his support for the compromise (S_3) (act 12). Before the break for dinner, the minister of foreign affairs concluded that all the speakers, apart from the minister of defense, supported a compromise solution (act 13). He further elaborated the compromise option by proposing that nonmilitary advisers in Indonesia be asked to seek clarification from the republicans (S_4), probably a move to placate the prime minister (act 14). He also suggested drafting a note about the points the advisers should discuss with the Indonesian vice president (acts 15 and 16). The speakers in this meeting were mainly key ministers. In fact, the deputy prime minister was the only key minister to keep silent. After this, the meeting was interrupted for dinner.

November 15, Second Session (Evening)

The second session began later the same evening and it may be assumed that there had been sufficient time for informal consultation not mentioned in the minutes. The group process of this session is summarized in Figure 7.3.

The second negotiator again opened the discussion, supporting the amended compromise option (S_4) (act 1). Then the minister of overseas territories, referring to the prime minister's argument of the first session, also rejected military action for the moment and supported the compromise option as amended by the minister of foreign affairs in the first session (S_4) (act 2).

Thereafter the prime minister also rejected the military action (S_1) for the time being, arguing that it would have serious repercussions in Indonesia and abroad, and stating that military action would only be acceptable in the foreign arena if violations of the truce continued (acts 3 and 4). He then indicated his preference for the continuation of negotiations as the minister of foreign affairs had earlier advised (S_2) (act 5).

Although there seems to be little difference between S_2 and S_4, probably out of fear of the consequences inflicted by the foreign powers, the prime minister preferred to have proof to offer them should negotiations fail to stop violations of the truce, the only admissible strategy which would in his opinion carry weight.

Figure 7.3
November 15, Second Session (Evening)

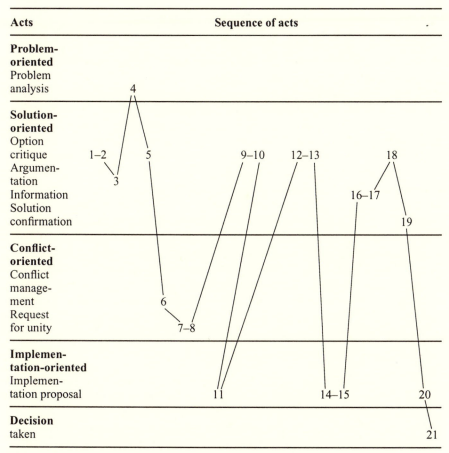

Acts	Sequence of acts	.

Problem-oriented
Problem analysis

Solution-oriented
Option critique
Argumentation
Information
Solution confirmation

Conflict-oriented
Conflict management
Request for unity

Implementation-oriented
Implementation proposal

Decision taken

Source: Minutes of a meeting of the Council of Ministers, Nov. 15, 1948, in P. J. Drooglever and M. J. van Schouten, eds., *Officiële bescheiden betreffende de Nederlands Indonesische betrekkingen, 1945–1950,* vol. 15, no. 328, pp. 662–667, (The Hague: Nijhoff, 1989).

Apparently in an effort to avoid a revival of disagreement, the deputy prime minister immediately stated that in his opinion the views of the prime minister and the minister of overseas territories were quite close, and again requested that the other members join him in supporting the compromise solution whereby clarification would be requested in a diplomatic way (S_4) (acts 6 to 7). The minister of foreign affairs followed by requesting the members of the council to remain united in this difficult situation, while again supporting the compromise strategy (S_4) (acts 8 and 9).

The minister of the interior then gave his support for S_4 and made some suggestions about the contents of the clarification letter for the republican vice president (acts 10 and 11). Then the ministers of finance and social affairs gave their support to S_4 and made further suggestions for the clarification letter (acts 12, 13, 14, and 15). When the minister of social affairs asked his colleague of foreign affairs whether he would return to Indonesia for the negotiations, the latter replied that he preferred that advisers should conduct the negotiations since he would not like to interfere too much in overseas territories' matters (acts 16 and 17). Finally the prime minister gave his consent to S_4 and summarized the further procedures (acts 18 and 19). The ministers of foreign affairs and overseas territories were instructed to draft an aide-mémoire for the advisers the next morning, to ask for the necessary clarification (acts 20 and 21).

November 17, Cabinet Meeting (Morning)

On November 17, an extraordinary cabinet meeting was scheduled, (summarized in Figure 7.4). The prime minister opened the meeting and informed the group about a severe disagreement that had arisen between the minister of overseas territories and the minister of foreign affairs about the formulation of a paragraph in the aide-mémoire for the negotiators, and stated that the two ministers had sent different interpretations to Indonesia (act 1). He then asked the members for their opinion (act 2). The minister of overseas territories defended his formulation and denounced foreign affairs for making public the dissension in the cabinet, which was harmful for the latter and against the rules, which first require a discussion in the council (acts 3 and 4). The minister of the interior then asked the council for overseas territories' version of the aide-mémoire to be read, which was done (acts 5 and 6).

Thereafter the minister of foreign affairs informed the cabinet that after discovering last evening the problematic parts of the formulation, he had tried in vain to discuss it by telephone with his colleague in overseas territories. The discussion was not very constructive, however, since the latter did not wish to make any changes, but had finally agreed that foreign affairs could send his own version (act 7). He then denounced his colleague for not wanting to discuss serious points (act 8). Subsequently the prime minister reassured the two ministers that he did not consider it a serious difference (act 9). Nor did other ministers (interior, without portfolio, and vice prime minister) (acts 10 to 12).

The minister of the interior then suggested the compromise of informing the Dutch authorities in Indonesia that, although the formulation of foreign affairs seemed to be more correct, they could maintain the overseas territories' version for practical reasons, which was then agreed to (acts 13, 14, and 15).

Figure 7.4
November 17, Extraordinary Morning Meeting

Acts	Sequence of acts

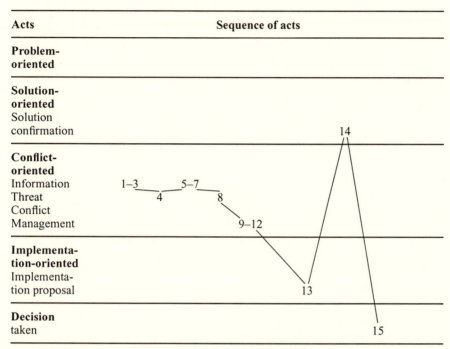

Source: Minutes of a meeting of the Council of Ministers, Nov. 17, 1948, in P. J. Drooglever and M. J. van Schouten eds., *Officiële bescheiden betreffende de Nederlands Indonesische betrekkingen, 1945–1950*, vol. 15, no. 341, pp. 689–691 (The Hague: Nijhoff, 1989).

November 17, Meeting with a Small Group of Key Ministers (Afternoon)

The differences between the ministers of foreign affairs and overseas territories persisted. On November 17 at 5 p.m., a meeting of a smaller group with the five key ministers most closely involved, that is, the prime minister, the deputy prime minister, and the ministers of overseas territories, foreign affairs, and defense, was held, in which the foreign affairs minister's objections to the aide-mémoire of the minister of overseas territories were discussed. There are no minutes of this meeting and we have to rely on the diary of a foreign affairs official and a private note from the minister of foreign affairs (Drooglever and van Schouten eds., 1989, vol. 16, note 1, pp. 692–693; no. 352, pp. 703–704). The aide-mémoire of the minister of overseas territories insisted that the republic would first have to comply with the truce conditions and only then could they negotiate step by step about other demands. The foreign affairs' minister's experience, however, based on earlier negotiations with the republic, told him that they should approach this problem in a more flexible way, or the international arena would be convinced that the Dutch did not really wish to negotiate but preferred to solve the problem militarily; this would bring the topic back on the agenda of the Security Council and would perhaps attract severe sanctions against the Dutch.

The result of this afternoon meeting was that the minister of overseas territories made a concession, agreeing not to submit this written aide-mémoire to the republic, but still insisting on the condition that the republic first had to respect the truce conditions and only afterward could they negotiate step by step about the eight demands. It was also agreed that he, together with the minister of foreign affairs, the second negotiator, and several other advisers and members of parliament, would go to Indonesia (S_5). However, he insisted that before implementing this strategy, he would have to consult his party leader. He was obviously employing a delaying tactic.

November 19, Meeting with a Small Group of Key Ministers (Afternoon)

After his meeting with the minister of overseas territories, the minister of foreign affairs was convinced that his colleague was doing his utmost to ensure the failure of the negotiations in order to proceed as quickly as possible to military action. The minister of foreign affairs, in contrast, was committed to flexible negotiations and therefore submitted his resignation to the prime minister. Since his resignation would also lead to a cabinet crisis, on November 19 at 3 P.M., a new meeting took place between the five key ministers.

According to the diary of the official of foreign affairs, who was also present, the atmosphere was very bad. Before the official meeting began, the minister of foreign affairs had some discussions with the deputy prime minister, who seems to have functioned as a mediator. When the five met, the minister of overseas territories presented a new list of instructions for the negotiators, which he wanted to submit in a plenary session of the cabinet. The prime minister objected and said that there was insufficient time for a plenary session because of the Security Council's impending measures and that the decision therefore had to be made on this day by this group. When the minister of overseas territories again insisted on observation of the truce conditions before entering into negotiations with the republic (S_5), the prime minister rejected this and threatened the dissolution of the cabinet. The minister of overseas territories agreed finally that the negotiators could decide themselves when to continue with other points. With a great deal of trouble a compromise was again reached and subsequently implemented: the ministers of overseas territories and foreign affairs, the second negotiator, some advisers, and some members of parliament would go to Indonesia, and the negotiators, the minister of foreign affairs, and the second negotiator, would be free to negotiate on the basis of the written instructions (S_6). We assume that the choice was unanimous since no cabinet crisis ensued.

Summary of Decision Phase 2

In this phase the disagreement between key ministers became overt. They resolved it with a great deal of trouble by developing three compromise options (S_2, S_3, and S_4) which contained both the negotiations and the military element. Apart from the high representative of the crown and the minister of foreign affairs, who gave their arguments in notes to the council, only the prime minister made an effort to consider consequences. However, since he was unable to convince the majority of his colleagues, he gave up the effort, and the other members concentrated on the search for a strategy which would be acceptable to all of them. It may be assumed that when struggling over the kind of delegation and the tone of the aide-mémoire, each minister would be visualizing the consequences he thought likely, but he avoided discussing them in order not to jeopardize the necessary consensus. Adherents of one of the factions may have thought that, once the brief clarification attempt had ended unsatisfactorily, they could begin military action and improve the situation in Indonesia, while members of the other faction may have hoped to reach an agreement with the Indonesians and to avoid international problems. They thus differed partially with respect to the perceived consequences and partially with respect to their likelihood of occurrence.

The decision-making process in this phase can be described, in our view, by incrementalism (Lindblom 1980), in the sense that only strategies slightly deviating from the status quo were considered, and by Maoz's (1990) cybernetic model, which specifies the review of a large number of options in order to find a consensus without looking explicitly at the consequences. Now there were also overt conflict and pressure for consensus, although the latter was not necessary but perhaps desirable because of the importance of the matter. The conflict was also due to considerable distrust. One faction thought that the other wanted the immediate use of force, while the other faction thought that the former wanted to pursue negotiations without limit.

DECISION PHASE 3; DECEMBER 8 TO DECEMBER 13, 1948

On December 8, the ministers of foreign affairs and overseas territories and the other negotiator were back in the Netherlands and reported to the cabinet in detail on their negotiation efforts. All three negotiators agreed that the republic had neither respected the cease-fire order nor submitted to their demands. At the end of the session the minister of foreign affairs handed his colleagues a note with the unanimous advice of the negotiators to begin the military action. They had considered two strategies: to initiate the military action (S_1) or to conclude an unsatisfactory agreement (S_2). If they concluded a peace treaty, the negotiators were certain that law and order could not be reestablished in Indonesia. If they went ahead with military action, the chance was high that it would lead to serious international sanctions and that the willingness of the remaining Indonesians to cooperate would diminish. A less negative outcome was also possible, albeit less likely, in which international sanctions would be less serious and the remaining Indonesians would be willing to cooperate.

December 9, First Session (Morning)

At the morning meeting of December 9, discussions began with an effort to reach a cabinet decision. Figure 7.5 illustrates the group process in this meeting. First the prime minister informed the council that the Americans had fortunately withdrawn a very harsh aide-mémoire prepared in the event of military action (act 1). But the minister of foreign affairs then informed the meeting that the new version only omitted the threat to withdraw aid under the Marshall Plan and still constituted a serious warning. The minister had also been approached by the British ambassador with a message from his prime minister, who tried to explain that the American view was to cooperate as much as possible with nationalist movements in this area in order to help them to resist communism. The ambassador had indicated verbally that the British did not really expect severe repercussions to follow Dutch military action (act 2). The discussion then turned to the course of action to follow.

All the ministers were by now aware of the advice of the minister of foreign affairs. The minister of social affairs rejected the advice of the negotiators (S_1); in his opinion, it would only lead to negative consequences such as international repercussions, less cooperation from the federalists, and also national difficulties (act 3). However, he did not care to conclude an unsatisfactory agreement (S_2, the other strategy the negotiators had considered). He then proposed a slightly different alternative, namely, first to send a message to the GOC and to the United States with the theoretical possibility that they might pressure the republic into accepting the primary demands, and if this did not succeed to begin military action (S_3) (act 4). In his opinion, their dependence on the Americans required that this should be done. But he did not look further at the consequences.

The minister of finance then analyzed the situation on the basis of recent experiences with the other three parties involved. In his opinion, the republic was unable to make an agreement because of an internal power struggle. The GOC was powerless, unable even, to ensure the observation of the truce. As for the major powers, the United States had its own ideas, and the Dutch could not expect much help from the British and French (act 5). In this situation, as he saw it, the government had to accept its responsibility and act (act 6). He then indicated that he was not sure whether the preliminary phase with the GOC, the alternative developed by the minister of social affairs (S_3), was a good solution, but he felt able to support it (act 7). The minister thus pointed in general terms to the direction in which the solution should be sought.

The minister of the interior subsequently considered three alternatives and gave his argument based on consequences. He rejected the strategy of the minister of social affairs (S_3) because in his opinion the Americans would force them to ease their demands. Then he introduced the option of doing nothing (S_4), only to reject it too, since it would only improve the position of the extremists in Indonesia. He supported military action (S_1) because it offered a good chance of achieving the cooperation of the population in the republican territory (act 8).

Following him, the minister of agriculture voiced his support for S_3 (act 9), but also developed a new alternative based on the assumption that the republic planned to initiate heavy guerrilla activities all over Indonesia on January 1. He suggested waiting until then and then taking military action (S_5), which would therefore be completely justified (act 10). The participants did not immediately react to this proposal.

Subsequently the minister without portfolio gave his support for S_3 and the minister of economics indicated his support for S_1 (acts 11 and 12). Three non-key ministers (social affairs, agriculture, and the minister without portfolio), therefore, had supported S_3. Five ministers favored S_1, including three key ministers, those of finance, foreign affairs, and overseas territories; the latter had indicated this preference in his advice to the cabinet. There was thus no agreement.

The deputy prime minister took this opportunity to develop a new strategy, namely, to evacuate from Indonesia (S_6). In his opinion, this would probably lead to an increase in terrorism and American military intervention. On the basis of these consequences, he immediately rejected it (act 13). He urged the council to unite, to fulfill its national duty, and to opt for S_3, but to take care that the phase with the GOC would be very brief in order not to jeopardize military action (acts 14 and 15). He evidently was trying to find a compromise that would allow the adherents of S_1 to support S_3.

Then the military ministers expressed their preferences. The minister of maritime affairs supported S_3 and rejected the minister of agriculture's proposal to delay military action until January 1 (S_5) on military grounds (act 16). He stated that they did not have sufficient capacity to fight against the republic on its territory and at the same time to guarantee law and order in the federal territories. The minister of defense rejected S_3 because, from a military point of view, valuable time would be lost (act 17). He supported S_1 (act 18).

Following this, the minister of reconstruction gave his support to S_3 but also developed a slightly different option, which consisted of bringing the case before the Security Council instead of before the GOC and of beginning the action (S_7) (acts 19 and 20). Since nobody reacted to this proposal, we can conclude that it did not appeal to his colleagues. The minister of justice supported S_1 and rejected S_3 because of the loss of time (acts 21 and 22). Then the minister of education gave his support to S_1 and rejected S_3 because he expected that the GOC would try to win time in order to prevent military action, which would increase the chaos in Indonesia (acts 23 and 24).

Finally, the prime minister gave his view. He considered three strategies: to continue with the negotiations with the aid of the GOC (S_8); to do nothing (S_4); or to send a message to the United States and the GOC with the theoretical possibility of putting pressure on the republic to accept the Dutch proposals, and

Figure 7.5
December 9, First Session (Morning)

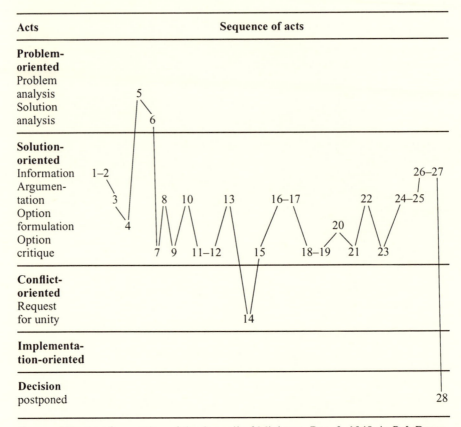

Source: Minutes of a meeting of the Council of Ministers, Dec. 9, 1948, in P. J. Droog-
    lever and M. J. van Schouten, eds., *Officiële bescheiden betreffende de Nederlands
    Indonesische betrekkingen, 1945–1950*, vol. 16, no. 41, pp. 73–82 (The Hague: Nijhoff,
    1991).

if they did not accept them to begin military action (S_3). If they continued with
the negotiations with the aid of the GOC (S_8), he was certain that no solution
would be achieved. If they did nothing (S_4), according to him, anarchy and
dictatorship would reign in Indonesia. If they sent a message to the United States
and the GOC to ask them to try to put pressure on the republic to accept the
primary Dutch demands (S_3), he estimated as very small the chance that the
republic would comply. Then they would have to resort to military measures, and
he felt there was a good chance that these would have only minor national and
international repercussions. Although such action could cost the lives of many
people and could cause a great deal of material damage, the chance was high that

anarchy and dictatorship would be avoided in Indonesia. On the basis of the consequences he had considered, he supported S_3 (act 25). But he also indicated that he needed more information about national consequences (act 26).

At this point in the meeting, three key ministers were supporting S_3 (the prime minister, the deputy prime minister, and the minister of maritime affairs), and four key ministers preferred S_1 (the ministers of foreign affairs, overseas territories, finance, and defense). The key ministers were divided along party lines, and the non-key ministers also expressed their preference according to party affiliation. The Labor ministers (the ministers of social affairs, agriculture, and reconstruction) supported S_3, while the Confessionals (the ministers of the interior, economics, justice, and education) preferred S_1.

The prime minister made it clear to the members of the Confessional parties, who mainly favored S_1 because of the loss of time if S_3 was chosen, that he would have to consult the council of the Labor party. He said that if the council did not agree with S_3, even though Labor cabinet ministers supported this strategy, the Labor ministers would not be able to continue in office (acts 27 and 28). The meeting was then adjourned until the afternoon for the lunch break.

December 9, Second Session (Afternoon)

When the meeting resumed, the minister of foreign affairs, who had earlier advised S_1, gave his support to S_3 (Figure 7.6). The reason he gave for this change of mind was that the arguments of the prime minister and the minister of finance had convinced him (act 1). (The finance minister's first preference had been S_1, but he had earlier indicated that he could also support S_3.) The minister of foreign affairs also informed the council that during the break he and the minister of overseas territories had drafted a note for the GOC and for the United States, which they read to the council (act 2). The minister of overseas territories subsequently gave his support to S_3, indicating that in essence he agreed with the prime minister (act 3). Referring to the evacuation alternative (S_6) brought up at the earlier meeting by the deputy prime minister, he stated that in his opinion the Americans would not intervene but that Indonesia would be infiltrated by Chinese communists (act 4). Finally, the minister of defense also supported S_3, but warned against wasting too much time (act 5). Now all key ministers supported S_3, and the nonspecialists (interior, economics, justice, and education) also gave their consent to S_3 when called upon to do so by the specialists (acts 6 to 9). The prime minister announced that the cabinet would make its final decision about commencing military action on December 13, thus leaving four days for the GOC and the United States to put pressure on the republic to comply with the primary demands (act 10). The entire cabinet thus accepted the first step of the compromise solution S_3.

Figure 7.6
December 9, Second Session (Afternoon)

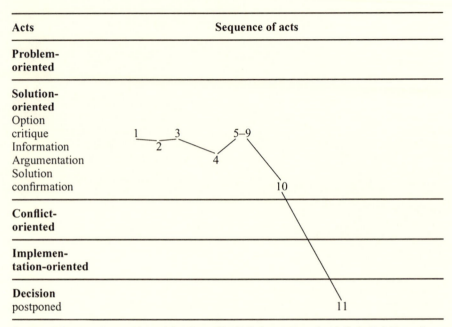

Acts	Sequence of acts
Problem- **oriented**	
Solution- **oriented** Option critique Information Argumentation Solution confirmation	
Conflict- **oriented**	
Implemen- **tation-oriented**	
Decision postponed	

Source: Minutes of a meeting of the Council of Ministers, Dec. 9, 1948, in P. J. Drooglever M. J. van Schouten, eds., *Officiële bescheiden betreffende de Nederlands Indonesische betrekkingen, 1945–1950*, vol. 16, no. 41, pp. 73–82 (The Hague: Nijhoff, 1991).

December 13, Cabinet Meeting

After the meeting of December 9, the Dutch government sent a note to the Americans summarizing the results of the negotiations and asking the Americans to put pressure on the republic to comply with the Dutch demands. When the meeting for the final decision about authorizing military action began on December 13 (Figure 7.7), the minister of overseas territories informed the cabinet that no new events had occurred that might change their view (act 1). The minister of foreign affairs informed his colleagues that their note had been sympathetically received by the U.S. State Department, which had indeed given instructions that their staff should put pressure on the republic (act 2). He further informed the cabinet that during his last meeting in Paris, the French had suggested that military action be planned for after December 16, because by then the Security Council would be in recess and measures against the Dutch could not be taken quickly (act 3).

The prime minister reported that he had also had satisfactory discussions with the trade unions and the council of the Labor party, although some members had been critical (act 4). He also mentioned that there were no signs that the United

Figure 7.7
December 13, Cabinet Meeting

Acts	Sequence of acts
Problem-oriented	
Solution-oriented Information 1–5 Solution confirmation 6	
Conflict-oriented	
Implementa-tion-oriented	
Decision taken 7	

Source: Minutes of a meeting of the Council of Ministers, Dec. 13, 1948, in P. J. Droog-lever M. J. van Schouten, eds., *Officiële bescheiden betreffende de Nederlands Indonesische betrekkingen, 1945–1950*, vol. 16, no. 73, pp. 114–119 (The Hague: Nijhoff, 1991).

States would force sanctions on them (act 5). He therefore proposed to authorize the high representative of the crown to prepare and initiate military action as quickly as possible, a proposal which was unanimously accepted (acts 6 and 7).

Summary of Decision Phase 3

Although there was some initial disagreement between key ministers and also among nonspecialists, the participants reviewed a large number of strategies (eight in total) in order to reach a decision. The compromise option S_3, which incorporated a delay of four days before authorizing military action in order to have more pressure exerted on the republic, was mainly promoted by the deputy prime minister. After he had supported it, other key ministers, including the minister of maritime affairs and the prime minister, also supported it. The prime minister also considered again the consequences for the two strategies, S_1 and S_3, which were supported by the different participants. After the lunch break, other key ministers gave their consent to S_3, stating that they had been convinced by the arguments of the prime minister. The sudden change of opinion of many ministers after the break is certainly remarkable. Most likely there had been discussions between them by which they became convinced that only the choice of S_3 could avoid a serious conflict. Once there was agreement among the key ministers, the nonspecialists also gave their consent at the request of the specialists, so that a unanimous decision could be made. The decision process in this phase was made by argumentation and bargaining, in the sense of forging out a compromise option, which in our view approximates Maoz's (1990) analytic model.

CONCLUSIONS

This case study showed a quite normal decision-making process within a multiple autonomous group. From the very beginning of the process there was disagreement about the available options, consequences, and their probabilities of occurrence among the participants. However, they wished to achieve a consensus, and this was done by a stepwise and incremental procedure, which means that they followed a cybernetic process (Maoz 1990). Regarding the sequences of interaction, in the first phase the process was only solution-oriented, while in the second and third phases it became slightly more complex, consisting of solution-, conflict-, and problem-oriented phases between which the participants oscillated back and forth. Later, less conflict occurred because it was resolved by the second visit to Indonesia, which had convinced the strongest opponents of the same choice. The last phase therefore consisted only of finding a solution.

The next chapter studies the decision-making process of the same heterogeneous group with severe conflicts.

Chapter 8

The Dutch Cabinet Decision to Carry Out Military Action in Indonesia, December 1948: A Cabinet on the Brink of Tendering Its Resignation

This chapter again describes the decision-making process in a multiple autonomous unit, but this time in a situation where the participants who are divided in two factions along party lines distrust each other increasingly and are highly prone to conflict. In these circumstances, the norm of consensus is no longer achievable; they therefore try to arrive at a decision by a stepwise procedure to find an option on which they vote in order to achieve a majority. They thus also use a different aggregation procedure. The substantive issue relates to the final decisions of whether or not to carry out military action in Indonesia in December 1948.

DECISION PHASE 1; DECEMBER 14 TO DECEMBER 15, 1948

On the night of December 13, the high representative of the crown cabled a telegram to The Hague containing a letter from the republican vice president in which the latter expressed his personal views about some concessions that could be made to the Dutch. The high representative of the crown advised that the letter be ignored since it contained no genuine concessions and had been dictated, according to him, by the American delegate of the GOC; he advised that they go ahead with military action (S_1). The same night, the prime minister contacted the ministers of foreign affairs, overseas territories, and defense and the deputy prime minister in order to discuss this event.

December 14, First Meeting (Morning)

On the morning of December 14 an extraordinary cabinet meeting was held at which the other members of the cabinet were informed of the latest development. The question now was whether or not they would have to reconsider the decision of December 13. The group process of this session is summarized in Figure 8.1. The minister of overseas territories discussed the letter, which was shown to the other members, and concluded that there was no reason to reconsider the decision of the previous day; he supported the advice of the high representative of the crown to ignore the letter and begin the military action (S_1) (acts 1, 2, and 3). He also asked the council to remain united (act 4).

Subsequently, the prime minister gave his interpretation of the letter; he found it a positive development (act 5). He rejected the advice of the high representative of the crown (S_1) because it would certainly lead to great international trouble and it would also be unacceptable nationally (act 6). He then developed a new strategy, to negotiate now step by step (S_2), which he supported by arguing that it would certainly avoid international and national difficulties (act 7). Then the minister of foreign affairs spoke and established that there were again two factions in the cabinet. He too asked the members for unity, because if the cabinet had to resign there would be complete deadlock; they would be unable either to begin the military action or to negotiate (acts 8 and 9). With regard to the content of the republican letter, he agreed with his colleague, the minister of overseas territories, that it was unsatisfactory (act 10).

The minister of social affairs, on the other hand, interpreted the letter in a positive way and rejected S_1 because of the great national and international problems which it would certainly provoke and because it would increase the breeding ground for communism in Indonesia (acts 11 and 12). He supported S_2 because it would certainly avert international and national problems with only the loss of Indonesia which, in his opinion, would be less disastrous (act 13). The minister of maritime affairs, an Independent, asked for a compromise and suggested asking again for clarification and beginning action only if the answer were unsatisfactory (S_3) (acts 14 and 15).

Then the minister of the interior intervened in the discussion to ask for unity and accommodation (acts 16 and 17). According to him, the majority favored initiating military action (S_1) and the rest should accommodate to this view. He himself would be ready to do so. At this point in the discussion, only a few ministers had spoken, but he probably knew that his fellow ministers of the Confessional parties, who were seven in total, together with the minister of foreign affairs (who had already agreed in this session that the letter was unsatisfactory), would support S_1.

The minister of finance now intervened, interpreting the letter as containing some positive elements and indicating that a phase prior to action would be appropriate in order not to annoy the Americans too much (act 18). He then further elaborated the compromise option suggested by the minister of maritime affairs, saying that they should ask the republican government in the tone of an ultimatum for clarification of the letter's content, and if the answer were unsatisfactory they should go ahead with the military action (S_3) (act 19). He clearly rejected the negotiation alternative (S_2) proposed by the prime minister (act 20).

The deputy prime minister subsequently agreed that because of possible

Figure 8.1
December 14, First Meeting (Morning)

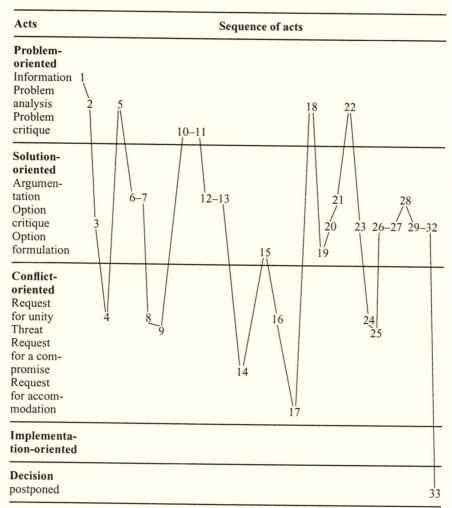

Source: Minutes of a meeting of the Council of Ministers, Dec. 14, 1948, in P. J. Drooglever and M. J. van Scouten, eds., *Officiële bescheiden betreffende de Nederlands
Indonesische betrekkingen, 1945–1950*, vol. 16, no. 88, pp. 141–147 (The Hague: Nijhoff, 1991).

international reactions it would be difficult to proceed immediately with military
action, qualifying the letter as a ploy to win time, and therefore he supported S_1
(acts 21, 22, and 23). He then asked the remaining members to show unity
because of the seriousness of the external situation (act 24). He also warned that
if the cabinet had to resign, a new and more conservative cabinet would not get

the necessary parliamentary majority to implement such serious decisions (act 25).

Following this, the ministers of agriculture and justice immediately supported the compromise option (S_3) (acts 26 and 27). The prime minister argued again that they should negotiate step by step (S_2) and rejected the compromise alternative (S_3), because the chance of a satisfactory answer was small, whereas there was a considerable chance that it would lead to serious international trouble (act 28). Several other ministers (defense, economics, reconstruction, and without portfolio) then supported the compromise alternative (acts 29, 30, 31, and 32). At this point, the session was postponed for the lunch break (act 33).

The advice of the high representative of the crown to initiate military action (S_1) was supported by two key ministers from the Confessional parties, namely, the minister of overseas territories and the deputy prime minister. They did not indicate consequences since they had discussed the question the day before and in their view the situation had not changed with the Indonesian vice president's letter. The prime minister and the minister of social affairs rejected this strategy and supported S_2, the negotiation alternative. For both strategies they considered the consequences since, in their opinion, the situation had changed as a result of the letter.

Since there was disagreement in the cabinet and the requests for unity and accommodation seemed to be in vain, the ministers of maritime affairs and finance introduced a compromise option (S_3). This strategy contained a prior phase for clarification which might meet the wishes of those who did not want to begin military action immediately. But the clarification questions were to be put in the manner of an ultimatum, which should satisfy those in the council who feared the loss of time and its implications for the implementation of the military action. S_3 was finally supported by six ministers, three Confessionals, two Labor ministers, and one Independent, among whom were three key ministers, those of maritime affairs, finance, and defense. The prime minister, however, rejected S_3 because of the negative consequences he expected to follow from this brief, aggressive phase. Both the minister of overseas territories and the minister of foreign affairs maintained silence and offered no comment on the compromise.

December 14, Second Meeting (Afternoon)

During the afternoon meeting the disagreement became exacerbated. Figure 8.2 summarizes the group process. The minister of overseas territories again gave the reasons why he found the letter unsatisfactory and rejected the compromise option (S_3) and the negotiation strategy (S_2) because they would certainly lead to the loss of Indonesia. He again voiced his support for the military action (S_1), because in this case he saw a possibility of holding on to Indonesia (acts 1 and 2). Subsequently, the prime minister repeated his interpretation of the letter (act 3). He also stated that military action was not justified simply because America and England were now supporting the Netherlands and pressuring the republic to

Figure 8.2
December 14, Second Meeting (Afternoon)

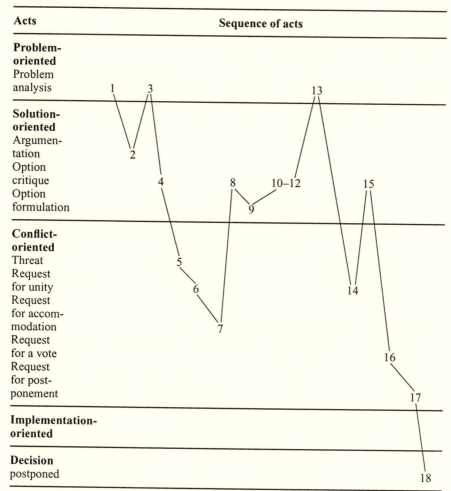

Acts	Sequence of acts

Source: Minutes of a meeting of the Council of Ministers, Dec. 14, 1948, in P. J. Drooglever and M. J. van Schouten, eds. *Officiële bescheiden betreffende de Nederlands
Indonesische betrekkingen, 1945–1950*, vol. 16, no. 88, pp. 141–147 (The Hague: Nijhoff, 1991).

give in (act 4). He also said he felt that further discussion between him and the
minister of overseas territories would be futile (act 5). The atmosphere became
highly charged and the minister of social affairs intervened to ask for unity and
accommodation and again supported the negotiation strategy (S_2) (acts 6, 7, and 8).
The minister of finance further elaborated the compromise alternative (S_3) by

stating that they should ask the republican government for clarification and give them time to answer by postponing the military action for several days (S_4) (act 9). By increasing the time for an answer he probably intended to go somewhere toward meeting the wishes of the prime minister. The minister of maritime affairs immediately supported this version (S_4), but the deputy prime minister and the minister of defense rejected it because they did not trust either the Americans or the republic (acts 10, 11, and 12). The deputy prime minister suggested it might be an American maneuver to prevent them from proceeding with military action (act 13). After the minister of foreign affairs had again asked his colleagues in vain to remain united and had given his support to the new version of the compromise (S_4), the prime minister requested a vote on immediate military action (S_1) (acts 14, 15, and 16).

The result of this vote for S_1 was a draw: the five Labor ministers and the minister of foreign affairs (the only Liberal in the cabinet) and the minister of maritime affairs (an Independent) voted against, while the six Confessional ministers who were present in the meeting and the minister without portfolio (another Independent) voted for the action. Since the minister of education was absent, the rules required them to vote again in his presence. Therefore, the prime minister suggested a break of forty-five minutes (acts 17 and 18).

In this session the minister of overseas territories tried this time to convince the council by pointing out the consequences that he foresaw for the first three alternatives, but without success. The intermediate result of this session was that three Confessional key ministers supported S_1. The prime minister supported S_2, along with the minister of social affairs, one of the few nonspecialists who spoke in the meeting. Two other key ministers, those of finance and foreign affairs, supported the refined compromise S_4. Despite several requests for unity, it is clear that the members were not at all afflicted by the groupthink syndrome (see, e.g., Janis 1982) and did not adjust their preferences to a consensus. Far from it; in fact, the prime minister resorted to a vote on S_1. The result shows that the participants voted mainly along party lines. The choice of the ministers of foreign affairs and maritime affairs against S_1, despite their not being Labor members, might be explained by their preference for the compromise strategy with the prior phase.

December 14, Third Meeting (Late Afternoon)

When the afternoon meeting resumed (Figure 8.3), the minister of education was also present. The minister of finance said that he had heard from several members during the break that the formulation of the option they had voted on (S_1) did not express exactly what they wanted (act 1). He tried again to mediate and therefore proposed a vote on his compromise strategy, which was to ask the republican government for clarification and to postpone military action for seventy-two hours (a new time limit) while waiting for an answer (S_4) (act 2). The prime minister rejected this proposal because, in his opinion, they would not

Figure 8.3
December 14, Third Meeting (Late Afternoon)

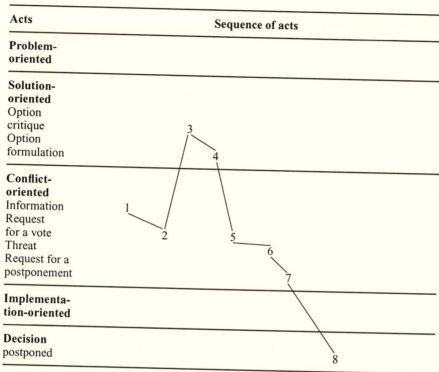

Acts	Sequence of acts
Problem-oriented	
Solution-oriented Option critique Option formulation	
Conflict-oriented Information Request for a vote Threat Request for a postponement	
Implementation-oriented	
Decision postponed	

Source: Minutes of a meeting of Council of Ministers, Dec. 14, 1948, in P. J. Drooglever and M. J. van Schouten, eds. *Officiële bescheiden betreffende de Nederlands Indonesische betrekkingen, 1945–1950*, vol. 16, no. 88, pp. 141–147 (The Hague: Nijhoff, 1991).

be able to proceed with the military action immediately after this deadline, since they would need several more days for deliberations to come to a conclusion, and this was not what the minister of overseas territories wanted (act 3). After this, the minister of overseas territories reformulated the second voting proposal in a very clear way, indicating the difference of opinion (acts 4 and 5).

The cabinet then voted on whether or not they would be willing to continue with further negotiations if the republican government agreed with its vice president's letter (S_5). In essence, this proposal combined the negotiation strategy, S_2, supported by the prime minister, with elements of S_4. The result of this vote was that nine ministers were against S_5, namely, all the Confessionals, the minister without portfolio, and even the minister of foreign affairs. The six who voted for the proposal were the five Labor ministers and the minister of maritime affairs. The proposal was thus rejected by a majority. The prime minister then discussed several resignation procedures, that is, whether the entire cabinet should resign or only the minority (act 6). Finally it was decided to postpone this discussion till the meeting the next morning (acts 7 and 8).

December 15, First Meeting (Morning)

At the morning meeting the prime minister informed his colleagues that the previous evening he and the vice prime minister had reported to the head of state, the queen, the events of the last cabinet meeting (act 1). The minister of foreign affairs then announced that the ministers of overseas territories and finance were still with the queen, trying to find a compromise (act 2). Apparently the queen had refused to accept their resignation because of the external crisis situation, but nothing was mentioned in the minutes about this. The prime minister immediately rejected all compromises, since after receiving the republican answer they would face the same problems in interpreting the answer as they were facing now (act 3). He discussed procedures for announcing the resignation of the cabinet,

Figure 8.4
December 15, First Meeting (Morning)

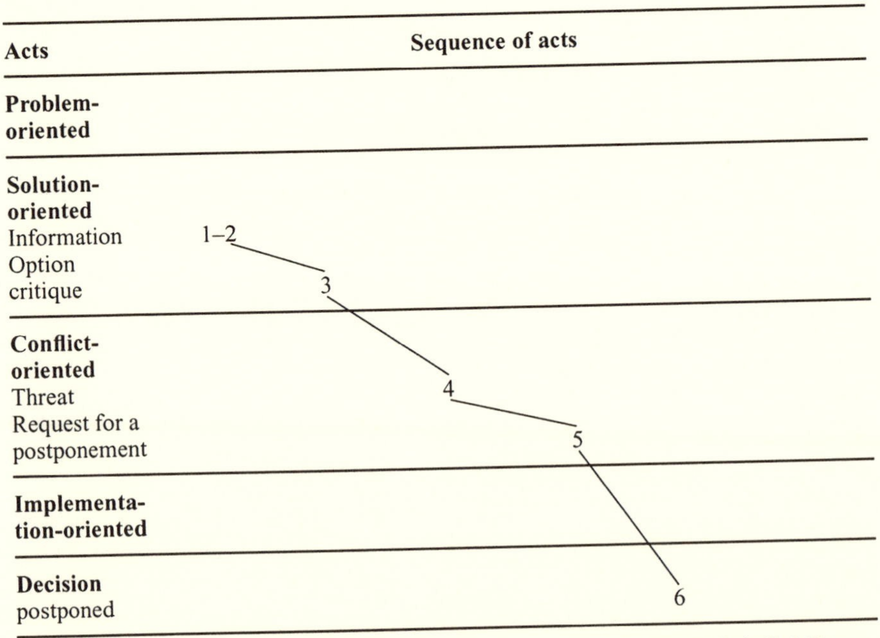

Source: Minutes of a meeting of the Council of Ministers, Dec. 15, 1948, in P. J. Drooglever and M. J. van Schouten, eds., *Officiële bescheiden betreffende de Nederlands Indonesische betrekkingen, 1945–1950*, vol. 16, no. 96, pp. 150–164 (The Hague: Nijhoff, 1991).

and the meeting was adjourned until the afternoon (acts 4 and 5). Figure 8.4 summarizes this meeting.

December 15, Second Meeting (Afternoon)

At the afternoon meeting the entire cabinet was present, with the exception of the minister of maritime affairs. The group process is summarized in Figure 8.5.

Figure 8.5
December 15, Second Meeting (Afternoon)

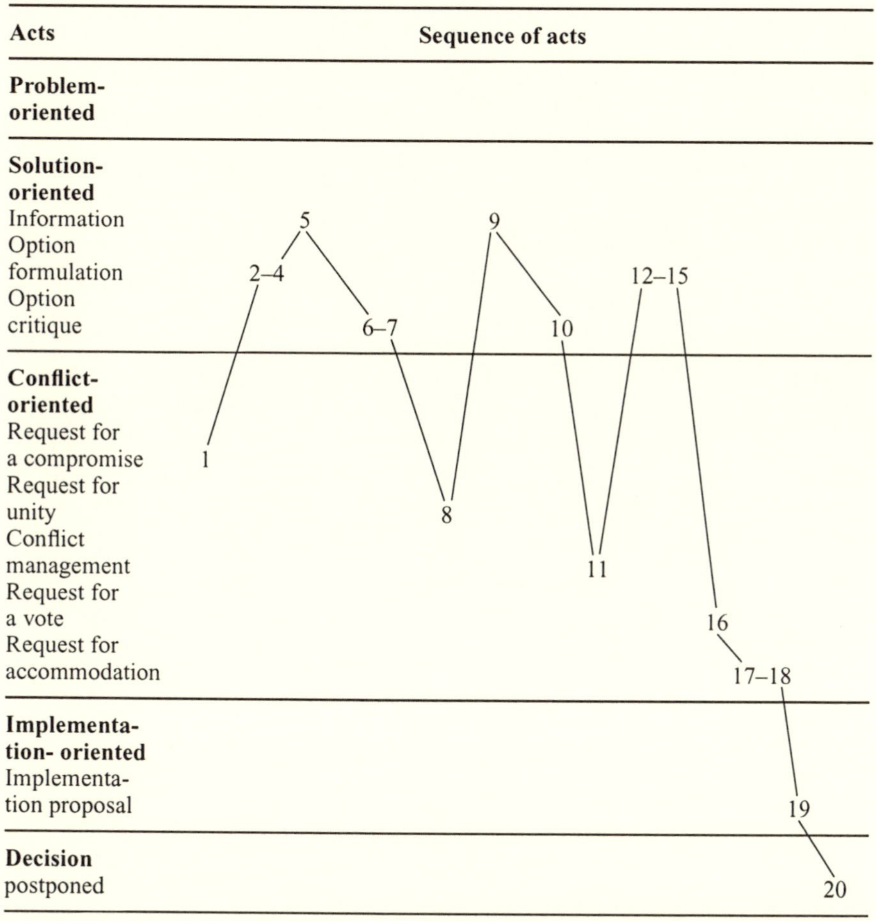
Acts
Sequence of acts
Problem-oriented
Solution-oriented
Information
Option formulation
Option critique
Conflict-oriented
Request for a compromise
Request for unity
Conflict management
Request for a vote
Request for accommodation
Implementation-oriented
Implementation proposal
Decision
postponed
1
2–4
5
6–7
8
9
10
11
12–15
16
17–18
19
20

Source: Minutes of a meeting of the Council of Ministers, Dec. 15, 1948, in P. J. Drooglever and M. J. van Schouten, eds., *Officiële bescheiden betreffende de Nederlands Indonesische betrekkingen, 1945–1950*, vol. 16, no. 96, pp. 150–164 (The Hague: Nijhoff, 1991).

The first suggestion for a compromise came from the minister of overseas territories. He suggested that a letter in the form of an ultimatum should be written to the republican government. This suggestion for the prior phase closely resembled the finance minister's proposal in earlier sessions, and therefore, we again label it S_3 (acts 1 and 2). However, the minister of overseas territories had previously rejected it at the second afternoon meeting of December 14, which means that this key minister now had made some concessions.

The minister of finance asked the council if they would be prepared to postpone the action for several days, as proposed in S_4 (act 3). The minister of foreign affairs added that the letter should not take the form of an ultimatum (S_6, prior phase of S_4 and S_5) in order to keep open the possibility of resolving the external conflict peacefully. He added that they could even now ask for clarification about some points, as within the last few hours he had received a positive message that the Americans and British were on their side. He also agreed on the necessity of postponing the action (acts 4, 5, and 6).

The deputy prime minister supported the proposal of the minister of foreign affairs (S_6) and said that the decision should be unanimous (acts 7 and 8). The minister of defense then mentioned that he had information from the military that the action could be postponed for two or three days, and he also supported the foreign minister's adjusted proposal (S_6) (acts 9 and 10). Finally, the prime minister spoke, stating that he valued the efforts to reach agreement within the cabinet and indicating that the letter should not be an ultimatum and should be drafted by the minister of foreign affairs (acts 11 and 12). Some nonspecialist Confessional ministers (justice and economics) made further constructive suggestions about the content of the letter (acts 13 and 14).

The prime minister then formulated the following proposal to vote on: a letter that did not take the form of an ultimatum, with a reasonable time limit for an answer (S_7) (acts 15 and 16). Twelve ministers were for this proposal and two against (the minister of overseas territories and the minister of the interior). This time the vote did not go along party lines. While the minister of defense unsuccessfully tried to get the minister of the interior to accept the proposal, the minister of overseas territories did acquiesce, merely mentioning that he would like to see the letter in advance (acts 17 and 18). The minister of foreign affairs was charged with drafting the letter, and the meeting was adjourned till the evening (acts 19 and 20).

The strategies considered in this difficult meeting relate mainly to the prior phase. The decision-makers broke these strategies down into several components and slowly pieced them together. The minister of overseas territories proposed an ultimatum-like letter (S_3, prior phase). The ministers of finance and defense immediately suggested that a postponement of the action seemed necessary. This was omitted by the minister of overseas territories, perhaps on purpose (see next meeting). The minister of foreign affairs and the prime minister supported a letter that did not convey the tone of an ultimatum (S_6, S_7). This component was then linked by the minister of foreign affairs to the postponement of military action in S_6. Then the prime minister introduced another element. As well as a non-ultimatum-like letter he demanded a reasonable time for the answer (S_7). He did not speak about postponing military action, but it can be assumed that this was self-evident. He then put this proposal to a vote and the majority agreed with it. The only key minister who disagreed was the minister of overseas territories, but after the vote he too acquiesced. Nobody considered consequences anymore; they disagreed so much on them that their main effort was to build an acceptable compromise, a process which can be described by the cybernetic model (Maoz 1990).

Figure 8.6
December 15, Third Meeting (Evening, 8 P.M.)

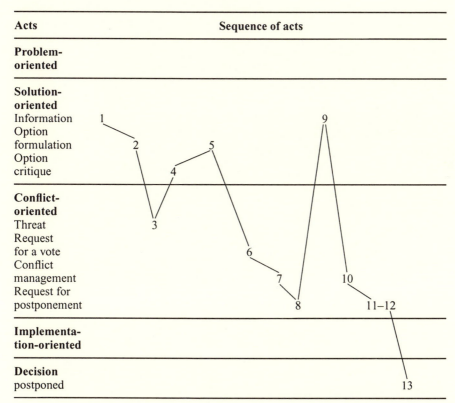

Source: Minutes of a meeting of the Council of Ministers, Dec. 15, 1948, in P. J. Drooglever and M. J. van Schouten, eds., *Officiële bescheiden betreffende de Nederlands Indonesische betrekkingen, 1945–1950*, vol. 16, no. 96, pp. 150–164 (The Hague: Nijhoff, 1991).

December 15, Third Meeting (Evening, 8 P.M.)

When the first evening session resumed, the prime minister announced that they were under time pressure, as he now knew that military action was scheduled after four days by the Dutch authorities in Indonesia, in accordance with the earlier cabinet decision (see phase 3) (act 1). Figure 8.6 summarizes the group process of this session.

The minister of overseas territories then said that he had drafted a letter which would not require postponement of military action (act 2). This maneuver by the minister of overseas territories greatly annoyed the prime minister, who said it went against the afternoon vote where a large majority had agreed on a non-ultimatum-like letter (to be drafted by the minister of foreign affairs) that would allow a reasonable time for an answer (S_7) (acts 3 and 4). The foreign minister's letter was not actually discussed at this session.

The prime minister immediately began to formulate another proposal to vote on, which was whether they wanted to prevent the republican vice president from answering the letter and to allow military action to begin without the consent of the cabinet (S_8) (acts 5 and 6). The deputy prime minister and the minister of defense tried to appease the prime minister and asked for a postponement of the session in order to let the cabinet hear military advisers on the possibility of postponing the action (acts 7, 8, 9, and 10). The minister of finance immediately agreed with the postponement proposal, after which the prime minister also accepted it (acts 11, 12, and 13).

December 15, Fourth Meeting (Evening, 9:45 P.M.)

At the beginning of this meeting (summarized in Figure 8.7) the prime minister welcomed the two advisers: a lieutenant general who had participated in the first military action and the second Dutch negotiator involved in the recent peace efforts with the republic. According to the military expert a postponement of seventy two hours was possible, but there was a strong chance that the surprise element of the attack would be lost (act 1). The other expert also agreed with this view (act 2). The minister of overseas territories then asked whether the military leaders in Indonesia could halt preparations for the action. This was confirmed by the experts (acts 3 and 4). To the defense minister's question of whether the troops could hold on in their positions the experts replied that it depended on the troops' discipline, but they estimated that a delay of three days would be possible (acts 5 and 6).

After the experts had left, the prime minister then proposed to discuss his voting proposal (S_8) from the earlier session that had brought the minister of overseas territories to formulate a compromise proposal, namely, to send his letter requesting clarification and to postpone the military action for seventy-two hours (S_9) (acts 7 and 8). The minister of finance immediately rejected this proposal because it lacked a time limit for the republican answer and maintained a time limit for the initiation of the military action (act 9). The discussion was

Figure 8.7
December 15, Fourth Meeting (Evening, 9:45 P.M.)

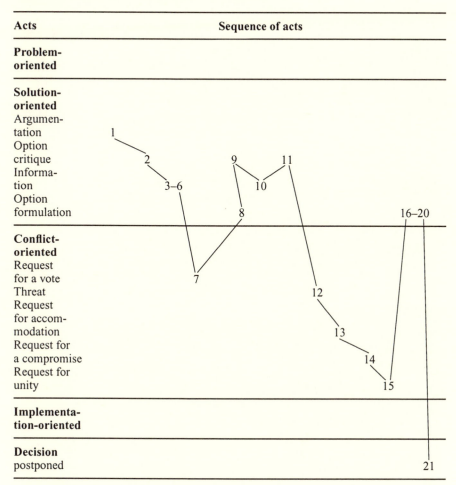

Source: Minutes of a meeting of the Council of Ministers, Dec. 15, 1948, in P. J. Drooglever and M. J. van Schouten, eds., *Officiële bescheiden betreffende de Nederlands Indonesische betrekkingen, 1945–1950*, vol. 16, no. 96, pp. 150–164 (The Hague: Nijhoff, 1991).

briefly interrupted because a cable had arrived from the high representative of the crown, which was read by the prime minister. The former communicated that a delay of the military action was not possible since it would lead to the loss of the surprise element (act 10).

Thereafter the discussion resumed and the prime minister rejected the overseas territories minister's last proposal, mentioning that his own views were diametrically opposed to those of his colleague. He himself wanted to prevent the military action, while the minister of overseas territories wanted to initiate it as quickly as possible (acts 11 and 12). The minister of overseas territories immediately accommodated by withdrawing his proposal, and both the minister of foreign affairs and the minister of defense asked for a compromise (acts 13 and 14). The latter asked the members to maintain unity and suggested they seek clarification with the letter of the minister of overseas territories, indicating a time limit for an answer and postponing the action for seventy-two hours (S_{10}) (acts 15 and 16).

Since the atmosphere again became rather charged, the minister of finance tried anew to mediate by adding a clear time limit for the republican answer to defense's proposal (act 17). Other ministers (social affairs and traffic) proposed skipping the deadline for military action, while a minister without portfolio wanted to maintain it (acts 18, 19, and 20). Still no agreement was reached, but a break was necessary since a member of the American embassy wanted to speak to the minister of foreign affairs (act 21).

December 15, Fifth Meeting (Evening, 11:15 P.M.)

When the meeting resumed (Figure 8.8), the minister of foreign affairs informed his colleagues that the Americans agreed with the Dutch point of view as far as the essential demands to the republic were concerned, but they advised the Dutch to resolve the problems by negotiation and warned of the risks of other measures (act 1). Then the minister of defense discussed the letter of the minister of overseas territories and proposed including a deadline for the republican answer (S_{10}) (acts 2 and 3).

The prime minister, however, asked again for a vote on his proposal to ask for clarification with the letter drafted by the minister of foreign affairs and to allow a reasonable time for an answer (S_7); this proposal had been accepted at the end of the second meeting that day by all ministers except those of overseas territories and the interior (act 4). The letter drafted by the minister of foreign affairs was actually never discussed in the plenary cabinet sessions. It is unclear why the prime minister proposed to vote on it again. Was it to push his will through or merely to get an indication of whether, after all these discussions with breaks in between, the former vote was still valid? In any case, the result this time was a draw. Seven ministers voted for it: all the Labor ministers and the ministers of maritime affairs and foreign affairs. The six Confessional ministers present voted against, as did the minister without portfolio. The prime minister then withdrew the proposal, since if the minister of the interior had been present, it would have been rejected anyway (act 5).

They then voted on the compromise suggested by the minister of defense, namely, to seek clarification with the letter of the minister of overseas territories, to indicate a time limit for the answer, and to postpone action for seventy-two hours (S_{10}) (act 6). This compromise was quite similar to the proposal of the

Figure 8.8
December 15, Fifth Meeting (Evening, 11:15 P.M.)

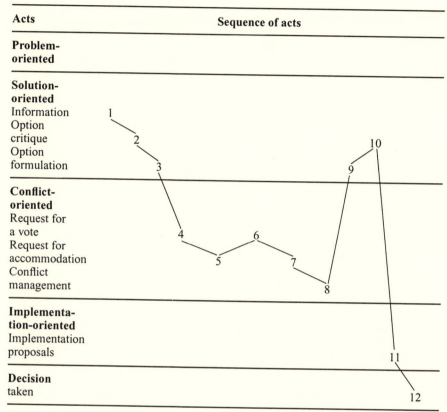

Acts	Sequence of acts
Problem-oriented	
Solution-oriented Information Option critique Option formulation	
Conflict-oriented Request for a vote Request for accommodation Conflict management	
Implementa-tion-oriented Implementation proposals	
Decision taken	

Source: Minutes of a meeting of the Council of Ministers, Dec. 15, 1948, in P. J. Droog-lever and M. J. van Schouten, eds., *Officiële bescheiden betreffende de Nederlands Indonesische betrekkingen, 1945–1950*, vol. 16, no. 96, pp. 150–164 (The Hague: Nij-hoff, 1991).

minister of overseas territories (S_9) but contained in addition the time limit for a republican answer, which seemed to meet the wishes of the Confessionals. Final-ly, twelve ministers agreed with this proposal, but the prime minister and the minister of social affairs were against. The prime minister then acquiesced (act 7). The minister of social affairs, however, remained silent.

Subsequently, the deputy prime minister expressed his relief with this result and suggested that the queen be told that the cabinet had reached agreement and that its resignation had been averted (acts 8 and 9). The prime minister agreed (act 10). The participants then began to draft a telegram to the high representa-tive of the crown and then, after a short break, in reasonable harmony, they revised the clarification letter drafted by the minister of overseas territories, which was cabled the same night to the high representative of the crown (acts 11 and 12).

Summary of Decision Phase 1

This phase was characterized from the very beginning by strong disagreement among the key decision-makers. They also employed different means to resolve the conflict. One of them was to search for an acceptable compromise by reviewing a large number of strategies, mostly without considering consequences since there was disagreement about these too. In the first meeting (Figure 8.1), only the prime minister systematically considered the consequences he perceived for the three strategies discussed. The minister of social affairs repeated them for two strategies and even indicated that he would support an option whereby they would lose Indonesia. On the other side, the Confessional ministers restricted themselves to supporting or rejecting an alternative, accompanied by requests for unity, accommodation, and compromise.

At the second meeting (Figure 8.2), the minister of overseas territories made one last attempt to analyze the consequences of the above mentioned three strategies, but it became very obvious that the cabinet members also disagreed about these consequences. The prime minister adopted a highly antagonistic stance and said he wanted no more discussion with the minister of overseas territories. It is clear that the Labor ministers were mainly concerned about international and national consequences, while the main concern of the Confessionals was to hold on to Indonesia.

Since a compromise supported by a large majority in the cabinet could not be found, they resorted to voting, which is the second means to employ in such a situation. The first vote produced a draw (Figure 8.2) and showed the ministers divided along party lines. They continued with the voting (Figure 8.3), but although the second vote produced a majority decision to reject further negotiations even if the republican government stood behind its vice president's letter, they were unable to continue searching for an acceptable strategy based on this result because the voting clearly split the two major coalition partners. The only step they could take was to tender their resignation.

When the queen refused to accept the resignation, they continued with voting to find a solution. They voted on the prior phase strategy S_7 (Figure 8.5), which was accepted this time by a majority. However, this was again followed by overt disagreement between the prime minister and the minister of overseas territories, so they repeated the vote on S_7 (Figure 8.8) and this again led to an even split along party lines. The last vote was cast on a tailor-made compromise (S_{10}, Figure 8.8) which was finally accepted by a large majority.

From the above it is clear that voting occurs when there is no other way left to reach a decision, but it is also used frequently simply to test the direction in which a compromise might be hammered out, since votes were taken several times on just one part of a strategy. Only the final vote was on an entire strategy. It also became obvious that, during voting, party affiliation plays a role, with nonspecialists appearing to line up behind their key ministers.

When time pressure increased on December 15, because of the schedule for military action, the number of meetings increased, with short postponements in between, in order to reach a decision. Because of the lack of time, they also accepted an almost unanimous decision (the prime minister and the minister of social affairs were against), although perfect unanimity would have been preferable.

DECISION PHASE 2; DECEMBER 17 TO DECEMBER 18, 1948

On the morning of December 17 the prime minister convened the cabinet for an extraordinary meeting, because the situation had changed once again; the high representative of the crown had only partially carried out the instructions and had taken some actions of his own.

December 17, Cabinet Meeting

The prime minister first informed his colleagues that the high representative of the crown had sent the government's letter to the American delegate of the GOC at a later date than instructed. He had also added a shorter time limit for the republican answer, which gave it a more ultimatum-like tone, and he had postponed the military action for only twenty-four hours. He had justified his measures in a telegram (Drooglever and van Schouten 1991, vol. 16, Dec. 17, no. 137, pp. 213–214), claiming that the postponement should remain limited to twenty-four hours and that he should be allowed to decide whether or not to initiate military action on the basis of the answer (S_1) (act 1). The prime minister expressed his fears that these maneuvers would make a very bad impression on the Americans (act 2). Figure 8.9 summarizes the group process of this meeting.

These fears were confirmed by the minister of foreign affairs, who had received messages from the ambassador in Washington that the Americans were accusing them of playing a double game (act 3). The minister of foreign affairs could not see an immediate solution. He rejected the advice of the high representative of the crown that he should decide on his own (S_1) since then the military action would be a *fait accompli*, yet to postpone the action any longer for a decision from The Hague (S_2) did not seem feasible either, for military reasons (act 4).

The minister of overseas territories agreed that the decision should be made by the cabinet and he had therefore again consulted a military adviser, with the consent of the other key ministers, about a longer postponement of the action (acts 5 and 6). He said that according to the military adviser such a postponement was still possible (act 7). The minister of overseas territories, therefore, proposed to postpone the action twenty-four hours but to decide in The Hague within a few hours of receiving the republican answer on whether or not to begin military action (S_3) (acts 8 and 9). The prime minister rejected this option in the first instance because of lack of time (act 10).

The minister of economics stressed the correctness of the principle that the government should make the decision, but because of the divergence of opinion between the military in Indonesia and the military in the Netherlands regarding the duration of the postponement of the military action, he was unsure whether to support S_2 or S_3 (acts 11 and 12). The minister of finance then declared his annoyance with the initiative of the high representative of the crown, stressed that

Figure 8.9
December 17, Cabinet Meeting

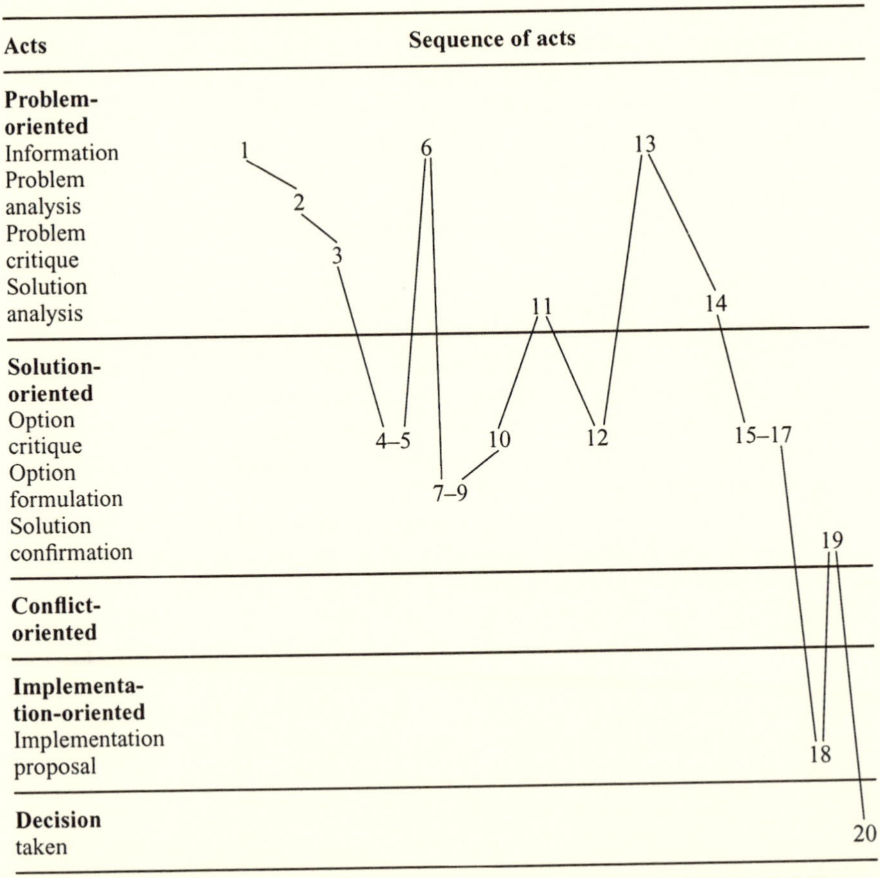

Source: Minutes of a meeting of the Council of Ministers, Dec. 17, 1948, in P. J. Drooglever and M. J. van Schouten, eds., *Officiële bescheiden betreffende de Nederlands Indonesische betrekkingen, 1945–1950,* vol. 16, no. 123, pp. 191–194 (The Hague: Nijhoff, 1991).

the government should make the decision and therefore supported S_3 (acts 13, 14, and 15). The minister of overseas territories then declared that the authorities in Indonesia were unanimous with respect to the duration of the postponement of the military action and therefore he supported S_3 (act 16). The deputy prime minister did the same (act 17).

Since the minister of foreign affairs had apparently already prepared a draft telegram to the high representative of the crown after an earlier informal meeting, in which he asked about the exact time for an answer, the prime minister read it to the members (act 18). Since they could see no other viable strategy whereby the cabinet could make the decision itself, they unanimously agreed (the prime minister too) on S_3, which was again a compromise: no further postponement of military action, as advised by the high representative of the crown, with the decision to be made by the cabinet in The Hague (acts 19 and 20).

In this session there was no longer disagreement. Some measures taken by the high representative of the crown were irreversible, and the cabinet had no choice but to accept them. The participants, therefore, were all searching for a viable solution. Figure 8.9 shows that it was mainly the key ministers who were involved in the discussions, with the exception of the minister of defense, who only supported S_3 at the end. Another key minister, the minister of maritime affairs, was not present at this meeting.

December 18, Cabinet Meeting

On December 18 the cabinet convened at 3:30 A.M., in anticipation of the republic's reply (Figure 8.10). They would have until 6:30 A.M. to reach a decision. Because of bad weather conditions, however, neither phone calls nor cables from Indonesia could reach The Hague.

At 5:15 A.M. the prime minister sent a telegram to the high representative of the crown as they had not yet received the republican answer (act 1). At 8:15 A.M. the high representative of the crown was able to reach The Hague by phone and inform the cabinet that he had not received an answer and that the American delegate of the GOC was highly annoyed about the letter and the procedure and did not wish to pressure the republican vice president (act 2). He also mentioned that a number of coded telegrams were on the way to The Hague (act 3). One of these was quickly decoded and reached the cabinet after the high representative's phone call. It said that the republican vice president was ill and therefore could not answer the letter personally. He would probably be ill for the next few days (act 4).

This message made it quite clear to the cabinet that they were waiting in vain for any reply from the republic. The prime minister suggested phoning the high representative of the crown again to ask him if there was anything essential for their decision in the telegrams which had not yet been decoded (act 5). If not, they could authorize him to begin the military action (act 6). The cabinet unanimously supported this procedure (act 7).

Figure 8.10
December 18, Cabinet Meeting

Acts	Sequence of acts

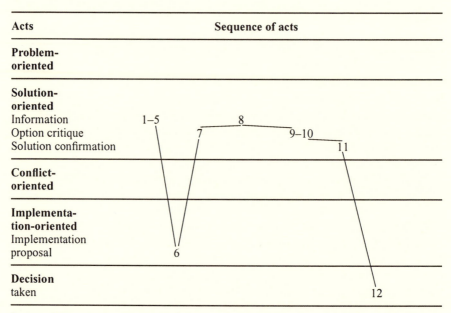

Source: Minutes of a meeting of the Council of Ministers, Dec. 18, 1948, in P. J. Drooglever and M. J. van Schouten, eds., *Officiële bescheiden betreffende de Nederlands
Indonesische betrekkingen, 1945–1950*, vol. 16, no. 141, pp. 219–222 (The Hague: Nijhoff, 1991).

At 9:15 A.M. the prime minister finally contacted the high representative of the
crown and asked him before the entire cabinet if there were any new messages
(act 8). Since there were none, the prime minister asked him if he still stood by
his advice (act 9). Since the high representative of the crown answered affir-
matively, the prime minister told him that the cabinet now also supported this
advice (acts 10, 11, and 12).

In his memoirs (Drees 1963, 241), the prime minister said that he found the
military action morally justified because the republic had not observed the truce.
It had also got itself into a situation where it could not give an answer, nor had it
asked for a delay. Politically, he added, he was very worried about the consequences.

Summary of Decision Phase 2

In this last phase, there was no further disagreement among the participants,
although the high-handed actions of the high representative of the crown, a
former prime minister, coincided in some way with the wishes of the conser-

vative faction in the cabinet, but not at all with those of the Labor faction. It seemed that the ministers all accepted the situation and agreed that the final decision, whether or not to initiate military action, should be made by the government after having received the republican answer.

CONCLUSIONS

This case study clearly demonstrates that the decision-making process in a heterogeneous group with a high level of disagreement is quite complicated. The group really needed different preference aggregation procedures to arrive at choices. Since there was strong disagreement, the conflict-oriented interactions, such as voting and requests for unity and accommodation, indicated that they switched the choice rule; that is, unanimity was no longer available and therefore, a majority decision had to be hammered out. In order to achieve this, they held a lot of meetings, with only short breaks in between, because there was not enough time available in this crisis situation to postpone the decisions indefinitely. Since the participants disagreed strongly about available options, their consequences, and their probabilities of occurrence, they mainly concentrated on the search for a strategy on which all or most of them could agree, which means that they followed a cybernetic process (Maoz 1990). The strategies on which they could reach agreement mainly consisted of compromises, which means that they found a middle ground between their initial proposals. With regard to the sequences of the interaction processes, the solution- and conflict-oriented sequences were quite long in the first phase, since this was the phase with the most conflict. The second phase was characterized by problem- and solution-oriented sequences ending with implementation.

The Practice of Collective Choice

CHOICE OF A THEORETICAL FRAMEWORK

In Chapter 1, where we discussed several theoretical frameworks for collective decision-making, a distinction was made between frameworks that assume groups make optimal choices (objective rationality) and those that assume that groups are limited in their knowledge of the situation and in their computing capacities and may therefore only achieve satisfactory choices (bounded rationality). Since, in our opinion, these later, descriptive frameworks highlighted only some of the different components, a framework was developed for our study in Chapter 2. This framework has been summarized in three basic assumptions and four propositions with respect to the decision-making in different decision units. These assumptions and propositions are summarized again.

Basic assumption 1: The process contains mostly three steps:

1. The specification of the problem and the general orientation about available solutions
2. The specification by one or more persons of arguments in favor of one of the options
3. A process of aggregation of individual preferences into a group preference

These three steps need not be carried out in sequence; the first two steps especially can be combined. There may be different people who provide information during the steps 1 and 2. In general, however, these two steps will be made before step 3. But when step 3 is unsuccessful, participants can also return to the earlier steps in order to proceed again with step 3.

Basic assumption 2: The way in which the three steps are taken depends on the type of decision-making group. A distinction is made between the following types of groups:

1. Groups with a predominant leader who is insensitive to advice from others
2. Groups with a predominant leader who is sensitive to advice
3. Homogeneous or single groups whose members have more or less the same opinions with regard to the topic of the decision
4. Heterogeneous or multiple autonomous groups with participants holding different opinions regarding the topic of decision.

We expected the differences in opinion to arise especially in group 4.

Basic assumption 3: The situation the group finds itself in will affect the decision-making process. The characteristic of the situation most expected to influence the decision-making process is whether or not there is a crisis situation. By "crisis" we understand a situation with limited decision time, where a decision is necessary because the problem poses a serious threat to the country's interests and an increased likelihood of war.

On the basis of these distinctions, the following propositions were specified concerning groups with a predominant leader and homogeneous groups. The propositions concerning the heterogeneous group are not summarized here since they will be tested by means of a quantitative study in the second part of this book.

Proposition 1: In homogeneous groups and groups with a predominant leader, the decision-making process will be much shorter than in heterogeneous groups because of fewer differences of opinion. The process will consist mainly of a presentation of the problem and one or a few arguments, after which the decision can be made. It will be clear that the process can only be as short as this where there are virtually no differences of opinion indicated. Because of this, it may appear that these groups make their decisions solely on the basis of arguments and that other procedures such as compromising or voting become redundant. This is, however, only due to agreement between participants. As soon as this agreement disappears, these groups will behave in the same way as the heterogeneous groups.

Proposition 2: Groups with a predominant leader do not need aggregation rules because the predominant leader makes the decision himself. Aggregation rules are needed in homogeneous and heterogeneous groups.

Proposition 3: In groups with a predominant leader there is no reason for conflict because the advisers do not make the decision. Therefore, conflict-oriented behavior will not occur, or will occur only minimally and normally not in public.

Proposition 4: In homogeneous groups conflicts can occur occasionally, especially when the group has to arrive at a unanimous decision. In such cases a dissenter can cause considerable problems requiring intense efforts at conflict management.

TEXT ANALYSIS OF PROCESS DESCRIPTIONS OF COLLECTIVE CHOICE

In order to study in detail the decision-making process, the underlying model (see Chapter 2), and the aggregation rule used, the minutes of meetings had to be segmented into acts that could be classified into process phases. On the basis of the sequence of acts, interaction patterns have been found that give insight into the development of the choice; that is, whether it was straightforward, proceeding from problem orientation through problem solution to a decision, or complex, including conflict management and several cycles of problem analysis and problem solution before a decision was made.

CASE STUDIES OF DIFFERENT DECISION-MAKING UNITS

Subsequently, we studied the choice processes of four different decision-making units in situations that pertained to important foreign policy decisions and mostly also to major crises of this century.

Hitler's decision-making process exemplified a decision-making unit with a leader who was insensitive to advice. In this case, it was the leader who made the decision. He analyzed the problem, gave his arguments and instructions for implementation, and expected tacit agreement from his audience. This process was quite brief since most of the acts were performed by the leader.

Kennedy's decision-making process during the Cuban missile crisis showed a decision-making unit with a leader sensitive to advice. In Kennedy's case the task of the advisers was to develop and study different alternatives in terms of their consequences and to present them to the leader for choice. This process took longer since advisers had to collect a great deal of information and to discuss the several options among themselves before presenting them to the president, who had to make the choice. In this process, conflict never arose since the task of the advisers was not to choose.

The Austro-Hungarian cabinet (a homogeneous group), although there was one dissenter present, reached a choice more quickly than the Dutch government (a heterogeneous group). By persuasion, compromising, and a certain degree of coercion, the dissenter rather quickly fell into line with the others.

Regarding the heterogeneous group, a consensual decision-making process was shown (Chapter 7) in which the level of disagreement was manageable so that they could arrive, by a cybernetic process with considerable effort, at a unanimous choice.

Chapter 8, however, showed a heterogeneous group on the brink of tendering its resignation because of an extreme conflict. In this situation, consensual decision-making was no longer available, and in a very complicated cybernetic process, using threats, conflict management, several postponements, and also a switch in the aggregation rule, a majority choice was finally hammered out.

SOME GENERAL REMARKS

These examples showed very clearly the usefulness of assuming three steps in the decision-making process. We have also seen that the sequences of activities can be very different for the same unit and in the same decision-making process. In Part 2 these sequences are studied in more detail. The examples also showed that the distinction made by Hermann and her associates (1987) is a useful one. The groups with a predominant leader make their decisions in a different way from the homogeneous or the heterogeneous group. In addition, the distinction between a group with a predominant leader who is sensitive to advice and a group whose leader is not, makes sense because of the difference in decision-making. Although only one case has been studied for each type of decision unit, and only one decision-making process, we are nevertheless confident that the propositions concerning the effects of these differences also hold for other units of the same type and their decision-making processes.

On the basis of our studies only one proposition needs a reformulation—proposition 1, which should read as follows:

Proposition 1: In groups with a predominant leader the decision-making process will be much shorter than in heterogeneous groups because of fewer differences of opinion. The process will consist mainly of a presentation of the problem and one or a few arguments, after which the decision can be made.

Previously the homogeneous group was included in this statement, but it will be clear that the process can be as short as this only when there are virtually no differences of opinion indicated. The example of Austro-Hungarian cabinet showed that this need not be the case. If differences of opinion are not allowed or do not occur, it may appear that these groups make their decisions solely on the basis of arguments and that other procedures such as compromising or voting become redundant. As soon as this agreement disappears, these homogeneous groups will behave in the same way as heterogeneous groups.

Our study would seem to corroborate proposition 2 without amendment. Proposition 3 also requires no adjustment in the light of our case studies. In both case studies, no conflict management was needed. This does not mean, however, that it will never be necessary, but that the need will be less given the way in which the decision-making is carried out.

Finally, proposition 4 also seems to be corroborated with the empirical finding in this study.

The decision-making process in a heterogeneous group is so complex and also varies so much more from one occasion to another that a separate quantitative study was carried out for this decision unit, specifically for the Dutch cabinet.

The results of this study are summarized in the second part of this volume. But before we study this heterogeneous group, this summary concludes with some reflections about the quality of collective decision-making in the different units.

THE QUALITY OF DECISION-MAKING IN THE DIFFERENT UNITS

In this last section we discuss the quality of the decision-making in the different units. Janis and Mann (1977), Janis (1989), and George (1980) have developed standards for quality decision-making within the frame of bounded rationality. There have also been some attempts to test their validity (Herek, Janis, and Huth 1987; Burke and Greenstein 1989) in crisis decision-making. The results of these efforts are summarized, for instance, by Gaenslen (1992).

Since we want to evaluate in a more general way the quality of decision-making from the perspective of the units and its members, we use the following three criteria for this purpose, which coincide in the main with criteria from the literature. In our view the quality of collective decision-making depends on:

- The process model employed (analytic or cybernetic)
- The number of persons involved in the preparation of the decision
- The number of persons participating in the final decision

A good decision should be based as much as possible on an evaluation of the possible consequences of the options, including the probabilities and utilities of the outcomes. When a group employs such arguments it is called an analytic model (e.g., Maoz 1990). The alternative is that the group reviews sequentially a number of alternatives, neglecting the consequences and searching for a compromise that is acceptable to all members. This model is called cybernetic. The analytic model is also recommended by Janis's (1989) vigilant problem-solving strategy and by George (1980).

It will be clear that the analytic approach cannot always be used to reach a decision. In that case a switch to a cybernetic approach is commonly made. Such a switch is dangerous since the possible consequences of options are completely ignored. It would still be acceptable if incremental decision-making is used, where the decision is taken by a series of steps, sequentially. In that case one still has control over the possible consequences. This is, however, not the case if completely new options are formulated which have not been evaluated beforehand.

The second criterion concerns the number of people participating in the preparation of the decision. The decision can be prepared by one or several persons of the same homogeneous group or by several persons of different groups. We believe that the latter possibility gives the best assurance that no important aspect of the decision problem will be omitted. With homogeneous groups, and even less so with single decision-makers, one does not have this guarantee.

The number of people participating in the final decision is a third criterion of quality: is the final decision made by one predominant leader or by a group of decision-makers? Decision-making by a group of people with different backgrounds and affiliations can reduce the risk involved in the final decision because the decision is checked from different points of view. Decision-making by a single person carries the risk that this individual has ignored a relevant aspect which would have been considered if more participants had been involved. Along the same line of argument, one might expect the decision-making of a homogeneous group to be more risky than the decision-making by a heterogeneous group. The second and the third criteria coincide roughly with George's (1972, 1980) multiple advocacy.

Table S.1 classifies the different decision units according to these criteria. This table shows that the criteria 1 and 3 do not normally coincide: agreement in a heterogeneous group is rather exceptional. Therefore, these groups mostly have to rely on a cybernetic approach to reach a decision. On the other hand, the analytic model is mainly found in groups where only one person or a homogeneous group makes the final decision. In that case the analytic model can be employed to the end of the decision-making process if no serious disagreements arise within the group.

A very interesting intermediate approach is found in the United States when the president is a predominant leader sensitive to the opinions of others, as was shown in Chapter 5. In this case, he asked a large group of heterogeneous people to prepare the decision. They had no power to make the decision so there was no reason for conflict and consequently resort to a cybernetic approach. They provided the president with two completely elaborated options, specifying for each the consequences. On the basis of this overview of all necessary information the president could make his decision. It seems that this combination of one person making the decision with the preparation of the decision by representatives of different groups can yield high quality. Although the outcome of the decision might not be satisfactory, the decision itself cannot be criticized on the basis that too little information has been assembled.

Another question is whether one can overload one person with too much information. The literature (e.g., Simon 1957, 1985; Tversky and Kahneman 1974, 1988; Vertzberger 1990; Gallhofer and Saris 1996) showed that individual decision-makers are unable to process all this information in such a way that an optimal decision will be made on the basis of the existing information. Nevertheless, we think that the procedure used by the U.S. government in the Cuban missile crisis was effective.

This conclusion has also been made by McNamara (1995, 332) when he compared the decision-making during the Cuban missile crisis with the decision-making concerning Vietnam. As secretary of defense he had participated in both decision-making processes. Speaking about the decision-making concerning Vietnam, he stated:

Over and over again as my story of the decision-making process makes shockingly clear, we failed to address fundamental issues. As I have suggested, this resulted in part from our failure to organize properly. No senior person in Washington dealt solely with Vietnam. To avoid these, we should have established a full-time team at the highest level focused on Vietnam and nothing else. The meetings should have been characterized by the openness and candor of Executive Committee deliberations during the Cuban missile crisis which contributed to the avoidance of a catastrophe. Similar organizational arrangement should be established to direct all future military operations.

It will be clear that this manner of decision-making by a group of advisers and a sensitive predominant leader is fundamentally different from the procedure of the unit with an insensitive predominant leader, like Hitler, who takes all steps alone. This is probably the most dangerous approach of all, as history has already demonstrated on several occasions.

An acceptable alternative to the approach with a sensitive predominant leader is probably the deployment of a heterogeneous group as practiced in many Western European cabinets. In this process the whole cabinet is formally responsible for decisions and several people can prepare the decision, but because of frequent disagreement about important issues, the analytic approach will not work and will be replaced by the cybernetic mode. In this approach the quality control ensured by explicitly specifying all necessary information for the decision is replaced by a group process where the quality of the decision is controlled by the amount of support the proposal obtains from participants with different backgrounds and different affiliations. For heterogeneous governments, the requirement of a unanimous decision is one way to keep control over the decision-making quality. It is obvious, however, that this approach can cost the participants much time in case of serious problems. Chapters 7 and 8 made this clear. But without this automatic control mechanism, the heterogeneous group runs the same risk as other groups, that decisions are not adequately checked from different perspectives. On the other hand, the requirement of a unanimous decision will frequently make group decision-making impossible if the group is very large (twenty or more members). How this problem is solved by hetero-geneous groups is one of the issues dealt with in the next part of this book.

Table S.1

Classification of the Different Decision-Making Units with Reference to the Quality Criteria

Model	Analytic			Cybernetic		
Number of participants during the preparation	One	More and homogeneous	More and heterogeneous	One	More and homogeneous	More and heterogeneous
Number of participants during the final decision:						
One	Predominant leader insensitive to others' opinions: German case study		Predominant leader sensitive to others' opinions: U.S. case study			
More and homogeneous		Homogeneous group with agreement			Homogeneous group with disagreement: Austro-Hungarian case study	
More and heterogeneous			Heterogeneous group with agreement			Heterogeneous group with disagreement: Dutch case studies

Part 2

A Quantitative Study of Collective Decision-Making by a Heterogeneous Group

Part 2 looks at the collective decision-making of a heterogeneous group, on the basis of a sample of minutes of meetings of the Dutch council of ministers dealing with important foreign policy decisions during this century. Chapter 9 introduces the research design and methodology. Chapter 10 tests the propositions concerning the process. The propositions relating to the preference aggregation rules are then tested in Chapter 11. The volume concludes with an extension of the theoretical framework to other heterogeneous groups (Summary of Part 2).

Chapter 9

The Study of Decision-Making Processes

In this part, we investigate how a heterogeneous group, exemplified by the Dutch council of ministers, arrives at collective decisions. Earlier we postulated that, in order to arrive at a decision, a group has to go through three necessary phases or steps. We suggested the following steps:

1. The specification of the problem, the gathering of information, and the general orientation about available solutions
2. The specification by one or more people of arguments in favor of one of the options
3. A process of aggregation of individual preferences into a group choice

In our view these steps are essential to the process of arriving at a collective choice, although the sequence in which they are carried out may differ from situation to situation and from group to group. Participants may change the sequence, omit steps, and cycle back and forth. Part 1 (Chapters 4 through 8) illustrated decision-making processes in different units, and there it was already obvious that they did not strictly follow a linear sequence. In this part we will try to assess which sequences of interactions or process types are characteristic for a heterogeneous group, under what conditions certain aggregation rules are used, and which participants contribute most to the decision-making process.

SURVEY OF THE LITERATURE

In communication research, according to Ellis and Fisher (1994), the most frequently used approach to an understanding of the group decision-making process over time is to study the different acts of participants in sequence. This sequence shows different stages or phases in the group's interactions from the beginning until the reaching of a choice. A prominent early phase model is Bales's (1950) and Bales and Strodtbeck's (1951) Interaction Process Analysis (IPA) model, which contains three stages. Stage 1 can be described as a problem orientation phase, stage 2 as a problem evaluation phase, where the group specifies what approach should be taken toward the problem, and stage 3 as a phase relating to the control of the problem, where the group decides how to resolve it (Ellis and Fisher 1994, 152–154). Ellis and Fisher (1994, 154–156) also mention several other phase models and conclude that although they do not share identical definitions of each stage, they all have in common that they first postulate a search for a view of the problem; then in a middle phase, a phase of conflict, differences of opinion emerge; and in the final stage the participants concentrate on reaching a decision.

Besides these models that posit a more or less single sequence of phases, Poole and his associates, on the basis of empirical evidence, develop the idea that groups do not necessarily follow a single sequence path, but depending on their task, goals, and group characteristics, they can take different paths, what the authors call multiple sequence models. Poole and his associates (Poole and Roth 1989a, 1989b; Holmes and Poole 1991; Poole and Holmes 1995; Poole and Baldwin 1996) cited data to support three major paths that collective decision-making could take. One of these they call the *unitary problem-solving sequence or path*, which consists of a pattern from problem definition (P), through conflict management (C) to solution development (S), and finally to the decision-making (D). This path or sequence can be characterized using our notation: PCSD. This pattern more or less coincides with the classical IPA model and occurred in 30 percent of their data. In their data they found that this path occurred mostly with cohesive groups having unclear goals.

The second model they call *complex decision paths*, characterized by the omission of phases and/or cycling to previous phases. A repeated problem/solution cycle is most characteristic of complex paths. This complex path can be summarized as follows: PSPS...D. According to Poole and Roth (1989a), decisions which lack consensus on goals and interests produce complex cyclic paths. The third model, which they call the *solution-oriented path*, is characterized by moving immediately to a solution-oriented discussion and spending little time on other phases. In their view this most frequently occurs in groups with clear goals and tasks requiring little creativity. This solution-oriented path can be denoted as SD.

In our view, however, not all combinations of the mentioned variables have been made. Many other process patterns are conceivable in political decision-making. Although Poole and his associates studied a great variety of decision-making groups, we think that political decision-making groups, if at all present, constituted only a small fraction of their study. In the next section we will therefore introduce our own framework with propositions, based on the findings of communication research.

THEORETICAL FRAMEWORK AND PROPOSITIONS

On the basis of empirical research, Poole and Baldwin (1996, 228) identify three variables that affect sequences of decision-making processes: task characteristics, group characteristics, and the degree of conflict in the group. Task and group characteristics are useful in studies of various decision-making groups having such different tasks as problem solving, negotiating, and so on. Since the objective of this study is to detect the use of different sequences in decision-making processes in one kind of group, namely, a multiple autonomous or heterogeneous group whose task it always is to solve an existing political problem, the two earlier mentioned characteristics do not seem appropriate. Agreement or disagreement among decision-makers or especially among the key decision-makers (i.e., those participants who play a crucial role in decision-making), however, seems to be a useful characteristic. Next we think that the situational characteristic of crisis and the complexity of the decision-making problem might also have an impact on the decision-making process. Table 9.1 displays sequences in processes that might be expected on the basis of variation in these characteristics.

Table 9.1 shows that if the problem is simple and the key decision-makers agree about the available solutions, we expect a brief process consisting of a solution-oriented phase and finishing with a decision (SD). In this case, any crisis situation will play no role because decision-makers are able to make a decision quickly (see patterns 1 and 5 in the table). When key decision-makers agree and the problem is complex, both solution-oriented phases and problem-oriented phases will occur because there is a need to study the problem in more detail before deciding. If there is no crisis situation (pattern 2 in the table), there will be

Table 9.1
Expected Relationship between Patterns of Decision-Making Processes and the Variables of Crisis, Agreement among Key Decision-Makers, and Problem Complexity

Pattern number	Crisis	Agreement	Problem complexity	Process
1	no	yes	simple	SD
2	no	yes	complex	SPSPSP...D
3	no	no	simple	SCSCS...D
4	no	no	complex	PSCSPSCS...D
5	yes	yes	simple	SD
6	yes	yes	complex	SPSP...D
7	yes	no	simple	SCSCS...D
8	yes	no	complex	PSCSCSCS...D

relatively more problem-oriented phases than in a crisis situation because there is more time available for discussion than in crisis situations (pattern 6).

If the problem is simple but key decision-makers disagree about the solution, we expect a sequence in which solution-oriented acts will alternate with conflict-oriented acts in order to arrive at a decision (patterns 3 and 7).We expect similar sequences for both crisis and noncrisis situations. We expect the most elaborate process sequences when there is disagreement about a complex problem. Since the problem is complex, problem-oriented phases will alternate with solution- and conflict-oriented phases. In noncrisis situations more problem-oriented phases will occur because there is more time available for discussions (pattern 4) than in crisis situations (pattern 8).

On the basis of these assumptions we can now reformulate the propositions we intend to test. Since our empirical material does not allow problem complexity to be studied independently, the propositions concerning the differences in decision-making processes will make use of the following variables:

* Agreement between the key decision-makers
* Presence of a crisis situation

To these two variables one more variable is added, indicating whether the problem has been previously discussed or not. The introduction of this variable is necessary because the analysis does not cover all meetings on the same topic but only the separate meetings of the cabinet which have been found. Otherwise, the number of cases would be reduced too much. This means that we have to bear in mind that the process will differ according to whether one speaks about an issue for the first or the second or the third time. The consequence of this variable will be specified later.

The propositions concerning the decision-making process have already been formulated in Chapter 2 (Part 1) together with propositions concerning other units. For clarity's sake we will stick to the numbering of the propositions used in Chapter 2.

Proposition 5: Decision-makers will spend more time discussing problem-oriented acts in noncrisis situations because there is more time available for such discussions.

Proposition 6: There will be more conflict-oriented acts when the key decision-makers (i.e., those most involved in the decision) disagree about the course of action to choose. But if decision-makers disagree and if the topic has already been discussed several times, conflict-oriented acts will be employed less because the participants are aware of the conflict and try to control it.

Proposition 7: If disagreement arises in a crisis situation, positive conflict-oriented acts especially will be employed in order to arrive at a decision because of lack of time.

In addition to the propositions about the process, which will be evaluated in Chapter 10, propositions have also been formulated in Chapter 2 with respect to the preference aggregation rules. These propositions are also repeated here and will be tested in Chapter 11.

Proposition 8: We expect decision-making groups to strive for consensus as the most preferred aggregation rule in political decision-making.

Proposition 9: If no consensus can be achieved, a decision-making group has in principle three options available to solve the problem:

1. To postpone the decision in order to collect further information and/or to have bilateral discussions
2. To shift from argumentation to a procedure where the search concentrates solely on a course of action which is acceptable to all participants
3. To shift to an aggregation procedure which requires not consensus, but a less restrictive aggregation rule

Proposition 10: What solution or combination of solutions is adopted by a group, and how quickly the shift from one procedure to the next is made, depend first of all on the norms of the specific group.

Proposition 11: The aggregation rule employed will be affected not only by disagreement but also by the situation (whether or not there is a crisis).

Proposition 12: In case of lack of consensus the decision-making mode will change from an analytic approach to a cybernetic one. In the cybernetic mode more options will be evaluated sequentially without consideration of consequences. These options will usually deviate only slightly from the status quo.

Before we test these propositions, it would seem in order to discuss the research design and the methodology.

RESEARCH DESIGN

For the quantitative studies we have taken a sample of decisions made by the Dutch government concerning foreign policy during the twentieth century. Before the raw data of the decision cases could be collected, two problems were encountered that had to be resolved. First, there was no way of knowing the total number of foreign policy decisions between 1900 and 1955—the period for which we were allowed access to documents—because the ministry of general affairs did not keep systematic inventories of all the decisions made in the cabinet. Second, when all available means are used to gather as complete as possible an inventory of decisions, it is still possible that some cases will be omitted, since the records may be incomplete, not containing the detailed discussion of the participants during the meeting.

In order to eliminate these problems as far as possible, the study population of foreign policy decisions between 1900 and 1955 was defined as follows: only those decisions were selected that were described in historical or political studies in such a manner that one could assume that documents existed containing the relevant choice arguments. We thus collected the most important decisions for which material was available. With respect to the choice of historico-political studies from which we drew our raw data, we first consulted handbooks for an overview of the existing literature (e.g., Stapel 1943; Smit 1950, 1962; Leurdijk 1978; Voorhoeve 1979; Hommes 1980; Klein and van der Plaat 1981). We then consulted the most recent studies of historical periods, and complementary material was gathered from the diaries and memoirs of officials (e.g., Drees 1963; Stikker 1966; Beyen 1968; Van Kleffens 1983; De Jong 1988).

In this way we collected 136 decision situations. We defined "decision situation" as a situation in which a problem was signaled by persons either outside or inside the cabinet that needed discussion within the cabinet. These problems might be a change of the existing situation to a more preferred one or reactions to measures from outside actors. Table 9.2 summarizes the number of decision situations in the study population for the time periods under investigation.

The table shows that for the period before the end of World War II, relatively few decision situations (forty-two) were available. This was partly due to the fact that some archives were no longer intact and it was also partly caused by the practice of the council of ministers, which did not take verbatim minutes of the discussions during this time. For this period we intended to study all the available material, but an inspection of the documents showed that for thirty-eight situations the material was incomplete, leaving only four situations, covering nine cabinet meetings, to study. Table 9.3 summarizes the description of the decision situations studied.

The ninety-four decision situations after World War II (Table 9.2) consisted on average of 3.5 cabinet meetings, which means that approximately 329 minutes of meetings would have to be analyzed. Since this task would have been too time-consuming and too costly for the available research funds, a random sample without replacement of ten decision situations was drawn, containing forty-nine cabinet meetings. The selection of cabinet meetings in the period before World War II was not very good, but we decided to keep the cases in the study.

In the first period, one decision situation related to World War I and concerned the maintenance of Dutch neutrality during the impending invasion of neutral Belgium by the German Reich. The other three sets of situations related to World War II. These decision situations concerned the negotiation of a separate peace treaty between Hitler's Germany and the Dutch government in exile in London, transferring the seat of the government in exile to Indonesia and lending gold stocks to the British for their war effort.

The remaining ten decision situations concerned the War of Independence in

Table 9.2

Description of the Population of Decision Situations in the Given Time Periods

Time period	Number of decision situations
1900–1945 World War I-World War II	42
1945–1955 Indonesian War of Independence and postwar recovery in the Netherlands	94
Total	136

Table 9.3

Description of the Decision Situations Studied

Time period	Number of decision situations	Number of minutes of meetings	Mode of selection
1900–1945 World War I- World War II	4	9	All complete documents
1945–1955 Indonesian War of Independence and postwar recovery in the Netherlands	10	40	Random sample without replacement
Total	14	49	

Indonesia (1945–1949) and postwar recovery in the Netherlands (1945–1955). With respect to Indonesia we analyzed the two military interventions by the Netherlands and the two interventions by the United Nations in response to Dutch military efforts. The postwar recovery decisions concerned claims for war reparations from Germany, settling a dispute with Germany concerning the Rhine Navigation Act and taking part in negotiations to set up organizations such as the Western European Union, NATO, Benelux, and the European Economic Community (EEC). In matters concerning the EEC and NATO, it should be mentioned that only a few cabinet meetings were available, because the majority of documents were still classified.

In conclusion, the sample of cabinet meetings for the time period after World War II can be considered representative of the population of interest. The data collection for the earlier period is incomplete because of the lack of documents.

METHODOLOGY

In the following chapters two types of quantitative analyses will be conducted. One is an analysis of the sequences of activities or phases in the decision-making process. The other is an analysis of the use of preference aggregation rules in the decision-making. In order to do these analyses, we have to say something about the way the sequences of acts or phases are determined and how the aggregation rules have been disclosed.

For the forty-nine collective decision-making processes studied, the acts were coded using the coding scheme presented in Chapter 3 (Part 1). The coding reliability was very high (Scott's π >.82). Dijkstra's (1994) Sequence program has been used to simplify the sequences of individual acts to sequences of different phases of acts. This was done by two procedures called "mask" and "unite." If the following sequence of acts was found:

SI SA SI SC SOF PI PSA SA SC PA SI SA SOF DT

where SI reads solution-oriented phase act of information

SA solution-oriented phase act of argumentation

SC solution-oriented phase act of solution critique

SOF solution-oriented phase act of option formulation

PI problem-oriented phase act of information

PSA problem-oriented phase act of solution analysis

PA problem-oriented phase act of problem analysis

DT decision taken

the procedure "mask" would take away the code specific for the individual act, leading to the sequence:

S S S S S P P S S P S S S D

If one uses thereafter the procedure "unite," all uninterrupted identical codes are combined in one code so that only the codes for switches in phases remain. The result would be:

S P S P S D

The reduction of the sequences of individual acts to sequences of phases does not have to be carried out by the "mask and unite" procedure we have used. Poole and Roth (1989a, 1989b) and Holmes and Poole (1991), for instance, suggest using a three-step procedure. According to these authors, the act codes are first transformed into phase codes that provide a more general classification of the acts. Second, the sequences of phase codes are used to create shorter sequences of phase codes by creating larger units, which characterize periods of acts. Finally, the reduced sequences of phases are compared with each other in order to generate some kind of classification of the processes that generate decisions in real-life decision-making. Poole and his associates (Holmes and Poole 1991; Poole and Holmes 1995) suggest basing the classification of the acts in phases on a fixed number of consecutive acts with the same phase value (the first label: S, P, C, or D). For example, if there is a switch in the phase value of acts and the next two have the same phase code, they suggest introducing a code of a new phase. If different acts followed after a switch within the next two acts, a mixed code would be used. For our example of a sequence of acts, this would lead to the following phase coding according to Poole and Holmes's procedure:

S PS SP S D

where PS and SP stand for mixed phases. Since it will often happen that less than three acts of the same phase type follow each other, one would have to deal with many phases with mixed activities like PS and SP.

Our procedure can be seen as identical to that of Poole and his associates, but with a different criterion for the length of a phase. They require three acts of the same phase to define a pure new phase. We decided that one act with a different phase label would immediately define a different phase. Poole and Holmes (1995, 124, note 3) also indicate that the value of three consecutive acts is an arbitrary choice.

After reducing the sequences of acts to sequences of different phases, we have used the same Sequence program (Dijkstra 1994) for the classification of the different sequences. To classify patterns of interactions, agreement scores have been used. The program provides for three possibilities. The measures differ with respect to the weight they give to the two differences that exist between sequences: the absence of some codes in one sequence compared with the other and the difference in position of the different codes in the string. One measure in their program "α" gives more weight to the first aspect, one measure "γ" gives more weight to the second, while the third measure "β" is intermediate between the other two in weighting.

In such problems, the position of the elements is essential and, therefore, the same string at a different position does not lead to agreement. These measures have also been used in the social sciences for narrative stories and the analysis of music, and so on (Abbot 1995). These measures give very low agreement between strings of the following kinds:

S P C P S C S C S D
and
S C P S C S I C I S D

even though both contain the same string C P S C S. The problem lies in the different position of this string in both sequences.

In our view, an approach which looks for similar strings even at different positions in the sequence is relevant for our purpose, and we have therefore chosen Dijkstra's approach and have used the agreement measure "γ" to determine the clusters of sequences. For a discussion of the merits of the different approaches we refer to Dijkstra and Taris (1995) and Abbot (1995). The quality of the result is demonstrated in the next chapter. For the text analysis of the preference aggregation rule we refer to Chapter 3, Part 1.

CONCLUSIONS

This chapter has introduced the way we reduce the complex sequences of acts in the decision-making process to sequences of phases. In this approach we have used a slightly different procedure than was suggested by Holmes and Poole (1991). In the next chapter we see how successful this procedure was.

The data selection for this quantitative study has also been discussed. Unfortunately, we could not take a sample of studies of the period before World War II because in many minutes only the final decisions were registered and not the discussion. For the period from 1945 to 1951, a sample had to be drawn because too many minutes with enough information were available. No meetings after 1951 have been studied because of limited access to the archives at the time these data were collected. As a result of these limitations, this study can formally be seen as representative only for the period from 1945 to 1951. However, we think that the results to be presented are so general that the conclusions will not be limited to this period and to only one country. An argument along these lines is presented in the summary of this part.

Chapter 10

The Decision-Making Process (Results)

The first section of this chapter describes the sequences of phases identified in our data. In the second part, the tests concerning the process propositions are discussed.

DESCRIPTION OF CLUSTERS OF SEQUENCES

Table 10.1, presenting the clusters of sequences identified, shows that forty-eight out of forty-nine sequences could be classified reasonably well in nine classes of clusters. One sequence could not be well classified because of the deviating pattern: P C P S I S D. Even if the I, which stands for an implementation-oriented phase, is omitted, the string P C P S D cannot be matched very well due to the deviant combination P C P, which does not appear in any other standard sequence pattern.

Some sequences have been added to a class for substantive reasons, although they were not placed there by the program. This will be indicated later. That these clusters are quite good will also be demonstrated by presenting the individual sequences for each cluster. In the first cluster four sequences are found which are all identical to the standard. We have added one sequence which was S I S D. If we ignore the code I, this sequence reduces to the standard of cluster 1. In the second cluster the sequence S P S D is found three times, while one other sequence has been automatically included in this cluster, which is P S D. This sequence is so similar that no discussion is necessary. The third type of sequence, S P S P S D, occurs in exactly the same form seven times.

The fourth cluster contains several deviant sequences. This cluster is therefore presented in Table 10.2. It will be clear that all these sequences have the same feature: more or less frequently a problem analysis (P) sequence occurs. This means that the pattern is very similar in this cluster. The similarity expressed in

Table 10.1
Different Clusters Found in the Data of the Dutch Council of Ministers,
Using the Program Sequence

Cluster number	Number of sequences	Most characteristic sequence
1	5	S D
2	4	S P S D
3	7	S P S P S D
4	6	S P S P S P S P S P S D
5	4	S P S P S P S C S D
6	6	P S P S C S P S P S P S C S D
7	4	S C S C S D
8	7	S P S C S C S C S C S D
9	5	S C S C S C S C P S C S D

Table 10.2
The Sequences in Cluster 4

Sequence number	Standard sequence	S P S P S P S P S P S D	γ
40		S P S P S P S D	0.80
31		P S P S P S P S D	0.87
33		S P S P S P S P S D	0.91
44		S P S P S P S P S P S D	1.00
36		S P S P S P S P S P S P S D	0.89
39		S P S P S P S P S P S P S P S D	0.86

the similarity coefficient γ is also very high (Dijkstra and Taris 1995).

Cluster 5 also contains several deviations from the standard, which are shown in Table 10.3. In this cluster all sequences have a problem-oriented phase at the beginning, and just before the end they explicitly introduce conflict. This does not mean that conflict was not already present in the discussion. Probably all participants were aware of this conflict and for this reason spent so much time on preparing the decision.

Cluster 6 contains six sequences which are largely very similar, but differences occur, as can be seen in Table 10.4. In each sequence the activities look similar. The group starts mostly with a problem-oriented phase, but is quickly reminded that there is a conflict in the background. They then try to find a solution for a while. This activity is successful, possibly with the assistance of a little threat or one or more extra request(s) for cooperation (C). The number of conflict-creating

Table 10.3
The Sequences in Cluster 5

Sequence number	Standard sequence	S P S P S P S P S C S D	γ
37		S P S P S P S P S C S D	1.00
38		S P S P S P S P S C S D	1.00
16		S P S C S D	0.73
29		S P I S P S P S P S P S C S D	0.35

Table 10.4
The Sequences in Cluster 6

Sequence number	Standard sequence	P S P S C S P S P S P S C S D	γ
41		P S P S C S P S P S P S C S D	1.00
27		P S P S P S C S P S P S C S D	0.83
35		S P S C S C S P S P S P S C S D	0.87
46		P C S C S P S C S P S P S P S C S D	0.89
48		S C S C S C S C S P S P S C S D	0.76
34		P S C S P S P S P C S P S P S P S C S C S C S D	0.73

or -reducing activities increases, but in this case the number of problem-oriented activities also increases. This is no longer the case in the next clusters.

For cluster 7 the standard sequence is rather simple, that is, S C S C S D. In this pattern there is no problem-oriented phase present, even though a threat or a reconciliatory remark has twice been made (C). This sequence is found exactly three times, while once the sequence is S C S D. This means one sequence of S C less than the standard, but the pattern (no P but C) seems to be very similar.

Finally, in cluster 8 (Table 10.5) the standard sequence is an extension of the standard of cluster 7. This more complex sequence also leads to more deviations, as Table 10.5 shows. The frequent occurrence of conflict is characteristic for cluster 8. The participants very quickly initiate conflict behavior and probably also conflict management, but do not spend any time on reconsidering how to approach the problem (P), except in some cases at the very beginning of the discussions.

This phenomenon is even more extreme in the last cluster (Table 10.6), where each sequence contains at least four C phases, but often even more. Only very occasionally is an effort made, as before, to reanalyze the problem (P). If it did happen it was mainly at the beginning of the discussions.

Table 10.5
The Sequences in Cluster 8

Sequence number	Standard sequence	S P S C S C S C S C S D	γ
14		S C S C S C S I S I S I S D	0.71
19		S C S C S D	0.80
23		S C S C S C S D	0.80
22		C S C S C S C S D	0.86
7		S C S C S C S C S D	0.91
4		S P S C S C S C S C S D	1.00
5		S P S C S C S C S C S D	1.00

Table 10.6
The Sequences in Cluster 9

Sequence number	Standard sequence	S C S C S C S C P S C S D	γ
18		S C S C S C S C P S C S D	1.00
32		P C P C S C S C P C S P S D	0.89
1		P S P S C P S P C S C S C S D	0.82
47		S C S C S C S C S C S C S C S D	0.77
45		S C S C S C S C S C P S C S C S C S D	0.81

Our impression is that we have found very clear classes of processes although the borderlines are often very arbitrary. It is, for example, not clear why the sequence of cluster 3 is not added to cluster 4. The smaller sequences of cluster 4 could also have been classified in cluster 3. The same could have been done for the clusters that vary in the number of C acts in the sequence.

Table 10.1 showed that the following four basic clusters of sequences could be distinguished:

1. A cluster of sequences without P and C phases (cluster 1). These decisions consist of relatively simple and low-involvement problems, and therefore, no P and C acts appear.
2. Clusters with sequences without C acts (clusters 2, 3, and 4). These sequences vary in complexity while the decision-makers seem to work in a cooperative mood so that no C acts occur.
3. Clusters of sequences with many Ps and a few Cs (clusters 5 and 6).
4. Clusters of sequences with many C acts but no P acts (clusters 7, 8, and 9).

Figure 10.1
The Sequences of Types of Phases Beginning with an S Phase
Five Steps Deep

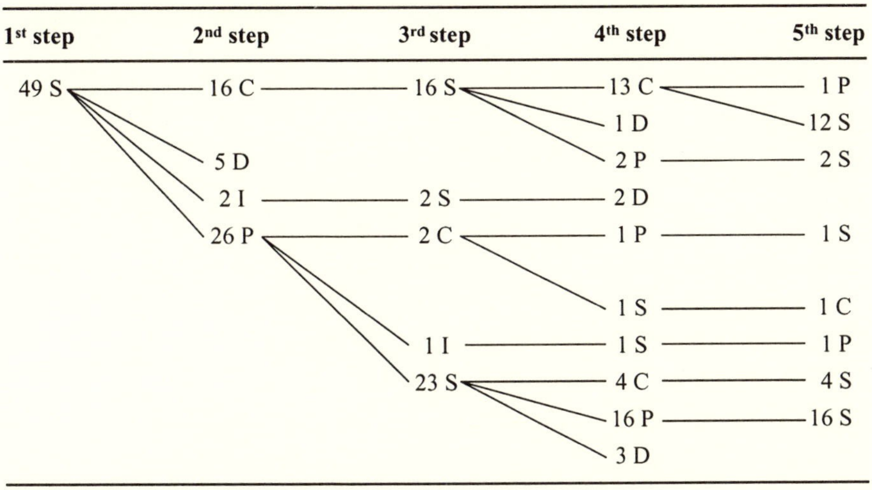

1st step	2nd step	3rd step	4th step	5th step
49 S	16 C	16 S	13 C	1 P
			1 D	12 S
	5 D		2 P	2 S
	2 I	2 S	2 D	
	26 P	2 C	1 P	1 S
			1 S	1 C
		1 I	1 S	1 P
		23 S	4 C	4 S
			16 P	16 S
			3 D	

The sequences we have found are rather restrictive. First of all, there are very few sequences where C and P follow each other. In fact, a C is followed in 90 percent of the cases by an S and in only 10 percent of the cases by a P, while a P is followed in 91 percent of the cases by an S and only in 9 percent of the cases by a C. This pattern reduces the number of possible sequences considerably. Another restriction in these data is that the order of the S P and S C pairs is also special. Both restrictions are illustrated in Figure 10.1.

Not all possible orders occur. There is one sequence where the S C pair occurs just before the decision is made, while before only S P pairs occur. There is another sequence where the group begins with S P pairs, then moves to S C, then again to S P, and finally, at the end, one S C pair appears again. These are two very special orders of S P and S C pairs. These empirical restrictions mean that many possible alternative clusters have also been excluded.

The reader should be aware that Figure 10.1 shows maximally five consecutive steps of the sequences. If they are shorter, the end of the sequence is indicated by a D phase. This figure clearly indicates that S P sequences are most frequently followed again by S P sequences, and in the same way S C sequences are mostly followed by S C sequences. Given the evidence for these restrictions it is to be expected that the number of possible sequences is also limited to the sets we have presented in Table 10.1.

To conclude this section on the validity of the identified sequences of phases, we would like to discuss the differences between the nine clusters we found in terms of the solution-oriented acts the participants employed. Independently of

Table 10.7
**Relationship between the Type of Sequence and the Way the Problem
Is Solved in Percentages for each Cluster**

Solution-oriented acts	1	Cluster 2	3	4	Numbers 5	6	7	8	9	Total %
Argument (SA)	18	25	24	21	21	27	0	11	31	23
Option critique (SCR)	44	12	17	15	20	12	6	33	20	20
Information (SI)	12	41	37	44	39	46	49	28	36	37
Option formulation (SOF)	16	15	13	15	13	10	34	17	8	14
Decision postponed (DP)	4	4	5	2	1	1	6	7	2	3
Decision taken (DT)	6	3	4	3	6	4	5	4	3	3
Total %	100	100	100	100	100	100	100	100	100	100
Total absolute	73	68	112	138	145	197	35	91	121	980

the occurrence of problem-oriented and conflict-oriented acts, the difference in decision-making processes can also be demonstrated by specific kinds of solution-oriented interactions that group members will use in the different situations. This result is shown in Table 10.7. This table shows that problem solving differs greatly for the different clusters. The differences are also statistically significant ($G^2 = 146.382$; df. = 45; prob. = 0.000). This result suggests to us the following interpretation.

In cluster 1, sequences are brought together for decision-making processes which are characterized by no problem analyses or conflict management. These sequences sometimes occur in cases of crisis, when people appear to refrain from any complex activities but go immediately to the point. In other cases, participants probably have little involvement; they solve their problems mainly by exhaustive criticism of mooted solutions, both positive and negative. Usual processes like provision of information and exchange of argument do occur less than normally. In the case of low involvement one can arrive in this way by majority decision at conclusions which in other situations would not be immediately acceptable to the participants.

Cluster 2 contains sequences indicative for situations where there is no crisis, the decision-makers disagree, and they know that from previous discussions. In such a situation their behavior is very different. A striking difference with the first cluster is the considerable reduction in the criticism of solutions and a considerable increase in such normal activities as exchange of information and arguments.

Cluster 3 is characterized by an approximately normal distribution of all problem-solving activities found in this study.

In situations of noncrisis and known disagreement (from previous discussions) between the decision-makers, cluster 4 sequences are frequently found, containing the greatest amount of problem analysis yet without conflict (management). As can be seen, cluster 4 sequences have more than average information exchange compared with the other situations.

We now move to these situations where conflict plays a role. As we have seen, this happens mostly when a topic is discussed for the first time. Cluster 5 is a strange situation because the key ministers agree. Conflict (management) nevertheless occurs, although at a very low level. As a result the problem-solving behavior still looks very much like that in clusters 3 and 4.

This is not the case in cluster 6, which occurs only in situations where the issue is discussed for the first time and the key ministers are in disagreement. In this case, the sequences contain more conflict (management), but at the same time (since these are noncrisis situations) the amount of effort spent on information and argumentation exchange also increases. This suggests a group that is still cooperative with sufficient time, trying to solve a (partially socially) complex decision problem.

Cluster 7 is found mainly in crisis situations where key ministers disagree. In cluster 7 the conflict is equally high but the problem analysis has disappeared because of lack of time. It seems that in such processes the problem-solving style also changes somewhat. The emphasis is not so much on argumentation and solution criticism, which can increase the tension, but on finding a compromise through increasing the exchange of information and suggesting available solutions.

In cluster 8 conflict is even further enhanced. It now appears that besides threatening each other and/or asking for cooperation, participants spend considerable effort making suggestions for solutions and criticizing each other's proposals. It would seem that they no longer have any hope that a solution can be found through information exchange and argumentation. Therefore, these activities have been reduced.

Finally, a surprising result can be seen in the last cluster, which is characterized by even more conflict. In this case the participants once again give arguments for their choices. One might wonder why they would do this, given the level of conflict and the finding that argumentation is reduced when the tension increases. In our view, the participants in these processes have given up any hope of a normal solution and therefore spend considerable time indicating for the record why they have chosen as they did. In the same mood a request for a vote is more frequently asked. This is not a last effort to solve the problem, however; the purpose is rather to put on record what their opinion was in this particular case. In the cases concerned, these decisions were so important that they expected that the government would have to resign if they did not reach an agreement; in that case they wanted their position to be clear.

This overview suggests again that the clusters of decision-making processes that were found are highly distinct, not only in their pattern of different activities, but also in the way the group deals with the problem-solving itself. This result lends strong support to the claim for the relevance of the distinctions made in these different sequences.

Poole and his associates (Poole and Roth 1989a, 1989b; Holmes and Poole 1991) also found a pattern similar to our cluster 1, but unlike them, we did not detect simple problem definition and solution clusters. Most of our patterns were in their terms quite complex decision paths characterized by repeated problem and solution cycles.

RESULTS REGARDING THE TESTS OF THE PROPOSITIONS

The first proposition to be tested here is proposition 5, which posits:

Decision-makers will spend more time on problem-oriented acts in noncrisis situations than in crisis situations because there is more time available for such discussions.

In table 10.8 the sequences of phases in crisis and noncrisis situations are presented. Comparing the third and the fourth columns of Table 10.8 shows the effect of crisis on the process. The table shows indeed that sequences with recurring problem-oriented phases (clusters 2, 3, 4, 5, and 6) occur relatively more frequently when there is no crisis situation, twenty-four out of thirty-four, than when there is a crisis, three out of fourteen. This difference is also statistically significant notwithstanding the small sample ($\chi^2 = 18.6$; df. = 8; prob. = .005). Our conclusion, therefore, is that proposition 5 is not falsified by our data.

Proposition 6 posits the following:

There will be more conflict-oriented acts when the key decision-makers (i.e., those most involved in the decision) disagree about the course of action to choose. But if decision-makers disagree and if the topic has already been discussed several times, conflict-oriented acts will be employed less frequently because the participants are aware of conflict and try to control it.

The first part of this proposition can also be evaluated on the basis of Table 10.8. The effect of disagreement among key decision-makers on the process can be seen by comparing the first and the second columns. It shows that there are relatively more conflict-oriented phases (clusters 7, 8, and 9) when the key decision-makers disagree (fourteen out of thirty-one) than when they agree (two out of seventeen). This difference is also significant on the 10 percent level ($\chi^2 = 14.7$; df. = 8; prob. = .06). The effect of crisis on the process cannot be explained by the disagreement or vice versa because these two variables turn out to be independent of each other in this research.

The last part of proposition 6 posited that conflict-oriented acts will occur less frequently if the topic has already been discussed several times, because participants are aware of the presence of conflict and try to control it. Table 10.9 presents the results to test this proposition. This table shows very clearly that this proposition is incorrect. It seems that in later discussions the decision-makers create more conflict and need more conflict management in order to come to a group decision. It would appear that it is not enough that all participants are aware of the conflict. In later meetings they are also explicitly busy with the management of these conflicts. This relationship is quite strong ($\chi^2 = 13.1$; df. = 7; prob. = .07) and it indicates that the second part of proposition 6 must be rejected on the basis of our data.

In this context it is interesting to see whether positive or negative conflict-oriented acts occur more frequently. Proposition 7 posited that:

Table 10.8
Relationship between the Clusters of Decision-Making Processes and the Variables of Crisis and Agreement among Key Decision-Makers

Cluster number	Agreement		Crisis	
	No	Yes	No	Yes
1 S D	3	2	3	2
2 S P S D	3	1	3	1
3 S P S P S D	3	4	6	1
4 S P S P S P S P S P S D	3	3	6	0
5 S P S P S P S C S D	0	4	3	1
6 P S P S C S P S P S P S C S D	5	1	6	0
7 S C S C S D	3	1	0	4
8 S P S C S C S C S C S D	6	1	3	4
9 S C S C S C S C P S C S D	5	0	4	1
Total	31	17	34	14

Table 10.9
The Effect of Previous Discussion on the Occurrence of Conflict-Oriented Interactions in Situations of Disagreement between the Key Ministers

Clusters	Topic No	Discussed before Yes	Total
Without conflict 1, 2, 3, 4	5	7	12
With conflict 5, 6, 7, 8, 9	1	18	19
Total	6	25	31

Table 10.10

Relationship between Crisis, Disagreement among Key Decision-Makers, and the Presence of Conflict-Oriented Acts

| | | | Conflict-oriented acts | | | | | |
| | | Positive | | | Neutral | Negative | | |
	Request for unity	Request for a compromise	Request for accommodation	Management of group tension	Request for a vote	Request for a postponement	Threat	Total number of acts
Crisis	6	4	5	5	5	3	5	33
Non-crisis	5	13	4	1	1	13	7	44

If disagreement arises in a crisis situation, positive conflict-oriented acts especially will be employed in order to arrive at a decision because of lack of time.

Table 10.10 displays data to test this proposition. In this table the different conflict-oriented acts which occur under the conditions of crisis and noncrisis have been indicated. It is not immediately clear whether proposition 7 is supported or not. In crisis situations there are twenty positive acts out of thirty-three conflict-oriented acts, while in noncrisis situations there are twenty-three positive acts out of forty-four conflict-oriented acts. This difference is not significant.

What is clear from this table is that decision-makers try to finish the decision in crisis situations if necessary by voting (five requests against one in noncrisis situations), whereas in noncrisis situations they are more inclined to postpone the decision (thirteen requests against three in crisis situations) in order to consider the problem afresh or to bring in new information. We continue with this issue in the next chapter. With respect to proposition 7, then, we conclude that the data do not provide evidence to support this hypothesis.

CONCLUSIONS

In this chapter we have discussed the empirical findings relating to the decision-making process. We found nine clusters of sequences which could describe the decision-making processes in a heterogeneous group. We have studied the validity of the identified clusters of sequences in different ways and we conclude that these sequences make sense because they indicate plausible behavior of decision-makers.

Next, different propositions concerning the decision-making process in a heterogeneous group were formulated and tested. It turned out that decision-makers devoted more time to problem-oriented phases in noncrisis situations, which is in agreement with proposition 5. Conflict-oriented phases were more frequent when key decision-makers disagreed. This finding supports the first part of proposition 6. We also found that decision-makers who disagreed and had already discussed the problem did not diminish conflict-oriented acts in later meetings. This finding contradicts the second part of proposition 6.

We also expected that decision-makers in crisis situations, because of the short decision time available, would show numerous positive conflict-oriented acts to arrive at a choice quickly, whereas in noncrisis situations, when they disagreed, the negative conflict-oriented acts might first predominate. However, our data did not show these expected differences. The participants were equally hostile and peaceful under the situations of crisis and noncrisis. Proposition 7 was therefore also not confirmed. However, it became obvious on the basis of our data that they tried to speed up the solution in a different way, which was to ask for a vote that would lead to a less restricted aggregation rule than consensus. This kind of process is studied in more detail in the next chapter.

Chapter 11

Preference Aggregation Rules (Results)

In this chapter we study the preference aggregation rules that are used by the Dutch government to make collective decisions. In Chapters 2 and 9 it was mentioned that different aggregation rules exist and that the choice of the rules depends on the norms employed in the decision group. Norms can be considered as behavioral standards which have been developed in order to reduce tension among participants. The members must conform to them or will be induced to do so. For a detailed discussion of norms we refer to Ellis and Fisher (1994, 128–132).

This chapter begins with an indication of how, in our opinion, these norms can be studied empirically. Thereafter we present the norms for preference aggregation rules that have been claimed in the literature to hold for the Dutch government. On the basis of this information, testable hypotheses with respect to the norms in the Netherlands will be formulated, and subsequently we test the formulated propositions about the use of these aggregation rules.

THE STUDY OF NORMS

It was earlier suggested that a basic rule for most governments is proposition 8:

We expect decision-making groups to strive for consensus as the most preferred aggregation rule for political decision-making.

An earlier version of this chapter was first published in the *Journal of European Research* 25 (1994), pp. 151–170. Kluwer Academic Publishers granted us permission to use the figures and the tables in this chapter.

Most of the time, one decision-maker reviews a range of strategies and indicates a preference on the basis of the consideration of possible consequences, probabilities, and evaluations of outcomes. If another decision-maker does not agree with this argument, he or she will also present an argument. If there is no difference of opinion and they can agree on a choice after these discussions, the decision is made by consensus. Proposition 8 says that this result is the one most preferred by the politicians.

However, this result is not always obtained. The participants may not succeed in convincing each other of a preferred course of action on substantive grounds because other decision-makers disagree about the strategy, the possible consequences, the probabilities, or the evaluative judgments of the consequences. In that case the argumentation phase will be terminated as being futile.

At that point, three different solutions are possible, which have been formulated in proposition 9:

If no consensus can be achieved, a decision-making group has in principle three options available to solve the problem:

1. To postpone the decision in order to collect further information and/or to have bilateral discussions
2. To shift from argumentation to a procedure where the search concentrates solely on a course of action which is acceptable to all participants
3. To shift to an aggregation procedure which requires not consensus, but a less restrictive aggregation rule.

Which solution will be chosen in any specific group depends on the norms of the group concerning the way decisions have to be made. This point was specified in proposition 10:

What solution or combination of solutions is adopted by a group, and how quickly the shift from one procedure to the next is made, depend first of all on the norms of the specific group.

If a group is strongly oriented toward decision-making on the basis of consensus, then it seems logical that after the argumentation phase a phase should follow in which they no longer argue but try to reach consensus by formulating different compromises between the competing proposals. If they succeed in finding such a compromise, they can still make a unanimous decision. This means that we expect a group which is striving for consensus to try first out the solution mentioned in proposition 9.2.

If these efforts prove unsuccessful, the decision-makers can choose between postponing the decision or relaxing the requirements of group consensus (propositions 9.1 and 9.3). This is mostly done by the chairman of the meeting (the prime minister), who may ask the opponents of a specific proposal whether they are willing to accept the proposal even though they disagree with it. If this

Figure 11.1

The Preference Aggregation Process in One Session, Indicating the Probabilities of the Different Events

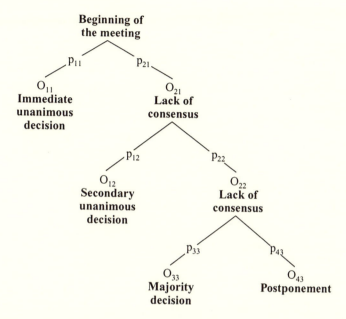

Symbols: P_{ij} probability of the ith number of outcome in the jth branch of the tree; O_{ij} the ith number of outcome in the jth branch of the tree. Outcomes which indicate the same content are given the same numerical value and differ only with respect to the index of the branch.

proposal is rejected, then the only solution left is a postponement of the decision in order to get a unanimous decision at a later date.

The three stages in the process discussed above are formally represented in the decision tree in Figure 11.1. The figure shows that there is a chance of an immediate unanimous decision (p_{11}) on the basis of the argumentation phase. If there remains disagreement among the ministers about the arguments in the first instance, the decision cannot immediately be made unanimously (p_{21}). But in the second stage there is a second chance to achieve a unanimous decision by a compromise (p_{12}). It is, however, possible that this process may also not be successful (p_{22}).

If there is still lack of agreement after the second phase, the requirements with respect to the aggregation rule can be relaxed to make a (weighted) majority decision possible (p_{33}), or the decision can be postponed again (p_{43}) in order to reach a consensus or a majority decision at a later date. This preference aggregation process can, of course, be repeated several times. It would be interesting to study it from meeting to meeting, but the number of cases studied does not allow for this. As in Chapter 10 where we studied the sequences of the process within one session, we will in this study similarly look at the preference aggregation rules.

On the basis of proposition 8 we expect that in case of disagreement after the first phase the government will always try to find a compromise in order to reach consensus. This is studied when we investigate the use of the different decision models. Another prediction that can be derived is that in case of continued lack of consensus, even after the second phase, the government would prefer postponement above majority decision-making; therefore, we would expect in general that $p_{33} < p_{43}$.

Using this decision tree we can make similar predictions about outcomes under different norms with respect to the use of aggregation rules. These predictions can be tested to evaluate the norms of different groups. In the next section such predictions are derived for the Dutch cabinet on the basis of the literature. Later in this chapter these predictions are tested.

NORMS OF THE DUTCH COUNCIL OF MINISTERS

In order to define the norms of the Dutch cabinet we concentrate first on the literature that refers to these norms. With respect to preference aggregation rules, Lijphart (1968) and Timmermans and Bakema (1990) suggest that the consensus principle is preferred to majority rule, although the latter would be formally sufficient. The authors claim that voting is very infrequent because of the danger of precipitating a cabinet crisis. In this respect, the norm seems to be in line with proposition 8.

Lijphart (1968), however, also characterized the decision-making process as a process of "accommodation" to divisive issues and conflicts when there is no consensus. The process of accommodation generally means that a compromise acceptable to all participants is hammered out, which would agree with our suggestion that governments striving for consensus will try to find compromises (proposition 9.2) when argumentation no longer works.

If a compromise cannot be reached because of the opposition of certain groups, the other groups do their best not to antagonize them and will be prepared to postpone the issue if it does not require an immediate solution (Lijphart 1968). This would be in agreement with our suggestion that for governments which strive for consensus, $p_{33} < p_{43}$. This theory suggests that the Dutch government makes decisions along the line we have previously indicated for a government which strives for unanimous decisions.

According to another author, however, a unanimous decision is not always necessary. There is also the norm of "noninterference" (Andeweg 1990, 27). According to this norm, the decisions can be made by the ministers whose departments are directly involved in the issue (we call them key ministers), while other ministers, whose departments are not concerned with the specific issue, refrain from interference. In essence, this principle of noninterference contradicts the norm of unanimity, since the decision is made by key ministers who might even be a minority in the cabinet. In terms of the probabilities in the decision tree, this would mean that in case of agreement between the key ministers, we expect that $p_{33} > p_{43}$. This is the opposite hypothesis of what was suggested earlier in the case of consensus norm. The critical test is, however, not this comparison. The reason will be mentioned later.

If it is true that the key ministers have the possibility of pushing ahead their choice without "interference" from others, it is up to them whether to strive for consensus or not. If the norm of consensus is stronger than the norm of noninterference, then the key ministers will try to find a strategy that is supported by all ministers and not only by themselves. If they do so, p_{12} should be larger than p_{22} in the case of agreement among the key ministers. Thus, the critical test of the strength of the two norms should be made on the probabilities p_{12} and p_{22}. If $p_{12} > p_{22}$ in the case of agreement among the key ministers, then we can conclude also that for them the norm of consensus is more important than the norm of noninterference.

Just as interesting as the strength of these two norms is the question of what happens if the key ministers disagree. The literature does not give an answer to this question. It is, however, compatible with this literature to expect that no decision could be made without their agreement because of their influence on the process. We therefore expect in the case of lack of consensus among the key ministers that no majority decision will be made, but postponement to a next meeting will be preferred. In the case of disagreement among the key ministers, then we expect that $p_{33} < p_{43}$. The last result also indicates why one cannot simply use a comparison of p_{33} and p_{43} for a test of proposition 8. If there are more cases where the key ministers disagree, one will already have $p_{33} < p_{43}$ while it still might be the case that the noninterference norm is stronger than the consensus norm. Therefore, the test will be conducted on the basis of the probabilities p_{12} and p_{22}.

But before we can do so we have to answer the question: who are these ministers who feature so prominently in the decision-making process? Bakema and Secker (1988) and Bakema (1990) have shown that ministers are mostly technical experts in their departmental policy area. Van den Berg (1990) and Toirkens (1990) focused on the positions of certain ministers in the cabinet and found that there are identifiable norms of ministerial importance. Although these ministers may not necessarily be experts in the field of foreign affairs, they nevertheless hold key positions in the decision-making process. According to the above authors, the Dutch prime minister, although formally having fewer powers than his counterparts in other European countries, can nevertheless be considered as carrying most weight in the cabinet. Second in importance is the minister of finance, who allocates the budgets to all departments. The deputy prime minister, usually the leader of a coalition party in the cabinet, becomes important when there are conflicts between the coalition partners. In foreign policy decisions it follows that the key decision-makers will always include the prime minister, the minister of finance, the minister of foreign affairs, and, depending on the issue, other expert ministers such as the minister of overseas territories, the minister of defense, the minister of economics, or the deputy prime minister.

THE CONTRIBUTIONS TO THE DEBATE

In order to gain insight into individuals' contributions to the debate, the participants of the cabinet meetings were categorized into three groups: key ministers, non-key ministers, and experts. The latter were advisers from outside the council of ministers, who were mainly asked in crisis situations to attend the meeting and give their advice. The following tables will show whether the key ministers indeed play a different role in these meetings. We expect key ministers more frequently to present arguments with specified consequences for the different options; we expect them to introduce more new options, more new outcomes; and we also expect them to play a more active role in the group process with respect to conflict (management).

The first expectation can be tested on the data of Table 11.1. The cases in this table relate to the total number of decision-makers present in a specific group of participants over the forty-nine meetings. The table shows that experts who were asked to attend the meeting made the greatest contribution to the discussion of strategies in terms of the assessment of outcomes (76 percent)—a result quite consistent with their task of giving advice. Next were the key ministers (39 percent), while the non-key ministers only engaged in an extended argument in 16 percent of the cases. The table also shows that the non-key ministers mainly accept and reject the proposals of key ministers.

Another way of investigating the contributions to the solution finding of the different ministers is to assess who put forward most of the new strategies and outcomes; in other words, who was the most creative or innovative in the discussion. Tables 11.2 and 11.3 display the results for strategies and outcomes respectively. The data in both tables relate to discussions of Indonesian independence, the issue which led to the most elaborate discussions in the council of ministers and which is therefore the largest in our data collection. Restricting the analysis to only one substantive issue means that the function of the key ministers is always the same and that they are easy to identify.

Both tables show that experts developed most of the new strategies and outcomes, followed by the prime ministers and then the ministers of overseas territories, which is hardly surprising since it is their speciality. Next in sequence are the remaining key ministers, those of foreign affairs, and finance and the deputy prime minister. Furthermore, we can see that nonspecialists make an extremely small contribution. They mainly reject or accept strategies put forward by the specialists, and if they assess outcomes (Table 11.3) they repeat, in essence, those already mentioned. This can also be interpreted as indicating their acceptance of the consequences. Again, it is clear that the discussion is mainly conducted by the specialists, with a great involvement of the prime minister.

The final question for analysis was who put forward the proposal which was eventually adopted. We found that 69 percent of these strategies were generated by key ministers, 19 percent by non-key ministers, and 12 percent by experts.

Finally, Chapter 10 showed that conflict-oriented acts occurred most frequently when key decision-makers disagreed (proposition 6). Table 11.4 displays which participants made most of these contributions and clearly shows that key ministers were again the most active in this respect. Non-key ministers made fewer contributions than expected. Experts made no contributions at all, which is not surprising since their task was only to give advice.

The analysis showed very clearly that the core group of Dutch decision-makers, consisting of the prime minister, the deputy prime minister (in cases of disagreement among coalition partners), the minister of finance, and the relevant

Table 11.1

Relationship between Contribution to the Argumentation and Function

| Function | Kind of argument | | | | Presence of decision-makers at meetings |
| | Assessment of outcomes | | Acceptance or rejection only | | |
	%	abs.	%	abs.	abs.
Experts	76	(19)	24	(6)	25
Key ministers	39	(81)	61	(125)	206
Non-key ministers	16	(57)	84	(309)	366

$\chi^2 = 71.60$; df. = 2; prob. = 0.00; CC = .33

Table 11.2

Relationship between the Strategies Mentioned and the Function of the Participants

| Function | Index of strategies | | Total strategies mentioned |
	Newly created strategies	Previously mentioned strategies repeated	
Experts	1.28	1.02	2.30
Prime minister	1.00	1.39	2.39
Overseas territories	0.79	1.48	2.27
Foreign affairs	0.40	1.26	1.66
Finance	0.38	1.18	1.56
Deputy prime minister	0.26	2.06	2.32
Remaining ministers	0.10	0.69	0.79

The various scores indicate the number of strategies mentioned divided by the number of meetings at which the participant was present.

Table 11.3
Relationship between the Outcomes Mentioned and the Function of the Participants

Function	Index of outcomes		
	Newly created outcomes	Previously mentioned outcomes repeated	Total outcomes mentioned
Experts	3.02	1.92	4.94
Prime minister	1.30	1.60	2.90
Overseas territories	1.00	1.34	2.34
Foreign affairs	0.82	0.71	1.53
Finance	0.59	0.65	1.24
Deputy prime minister	0.46	0.80	1.26
Remaining ministers	0.12	0.23	0.35

The various scores indicate the number of outcomes mentioned divided by the number of meetings at
    which the participant was present.

Table 11.4
Relationship between the Function of the Decision-Maker and His Contribution to Conflict-Oriented Acts

Function of decision-maker	Conflict-oriented acts						
	Request for unity	Request for accom-moda-tion	Request for a compro-mise	Manage-ment of group tension	Request for a post-pone-ment	Threat	Request for a vote
Key minister	.06	.03	.05	.07	.08	.04	.02
Non-key minister	.03	.01	.02	.04	.02	.01	.00
Expert	.00	.00	.00	.00	.00	.00	.00

The various scores indicate the number of interactions divided by the presence of the specific
    decision-maker at the forty-nine meetings.

specialists, generated most of the options, discussed their consequences, and if conflict broke out, also generated and handled it. This confirms, we think, that in this respect the definition of key ministers is correct.

The next question is whether these ministers could also force their opinion on the majority in cases where there was no consensus. Although we have shown that the critical test should be performed on the probabilities in the case of agreement between the key ministers, we first present the overall probabilities to give an idea of the results obtained. Following this, we will perform the critical test on the strength of the two contradictory norms. How the probabilities will change in case of crisis is hard to predict. We prefer, therefore, not to formulate hypotheses for this situation in advance, but rather to return to these results after we have studied the noncrisis situations.

NORMS OF PREFERENCE AGGREGATION RULES IN NONCRISIS SITUATIONS

Figure 11. 2 shows that there was considerable disagreement at the beginning of the decision-making process in the meetings studied ($p_{21} = .86$). Further, the possibility of reaching a unanimous decision in the second instance seems limited ($p_{12} = .33$). In such an undecided situation where there is a lack of consensus (twenty-eight cases), the probability that a majority choice will be accepted (p_{33}) is only .39, while the probability of postponement is greater ($p_{43} = .61$). The latter probability seems to indicate that ministers are, in general, apparently unwilling to accept a choice if it is not supported by the whole cabinet. In cases where there is disagreement, they clearly prefer postponement to a majority decision. It should be remarked, however, that this result may also be a consequence of the fact that there are more cases where the key ministers disagree with each other than situations when they agree with each other. This mere fact can already be the explanation of the obtained result if disagreement between the key ministers normally leads to postponement. This result cannot therefore be seen as a critical test of the norm that they strive for consensus. For this purpose, the situation where the key ministers agree with each other has to be studied, as we mentioned before.

Table 11.5 summarizes the same probabilities for the cases of presence and absence of agreement among key decision-makers. Although the sample on which the analysis is based is rather small, Table 11.5 shows a very clear result: $p_{33} = 1$ in the case of agreement between key ministers. This indicates that the key ministers in the cabinet have the power to make a decision on their own without consent of the other ministers.

This result lends greater interest to what happens in this case to p_{12}. Do these key ministers strive for consensus even though they have the power to continue without it? The answer to this question is a definite yes, because of the probabilities: $p_{12} = .71$ and $p_{22} = .29$. It seems that the key ministers indeed strive for consensus if that is possible. Only if that fails do they make the decision on the

Figure 11.2
The Preference Aggregation Process in One Session, Indicating the Probabilities of the Different Events

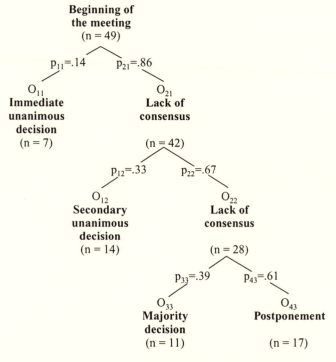

Symbols: P_{ij} probability of the ith number of outcome in the jth branch of the ree; O_{ij} the ith number of outcome in the jth branch of the tree. Outcomes which indicate the same content are given the same numerical value and differ only with respect to the index of the branch.

basis of the noninterference principle. The strength of the position of the key ministers is also very clear from the probabilities under the condition of lack of agreement among them. If the key ministers disagree with each other, it seems that the cabinet is unwilling to accept a majority decision and the decision is in most cases postponed (proposition 9.1).

The six cases which involved disagreement among key ministers and resulted in a majority decision need some further explanation. In these cases, the key ministers disagreed when initially presenting their arguments, but during the discussion this disagreement was resolved by finding a strategy on which they could agree. We could also have placed them in the category "agreement among key ministers," but since there was no agreement in the first instance, we preferred to present them in this way. If they had been placed in the category "agreement," the relationship would have been perfect.

Table 11.5
Estimates of the Probabilities under Condition of Agreement or
Disagreement between the Key Ministers

	Second level of Figure 11.1			Third level of Figure 11.1		
	Probability of a unanimous decision	Probability of lack of consensus		Probability of a majority decision	Probability of a postpone- ment	
	P_{12} (abs.)	P_{22} (abs.)	Total	P_{33} (abs.)	P_{43} (abs.)	Total
Agreement among key decision- makers	.71 (12)	.29 (5)	17	1.0 (5)	.00 (0)	5
Disagreement among key decision- makers	.08 (2)	.92 (23)	25	.26 (6)	.74 (17)	23
Total	14	28	42	11	17	28
	$\chi^2 = 17.83$; df. = 1; prob.= 0.00; CC = 0.55			$\chi^2 = 9.41$; df. = 1; prob. = 0.00; CC = 0.50		

The reader should note that this table consists of two parts which should be read separately.

In summary, the results indicate very clearly the power of the key ministers: without an agreement among them a decision is not possible. On the other hand, the key ministers strive for consensus with their colleagues according to proposition 8, but they can also make decisions on their own. They do not need this consensus. If there remains a lack of consensus while they have already reached an agreement, they can also make a decision on the basis of a weighted majority, which means that their preferences weigh more than those of other ministers. This observation is in line with the norm of noninterference. It is clear that in the Dutch cabinet both the consensus norm and the noninterference norm apply together: the group of key ministers which can exercise its power with implicit consent of the others (noninterference) refrains from doing so in order to strive for consensus as much as possible. Only if this consensus fails does this group use its power. Whether this combination of norms also occurs in other heterogeneous groups is discussed in the summary of this part.

Table 11.6
Estimates of the Probabilities in Crisis and Noncrisis Situations

| | Second level of Figure 11.1 | | | | | | Third level of Figure 11.1 | | | | | | |
| | Probability of a unanimous decision | | Probability of lack of consensus | | Total | | Probability of a majority decision | | Probability of a short postponement | | Probability of a long postponement | | Total |
	P_{12}	abs.	P_{22}	abs.		abs.	P_{33}	abs.	P_{43}	abs.	P_{53}	abs.	abs.
Crisis	.15	2	.85	11		13	.55	6	.46	5	.00	0	11
Noncrisis	.41	12	.59	17		29	.29	5	.00	0	.71	12	17
Total		14		28		42		11		5		12	28

$\chi^2 = 2.72$; df. = 1; prob. = .10; CC = .25 $\chi^2 = 16.5$; df. = 2; prob. = 0.00; CC = .61

NORMS OF PREFERENCE AGGREGATION RULES IN CRISIS SITUATIONS

Proposition 11 discusses the effect of the situation on the preference aggregation rules, although the proposition is not very explicit:

The aggregation rule employed will be affected not only by disagreement but also by the situation (whether or not there is a crisis).

The specification depends on the country studied. For the Dutch case, where consensus is the basic principle, we can now extend this proposition and state that crisis situations change the norm of unanimous decisions because there is less time for postponements and that, therefore, the majority rule will be more frequently employed than when there is no crisis.

Table 11.6 presents the results of this analysis. The first part of the table shows that the difference in secondary unanimous decisions between crisis and noncrisis situations lies in the expected direction, but is not significant at the 5 percent level. However, the difference in majority decisions between crisis and noncrisis (second part of the table) is significant at the 1 percent level. This table shows clearly that in crisis situations postponements are still possible, but they are much shorter than in noncrisis situations. In a crisis, one can also postpone decisions by a couple of hours; the case study in Chapter 8, Part 1 showed some evidence of this. The second part of proposition 11, namely, that majority decisions occur more frequently in crisis situations than in noncrisis situations, is thus corroborated.

It should be mentioned here that this finding cannot be explained by the fact that in crisis situations more agreement between the key ministers also occurs. Although this relationship could in principle explain the observed finding, it is not possible in this case because there is no relationship between the occurrence of crisis and agreement or disagreement between the key ministers. Therefore, this cannot be the explanation for the finding that more majority decisions are found in crisis situations. This must be an effect of the situation itself, a possibility which was suggested in proposition 11.

PROCESS MODELS

Proposition 9.2 posited that in the case of lack of consensus an effort can be made to reach consensus by formulating compromise proposals. In such a case, a switch from the analytic model to the cybernetic model is made. If that happens we might also expect that more options would be generated in cases of lack of consensus than in cases of consensus.

The strategies reviewed may be completely new ones, but more frequently, they are options which differ incrementally from the status quo, as suggested by Lindblom (1982). Compromise alternatives are frequently formulated which contain elements of options already suggested by different participants and which might be supported by all participants (see also Lijphart 1968; Timmermans and Bakema 1990). These arguments suggest proposition 12:

In the case of lack of consensus the decision-making mode will change from an analytic approach to a cybernetic one.
In the cybernetic mode options will be evaluated sequentially without consideration of consequences. These options will usually deviate only slightly from the status quo.

Table 11.7 presents the results of a test of this proposition with regard to the number of options evaluated. The table shows that when there is agreement among all the decision-makers, there is indeed a tendency to consider very few strategies. In only one case do they consider more than five alternatives. In situations of crisis and disagreement among key ministers and other decision-makers, two strategies are considered in only a very few cases: in 54 percent of the cases, between three and four options are considered, and not uncommonly more than five alternatives. If decision-makers are not in a crisis situation but are divided among themselves, they generate five or more alternatives in 55 percent of cases.

For a situation in which there is agreement among decision-makers or at least agreement among key ministers, we postulated (contrary to Maoz 1990) a more analytic type of decision-making process, which entails the choice of an option based on the consideration of consequences. For a situation in which there is

Table 11.7
Relationship between Crisis, Agreement, and the Number of Options Reviewed

Agreement	Number of options formulated						Total number of meetings
	2		3–4		5 or more		
	%	abs.	%	abs.	%	abs.	abs.
General agreement	30	2	55	4	16	1	7
Crisis and disagreement among key decision-makers	15	2	54	7	31	4	13
Noncrisis and disagreement among key decision-makers	10	3	35	10	55	16	29
Total		7		21		21	49

$\chi^2 = 17.57$; df. = 6; prob. = 0.00; CC = 0.51

disagreement, however, a cybernetic process was assumed in which a variety of strategies would be sequentially reviewed without considering consequences (proposition 12). Table 11.8 displays the results of this analysis.

The left side of Table 11.8 shows that out of a total of thirty-two choices (in seventeen of the forty-nine cases the decision was postponed), the outcomes of the chosen option were assessed in only twelve cases (38 percent). In the remaining twenty cases (62 percent), options were chosen without any evaluation of the possible consequences. Twenty-two of the chosen options (Table 11.8, right side) were formulated in such a way that they required action only in small steps, deviating only slightly from the status quo. In Lindblom's terms (Lindblom 1982), they would be called "incremental policies," policies which can always be adjusted at a later date if they prove to be unsatisfactory. Ten of them could also be characterized as compromises, containing elements of the chosen options preferred by several factions in the meeting. The remaining ten options were based on newly created strategies proposed by one of the participants.

Table 11.8 (left side) does indeed show that when decision-makers agree with the argument put forward, a strategy is selected on the basis of an evaluation of consequences. In this case, key ministers give complete arguments for the available options. If they agree on the option to select, even if there are differences in the perceived consequences, and if other ministers also give their approval, no further discussion takes place and an option is chosen on the basis, in some sense, of strategic evaluations, which approximates to the analytic model.

Table 11.8
Relationship between Disagreement and the Choice of an Option Based on the Assessment of Consequences

Disagreement	Choice process			Collectively chosen strategy		
	Analytic	Cybernetic	Total	Ssd	New	Total
No disagreement	7	0	7	3	4	7
Agreement among key ministers	5	5	10	4	6	10
Disagreement among key ministers	0	15	15	15	0	15
Total	12	20	32	22	10	32

$\chi^2 = 30.30$; df. = 2; prob. = 0.00; CC = .70 $\qquad$ $\chi^2 = 29.60$; df. = 2; prob. = 0.00; CC = .69

N = 32 because only the situation where a decision is made is taken into account. "Ssd" indicates an option differing slightly from the status quo and "new" refers to a newly created strategy.

If the key ministers agree but other ministers object to the selection of this option, there is frequently a brainstorming session to search for an acceptable strategy, and the evaluation of consequences is ignored because of the disagreement. If there is disagreement among the key decision-makers too, then the cabinet is only engaged in the generation of acceptable strategies, and the assessment of outcomes is completely disregarded. The ministers then review sequentially all kinds of strategies till a satisfactory one is found. Table 11.8 (right side) also clearly shows that the choice of incremental actions increases with disagreement. These results corroborate proposition 12, which predicts a preference for the cybernetic model and incremental strategies in cases of disagreement. This preference is understandable from a practical point of view, since it is often impossible to persuade other participants to change their minds, and therefore an effort has to be made to develop a course of action which all can accept whatever the consequences might be.

CONCLUSIONS

In this chapter propositions 8 through 12, formulated in Chapter 2 concerning the theory, have been tested. This test has been conducted on data taken from Dutch coalition cabinets, which are typical examples of heterogeneous groups.

First of all, it was posited that the meetings normally begin with the presentation of arguments for and against different options by a participant of the meeting. If all members of the meeting agree with the argument or the choice suggested, the decision is made unanimously. If some participants do not agree with the argument, a discussion will take place to convince each other on the basis of arguments. This analytic way of decision-making will continue for some time. It can lead to a unanimous decision, but it can also end in disagreement about the arguments among the decision-makers. In such a situation it makes no sense to continue in the same way, because it is impossible to convince the other party of estimates of probabilities and utilities of outcomes. In the second instance, therefore, if there is disagreement, the decision-makers have in principle the following possibilities: postponement (proposition 9.1), to look for a compromise (proposition 9.2), or to look for a less restrictive aggregation rule than consensus (proposition 9.3).

Which of these solutions is used depends on the norms of the group making the decisions (proposition 10). Proposition 8 stated that decision-making groups will try to reach consensus. This would mean that in cases of disagreement, the decision-makers will adopt a different procedure, known as the cybernetic model, in which they try to find a compromise on which all participants can agree without consideration of consequences. Second, it may be expected that the decision-making will be postponed if disagreement remains because the group prefers unanimous decisions above majority decisions.

In the Netherlands, the decision-making process is, however, different because the key ministers play a much more important role than the other ministers. Key ministers are the specialists with regard to the topic of the decision and those central figures in the cabinet like the prime minister. There is a norm, called noninterference, which allows the key ministers to make decisions by weighted majority if they agree with each other. Interestingly enough, this power is only used occasionally by the key ministers. In general, they (the key ministers) try to find a compromise on which all ministers can agree even if they have already agreed with each other on their course of action. This phenomenon, occurring in 63 percent of the cases that key ministers agreed with each other but not with the other ministers, clearly indicates that in this group the norm of consensus is also taken into account as far as possible.

Finally, it was shown that the key ministers are so important that if they disagree with each other, no decision can be made and the decision will almost certainly be postponed to the next meeting. This norm will be called the norm of postponement. This brings us to the following specification of proposition 10 for the Dutch cabinet:

- The norm of noninterference dictates that the key ministers can make a decision by a weighted majority if they agree with each other.
- The norm of consensus dictates that the key ministers will not immediately use this power but will always try to reach a unanimous decision first.
- The norm of postponement dictates that no decision can be made by the whole group if the key ministers have not found a compromise on which all of them agree.

Whether similar norms are also used in other Western-European countries is a question to be examined in the summary of this part.

We have also seen that in the Netherlands, where consensus has priority under normal conditions of noncrisis, a switch of the aggregation rule to a majority rule is possible if the government is confronted with a crisis situation. It will be clear that this happens in order to speed up the decision-making process under such conditions. It is also obvious that such a switch is only possible if the norm of consensus exists in a country; otherwise such a switch is unnecessary.

Lastly, it was shown that in the case of disagreement, especially among the key ministers, the mode of decision-making changes. The Dutch government normally begins with argumentation, known as the analytic model. If disagreement persists, a switch is made to a different mode, known as the cybernetic model, where one looks for compromises without considering the consequences of the proposed options. This process has been described in proposition 12.

We believe this study has provided us with the empirical evidence for a description of the decision-making in the Dutch cabinet which makes sense. In this description, we were able to apply the general framework specified in Chapter 2, and in this chapter to combine it with information about norms found in the literature for the Netherlands. Given the usefulness of our concepts, we shall in the summary of this part look to see whether we can also make general statements about the way other governments, consisting of heterogeneous groups, aggregate their individual preferences to formulate collective choices.

The Practice of Collective Choice in a Heterogeneous Group

EMPIRICAL ANALYSIS OF THE DECISION-MAKING PROCESS

This study showed that the sequences of acts in the decision-making process vary so much and that the structure is so complex that we have first had to simplify the patterns by introducing phases in order to analyze sequences of phases rather than sequences of individual acts. As a result, nine clusters of sequences were found which could describe the decision-making processes in this heterogeneous group. The validity of the detected clusters of sequences was studied in different ways and it was concluded that the detected sequences were valid; they indicated the plausible behavior of decision-makers.

Next, the different propositions concerning the decision-making process in a heterogeneous group have been formulated and tested. Proposition 5 posited that decision-makers would spend more time on problem-oriented acts in noncrisis situations because there was more time available for such discussions. It turned out that decision-makers indeed devoted more time to problem-oriented phases in noncrisis situations, which is in agreement with proposition 5.

Proposition 6 stated that there would be more conflict-oriented acts when decision-makers disagree about the course of action to choose. But if the topic had already been discussed several times, conflict-oriented acts would be employed less often because the participants knew about the presence of conflict and tried to control it. Our data showed that conflict-oriented phases were more frequent when decision-makers disagreed. This finding corroborated the first part of proposition 6. We also found that decision-makers who disagreed, and had already discussed the problem before, did not refrain from conflict-oriented acts in later meetings. This finding thus did not corroborate the second part of proposition 6. The second part of proposition 6 therefore needs to be reformulated as follows:

If decision-makers disagree about the course of action, they will resort to conflict-oriented acts.

We also expected (proposition 7) that decision-makers in crisis situations would show more positive conflict-oriented acts in order to arrive quickly at a choice, because of the shorter decision time available than in noncrisis situations. However, our data did not show these expected differences. The participants were equally hostile and peaceful under the situations of crisis and noncrisis. It became obvious, on the basis of our data, that they tried to speed up the solution in a different way, by asking for a vote, which meant that they allowed a less restricted aggregation rule than consensus. Proposition 7 was thus not confirmed and needs to be reformulated:

If disagreement arises in crisis situations, decision-makers do not behave more cooperatively than in noncrisis situations in pursuit of a quicker decision.

In this situation the problem was solved by altering the decision rule. This is the topic of the next section.

EMPIRICAL RESULTS CONCERNING THE AGGREGATION RULES

Where the use of aggregation rules was concerned, it was postulated that in addition to the situational characteristic of crisis and the presence or absence of disagreement, the norms of the cabinet played a major role (propositions 8 to 11). These norms were the striving for consensus, the norm of noninterference, which gave the key ministers (those most involved in the decision because of their position in the cabinet or the topic of decision) major power, and the norm of postponement.

The data showed that consensus was the basic principle for decision-making. When the core group of key ministers agreed on the course of action to follow and the nonspecialists did not object, a consensus was reached immediately. If the key ministers disagreed in noncrisis situations, the decision was postponed several times in order to reach a consensus, which consisted usually of a compromise. If the key ministers agreed in a noncrisis situation but other ministers had objections, the norm of consensus was stronger than the norm of noninterference, since the key ministers did not use their power to arrive at a weighted majority decision, but rather tried again to arrive at a consensus by formulating compromises acceptable to all participants. However, if there was a crisis situation and the key ministers disagreed, they postponed the decision, but only for a short time. In order to arrive at agreement among the core group and because of lack of time they switched from the consensus principle to a majority rule.

We also found that in general in this heterogeneous group, disagreement produced a change in the decision model. Instead of continuing with an analytic approach, they switched to a cybernetic one (proposition 12). When the decision-makers agreed, the analytic "type" of model was followed on the basis of the assessment of the consequences. The reader may note that we prefer to speak about an analytic "type" of model because it is impossible to prove that decision-makers actually made use of the available information about consequences when finally selecting an option. When disagreement occurred, a cybernetic approach was followed, which meant reviewing sequentially a large number of alternatives without paying attention to consequences. The problem in cases of disagreement was how to reach a solution; the remedy was mostly to seek an alternative that could win maximal support. These options were frequently formulated in such a way that they only required action in small steps, deviating slightly from the status quo (incremental decision-making; see Lindblom 1982), because the decision-makers were in disagreement either about the consequences or about the steps to take. Other options employed consisted of compromises between the initial proposals.

Now that we have studied in detail the collective decision-making in the Dutch council of ministers, the question remains whether this kind of decision-making, especially where the norms are concerned, is also used to any extent in other heterogeneous governing groups in Western Europe. In the next sections we investigate this question on the basis of the available literature.

HOW COUNTRY SPECIFIC ARE THE DUTCH NORMS?

The norms of the Dutch cabinet were specified in proposition 10 as follows:

- The norm of noninterference dictates that key ministers can make a decision by a weighted majority if they agree with each other.
- The norm of consensus dictates that the key ministers will not immediately use this power but will always try to reach a unanimous decision first.
- The norm of postponement dictates that no decision can be made if the key ministers have not found a solution on which all of them agree.

In one of the first comparative studies of the style of decision-making by Western European governments, Blondel (1988, 1) states: "For the first time in their history, Western European countries have been ruled during a substantial period by similar types of governments. All Western European governments have adopted the formula of parliamentary and cabinet rule." He further states (Blondel 1988, 1):

The formula of parliamentary and cabinet rule is organized, in contrast to the presidential system which prevails in the United States and Latin America, on the idea that the executive is linked to legislature. The government cannot remain in office if it ceases to have the confidence of Parliament.

Possibly more important for our discussion is the following observation (Blondel 1988, 1):

> The arrangement is also based on the notion that the government constitutes a collective body: the ministers form a cabinet which is more than the sum of its members as it is ultimately responsible as a body to Parliament and through Parliament to the nation for the conduct of the affairs of the country.

This last quotation indicates that in most Western European countries the government as a whole is responsible for the decisions it makes. This means that in all these countries, ministers with different backgrounds and affiliations at least to different ministries, and in coalition governments also to different parties, have to make decisions together. In this respect these governments can be described as heterogeneous groups. This situation is not different from the situation described for the Dutch government.

Within this context, of course, there is still room for a considerable variation in the way that cabinets will function. In this respect, one might think of the roles of the prime minister and the minister of finance, the responsibilities of the other ministers, and the norms regarding the way the decisions have to be made. Below we give some idea of the norms that have been claimed in the literature to hold in several Western European countries. We have chosen to discuss the norms for the three largest Western European countries—Great Britain, France, and Germany—and for another smaller country, Belgium. It should be noticed that we do not discuss routine decision-making in this section. The decision problems should be of such importance that they require at least communication with one other ministry.

NORMS REGARDING AGGREGATION RULES IN GREAT BRITAIN

The British government has attracted much attention in the literature in recent years (Burch 1988; James 1992; Rhodes and Dunleavy 1995). In Great Britain, the cabinet has grown from ten people at the beginning of this century to twenty people nowadays. This has required a different way of decision-making. James (1992, 87) mentions that "most decisions are taken by individual ministers or by bilateral agreement, or by clearing papers by correspondence." This means that the individual ministers have gained considerable power to decide many problems themselves.

With regard to foreign policy and economic decisions, the authors mention that the prime minister is also very much involved. These decisions are either resolved bilaterally with the prime minister and the specific minister, or if more departments are involved, committees are created, frequently chaired by the prime minister and having as members both experts and the relevant ministers. These committees have the power to make decisions. It is clear that because of the work of committees, the role of the cabinet is reduced. In fact (James 1992, 87 and 195):

The majority of significant decisions are now taken by committees. The Cabinet's role has shrunk: in the period 1945 to 1979 it became mainly a court of appeal against committee decisions, and since the 1980's it has exercised a general oversight, warning and commenting but no longer deciding. In essence, the Cabinet system exercises over individual ministers the same control that Parliament exercises over the government.

Previously, the cabinet had a task to perform if a committee did not come to a decision because of differences of opinion. In such cases the procedure was as follows (James 1992, 73–74):

A paper was circulated with the agenda by the lead minister: usually a short summary (two pages or so) with detailed supporting information relegated to appendices. The Prime minister asked either the chairman of the Cabinet committee or the lead minister to introduce the subject, preferably as tersely as possible. He would then invite opposing ministers, who may also have put in paper, to speak. If there were public spending implications and the Chancellor was not one of the main protagonists, he would be invited to speak next. After these set-piece contributions, the Prime minister would invite the views of other colleagues. These ministers were expected to screen the proposal for its good sense and public acceptability. As these "non-involved" ministers gave their views and the ministers in the conflict responded, a collective view slowly took shape.

According to the literature, such discussions became rare after 1980. Ministers even became annoyed by excessively long explanations of proposals by colleagues. This shows that the British system has developed more in the direction where the main norm is the noninterference rule, leaving the responsibility as much as possible with the ministers involved in the issue.

The concept of collective responsibility has, however, not completely disappeared, particularly where there are conflicts between the specialists. James (1992, 76–77) suggests that:

The delicate task of framing the Cabinet's decision was up to the Prime minister. The Cabinet did not vote. The Prime minister had to take into account not only the number on either side but also the weight of opinion (quoting Heath and Barker): and by weight I mean the views expressed by some senior members of the Cabinet, carrying more weight than the views that are put forward by others.

In terms of the previous chapter, we would conclude that in the British system the key ministers, if they agree with each other, have the right to make decisions on their own (without even hearing the cabinet). This is a strong form of the noninterference norm.

Only if the key ministers disagree is the problem put to the cabinet. Discussion takes place just as presented earlier in this book. The final decision is not necessarily a unanimous decision. According to the literature, the prime minister summarizes the conclusion, taking into account unequal weighting of the ministers. This might even be some kind of decision by interpretation, the aggregation rule discovered by Steiner and Dorff (1980a, 1980b). What this shows is that in Britain consensus is no longer so important.

We did not find any indication that postponement takes place if the ministers involved continue to disagree with each other. This might be a point for further research.

On the whole, it seems that in Great Britain the cabinet plays a less important role in the decision-making than in the Netherlands, due to the stronger norm of noninterference. However, when the cabinet comes together, the process seems to be similar to that in the Dutch cabinet.

NORMS REGARDING AGGREGATION RULES IN FRANCE

France has a dual executive based on the president and the prime minister with his government. Until 1986 the president had a supportive majority in parliament, which meant that the prime minister and the government were also of the same party. According to the literature (Thiébault 1988, 88), "the Prime minister acted under the umbrella of the leadership of the President. The relationship was a hierarchical one." But when this ceased in 1986 the prime minister was furnished by the majority party in parliament and he became a real head of government. Both the prime minister and the president rely on their parties. This means that we are dealing with a heterogeneous group. This group is hierarchical since the ministers are "wholly dependent on the prime minister and the President" and they "tend to relate to the president and the prime minister in a manner akin to that of civil servants" (Thiébault 1988, 90).

Decision proposals are discussed in interdepartmental committees which are chaired, if the issue is an important one, by the prime minister and which include the relevant ministers and their civil servants. "If the points of view differ, further meetings are scheduled in order to achieve consensus. If disagreement persists between the ministers the matter is referred to the Prime minister, who takes a decision. Such decisions are called arbitrages of the Prime minister" (Thiébault 1988, 98).

This procedure indicates, in our view, the following with regard to norms:

1. Noninterference of key ministers is practiced

2. Consensus is not required

3. Postponements are not employed. In cases of disagreement the decision is made by the prime minister.

The council of ministers has to approve decisions prepared elsewhere. It is chaired by the president and brings him together with the prime minister and his government. Since the literature does not mention what happens in the case where the president disagrees with a decision, further research is required on this topic.

NORMS REGARDING AGGREGATION RULES IN THE FEDERAL REPUBLIC OF GERMANY

The government in the Federal Republic of Germany is based on a parliamentary majority, which suggests that the group can be classified as heterogeneous. According to the literature (Müller-Rommel 1988), the chancellor, who is the head of government, plays a dominant role in cabinet decision-making by setting priorities in policy making. Next to him the minister of finance has a strong position, whereas the other ministers are considered as equal.

Individual ministers enjoy considerable autonomy in formulating policy proposals. Müller-Rommel (1988, 166) states that "all ministers have a vested interest in not interfering with, or criticizing, the proposals of fellow ministers and this way they protect their autonomy," which clearly indicates that a norm of noninterference exists. Proposals are discussed bilaterally with the chancellor or, if the topic relates to different departments, there are interdepartmental meetings where the subject is discussed and a consensus reached among the responsible ministers (Müller-Rommel 1988, 159, 166). Müller-Rommel, however, stresses that the decision-making in committees is only used to a limited extent in Germany.

According to the literature, the work of the cabinet consists of discussions of current political matters and the formal approval of submitted policy proposals. Since the consensual bargaining process has already taken place before the cabinet meeting:

Policy issues create conflicts among cabinet ministers only very rarely. In such cases the chancellor usually formulates what he perceives to be the majority view. If no cabinet member opposes, the Chancellor's suggestion becomes the cabinet decision. Formal voting in cabinet is very rare (Müller-Rommel 1988, 166).

This last observation stresses once again the strong position of the chancellor and indicates the switch of aggregation rule.

In conclusion, it can be said that the norm of noninterference is practiced in the German government. Concerning postponements a more detailed study probably also could reveal this norm.

NORMS REGARDING AGGREGATION RULES IN BELGIUM

Belgian cabinets are mostly coalition cabinets of the three main parties. The cabinets are considered hierarchical with the prime minister and two deputy prime ministers, who are drawn from the three parties, as the key decision-makers. The deputy prime ministers are also heads of the more important departments. "As the top elite of the parties they tend to meet as a group in order to discuss the main problems facing the cabinet. Once they have come to an agreement among themselves and with the Prime minister, this agreement is then proposed to the rest of the ministers" (Frognier 1988, 75–76).

The passage just quoted indicates clearly the presence of key ministers who do not tolerate interference in their affairs. Frognier (1988, 83) mentions that:

The Belgian cabinet is not only a place where matters which have already been prepared elsewhere are being formally approved. The cabinet often discusses delicate problems which divide the majority and the cabinet meeting becomes a forum for debate and negotiation. Debates are particularly awkward when the Prime minister and the Deputy prime ministers have not been able to reach agreement beforehand.

This quotation clearly indicates that this heterogeneous group is quite similar to the Dutch cabinet in using more or less the same norms for preference aggregation.

QUESTIONS THAT HAVE BEEN LEFT OPEN

These last sections show that those Western European governments we have briefly investigated on the basis of available literature all use to some extent the aggregation rules we discovered in our quantitative study of the Dutch cabinet. It appears that all the countries discussed use a system of delegation of power from the cabinet to a smaller group of key decision-makers. This core group of decision-makers, however, can be formed in different ways. They all have in common that they can make a decision on their own if they agree. This is characterized by the rule of noninterference. This also means that the quality of decision-making (see also Summary of Part 1) is largely delegated to these key decision-makers and it is not the responsibility of the entire cabinet. The countries differ in their emphasis on consensus in the cabinet. It seems that especially in the United Kingdom consensus no longer plays a major role. Since the literature does not describe this issue in detail, a systematic and highly detailed cross-national comparative study would be necessary to gain more insight into the exact differences and similarities.

References

LITERATURE

Abbot, A. 1995. "A Comment on Measuring the Agreement between Sequences." *Sociological Methods and Research* 24: 214–231.

Akten zur Deutschen Auswärtigen Politik, 1918–1945, Serie D, vol. 7. 1956. Baden-Baden: Imprimerie Nationale.

Allison, G. T. 1971. *The Essence of Decision: Explaining the Cuban Missile Crisis.* Boston: Little, Brown.

Allison, G. T., and H. M. Halperin. 1972. "Bureaucratic Politics: A Paradigm and Some Policy Implications." In R. Tanter and R. U. Ullman, eds., *Theory and Policy in International Relations,* 40–79. Princeton: Princeton University Press.

Anderson, P. A. 1983. "Decision-Making by Objection and the Cuban Missile Crisis." *Administrative Science Quarterly* 28: 201–222.

———. 1987. "What Do Decision-Makers Do When They Make a Foreign Policy Decision? The Implications for the Comparative Study of Foreign Policy." In C. F. Hermann, C. W. Kegley, Jr., and J. N. Rosenau, eds., *New Directions in the Study of Foreign Policy*, 285–308. Boston: Allen & Unwin.

Andeweg, R. B. 1988. "Centrifugal Forces and Collective Decision-Making: The Case of the Dutch Cabinet." *European Journal of Political Research* 16: 125–151.

———. 1990. "Tweeërlei Ministerraad." In R. B. Andeweg, ed., *Ministers en Minister-raad,* 17–41. The Hague: SDU Uitgeverij.

Arrow, K. J. 1951. *Social Choice and Individual Values.* New York: Wiley.

Bakema,W. E. 1990. "Vakbekwame Ministers." In R. B. Andeweg, ed., *Ministers en Mi-nisterraad,* 71–96. The Hague: SDU Uitgeverij.

Bakema, W. E., and I. P. Secker. 1988. "Ministerial Expertise and the Dutch Case." *European Journal of Political Research* 16: 152–169.

Bales, R. F. 1950. *Interaction Process Analysis: A Method for the Study of Small Groups.* Cambridge, Mass.: Addison Wesley.

Bales, R. F., and F. L. Strodtbeck. 1951. "Phases in Group Problem Solving." *Journal of Abnormal and Social Psychology* 46: 485–495.

Baybrooke, D., and C. E. Lindblom. 1963. *A Strategy of Decision Policy Evaluation as a Social Process.* New York: Free Press.

Beyen, J. W. 1968. *Het spel en de knikkers: Een Kroniek van Vijftig Jaren.* Rotterdam: Donker.

Bihl, W. 1989. *Von der Donaumonarchie zur Zweiten Republik: Daten zur Österreichischen Geschichte seit 1867.* Vienna: Böhlau Verlag.

Blight, J. G., B. J. Allyn, and D. A. Welch. 1993. *Cuba on the Brink: Fidel Castro, the Missile Crisis and the Collapse of Communism.* New York: Pantheon.

Blondel, J. 1988. Introduction to J. Blondel and F. Müller-Rommel, eds., *Cabinets in Western Europe,* 1–15. London: MacMillan.

Blondel, J., and F. Müller-Rommel, eds. 1988. *Cabinets in Western Europe.* London: MacMillan.

Brams, S. J. 1985. *Rational Politics: Decisions, Games and Strategy.* Boston: Academic Press.

Brecher, M. 1977. "Toward a Theory of International Crisis Behavior." *International Studies Quarterly* 21: 39–74.

Brecher, M., and B. Geist. 1980. *Decisions in Crisis: Israel, 1967 and 1973.* Berkeley: University of California Press.

Brecher, M., B. Steinberg, and J. Stein. 1969. "Foreign Policy Behavior." *Journal of Conflict Resolution* 13: 75–101.

Burch, M. 1988. "The United Kingdom." In J. Blondel and F. Müller-Rommel, eds., *Cabinets in Western Europe,* 16–32. London: MacMillan.

Burke, J., and F. I. Greenstein. 1989. *How Presidents Test Reality: Decisions on Vietnam, 1954 and 1965.* New York: Russell Sage Foundation.

Callahan, P., L. P. Brady, and M. G. Hermann, eds. 1982. *Describing Foreign Policy Behavior.* Beverly Hills, Calif.: Sage.

Chang, L., and P. Kornbluh. 1992. *The Cuban Missile Crisis, 1962: A National Security Documents Reader.* New York: Free Press.

Cohen, M. D., J. G. March, and J. P. Olsen. 1972. "A Garbage Can Model of Organizational Choice." *Administrative Science Quarterly* 17: 1–25.

Condorcet, J. A. 1979. *Sketch for a History for the Progress of the Human Mind.* Reprint. 1785. Westport, Conn.: Hyperion Press.

Craven, J. 1992. *Social Choice: A Framework for Collective Decisions and Individual Judgements.* Cambridge: Cambridge University Press.

De Jong, J. J. P. 1988. *Diplomatie en Strijd: het Nederlands Beleid tegenover de Indonesische Revolutie 1945–1947.* Meppel, Amsterdam: Boom.

Dijkstra, W., and A. W. Taris. 1994. *Sequence Manual.* Amsterdam: ProFile.

———. 1995. "Measuring the Agreement between Sequences." *Sociological Methods and Research* 24: 214–231.

Drees, W. 1963. *Zestig Jaar Levenservaring.* Amsterdam: Arbeiderspers.

Drooglever, P. J., and M. J. van Schouten, eds. 1981–1992. *Officiële bescheiden betreffende de Nederlands Indonesische betrekkingen, 1945–1950.* Vols. 15–17. The Hague: Nijhoff.

Ellis, D. G., and B. A. Fisher. 1994. *Small Group Decision-Making: Communication and the Group Process.* New York: McGraw-Hill.

Fisher, B. A. 1974. *Small Group Decision-Making: Communication and the Group Process.* New York: McGraw-Hill.

Frey, L. R., ed. 1994. *Group Communication in Context: Studies of Natural Groups.* Hillsdale, N.J.: Erlbaum.

Frognier, A. P. 1988. "Belgium." In J. Blondel and F. Müller-Rommel, eds., *Cabinets in Western Europe*, 68–85. London: MacMillan.

Gaenslen, F. 1992. "Decision-Making Groups." In E. Singer and V. Hudson eds., *Political Psychology and Foreign Policy*, 165–193. Boulder, Colo.: Westview Press.

Gallhofer, I. N., and W. E. Saris. 1996. *Foreign Policy Decision-Making: A Qualitative and Quantitative Analysis of Political Argumentation.* Westport, Conn.: Praeger.

Geiss, I. 1963. *Julikrise und Kriegsausbruch 1914.* Hannover: Verlag für Literatur und Zeitgeschichte.

George, A. L. 1972. "The Case for Multiple Advocacy in Making Foreign Policy." *American Political Science Review* 66: 751–794.

———. 1980. *Presidential Decision-Making in Foreign Policy: The Effective Use of Information and Advice.* Boulder, Colo.: Westview Press.

Gross-Stein, J., and R. Tanter. 1980. *Rational Decision-Making: Israel's Security Choices, 1967.* Columbus: Ohio University Press.

Halperin, M. H. 1974. *Bureaucratic Politics and Foreign Policy.* Washington, D.C.: Brookings Institution.

Hargreaves Heap, S. P., and Y. Varoufakis. 1995. *Game Theory: A Critical Introduction.* London: Routledge.

Herek, G. M., I. L. Janis, and P. Huth. 1987. "Decision-Making during International Crises: Is Quality of Process Related to Outcome?" *Journal of Conflict Resolution* 312: 203–226.

Hermann, C. F. 1978. "Decision Structures and Process Influences on Foreign Policy." In M. A. East, S. A. Salmore, and C. F. Hermann, eds., *Why Nations Act,* 69–102. Beverly Hills, Calif.: Sage.

Hermann, C. F., ed. 1972. *International Crisis.* New York: Free Press.

Hermann, C. F., C. W. Kegley, Jr., and J. N. Rosenau, eds., 1987. *New Directions in the Study of Foreign Policy.* Boston: Allen & Unwin.

Hermann, M. G., C. F. Hermann, and J. D. Hagan. 1987. "How Decision Units Shape Foreign Policy Behavior." In C. F. Hermann, C. W. Kegley, Jr., and J. N. Rosenau, eds., *New Directions in the Study of Foreign Policy,* 247–268. Boston: Allen & Unwin.

Hilsman, R. 1987. *The Politics of Policy Making in Defense and Foreign Affairs: Conceptual Models and Bureaucratic Politics.* Englewood Cliffs, N.J.: Prentice-Hall.

———. 1996. *The Cuban Missile Crisis: The Struggle over Policy.* Westport, Conn.: Praeger.

Hirokawa, R. Y., and M. S. Poole, eds., 1986. *Communication and Group Decision-Making.* Beverly Hills, Calif.: Sage.

———. 1996. *Communication and Group Decision-Making.* 2nd edition. Thousand Oaks, Calif.: Sage.

Holmes, M., and M. S. Poole. 1991. "The Longitudinal Analysis of Interaction." In B. Montgomery, and S. Duck, eds., *Studying Personal Interactions*, 286–302. New York: Guilford.

Holsti, O. R. 1969. *Content Analysis for the Social Sciences and Humanities.* Reading, Mass.: Addison Wesley.

———. 1979. "Theories of Crisis Decision-Making." In P. G. Lauren, ed., *Diplomacy: New Approaches in History, Theory and Policy,* 99–136. New York: Free Press.

Hommes, P. M. 1980. *Nederland en de Europese Eenwording.* The Hague: Nijhoff.

James, S. 1992. *British Cabinet Government.* London: Routledge.

Janis, I. L. 1972. *Victims of Groupthink.* Boston: Houghton Mifflin.

―――. 1989. *Crucial Decisions: Leadership in Policymaking and Crisis Management.* New York: Free Press.

Janis, I. L. and L. Mann. 1977. *Decision-Making: A Psychological Analysis of Conflict, Choice and Commitment.* New York: Free Press.

Jensen, A. D., and J. C. Chilberg. 1991. *Small Group Communication: Theory and Application.* Belmont, Calif.: Wadsworth.

Kahneman, D., and A. Tversky. 1979. "Prospect Theory: An Analysis of Decision under Risk." *Econometrica* 47: 263–291.

Kennedy, R. 1969. *Thirteen Days: A Memoir of the Cuban Missile Crisis.* New York: Norton.

Klein, P. W., and G. N. van der Plaat, eds. 1981. *Herrijzend Nederland.* The Hague: Nijhoff.

Komjáthy, M., ed. 1966. *Protokolle des Gemeinsamen Ministerrates der Österreichisch-Ungarischen Monarchie (1914–1918).* Budapest: Akadémiai Kiadó.

Larson, D. L. 1986. *The Cuban Missile Crisis of 1962: Selected Documents, Chronology and Bibliography.* Landham, Md.: University Press of America.

Leurdijk, J. H. 1978. *The Foreign Policy of the Netherlands.* Alphen aan den Rijn: Sijthoff.

Lijphart, A. 1968. *The Politics of Accommodation: Pluralism and Democracy in The Netherlands.* Berkeley: University of California Press.

Lindblom, C. E. 1959. "The Science of Muddling Through." *Public Administration Review* 19: 79–99.

Lindblom, C. E. 1980. *The Policy-Making Process.* Englewood Cliffs, N.J.: Prentice Hall.

Lindblom, C. E. 1982. "Still Muddling Not Yet Through." In A. G. McGrew and M. J. Wilson, eds., *Decision-Making Approaches and Analysis,* 125–138. Manchester: Manchester University Press.

Maidment, R., and A. McGrew. 1992. *The American Political Process.* London: Sage.

Manning, A. F., and A. E. Kersten, eds. 1976–1984. *Documenten betreffende de Buitenlandse Politiek van Nederland, 1940–1945.* Vols. 1–4. The Hague: Nijhoff.

Maoz, Z. 1990. *National Choices and International Processes.* Cambridge: Cambridge University Press.

McNamara, R. S. 1995. *In Retrospect: The Tragedy and Lessons of Vietnam.* New York: Random House.

Mor, B. D. 1993. *Decision and Interaction in Crisis: A Model of International Crisis Behavior.* Westport, Conn.: Praeger.

Moscovici, S., and W. Doise. 1994. *Conflict and Consensus: A General Theory of Collective Decisions.* London: Sage.

Müller-Rommel, F. 1988. "Federal Republic of Germany." In J. Blondel and F. Müller-Rommel, eds., *Cabinets in Western Europe,* 151–166. London: MacMillan.

Papp, D. S., ed. 1990. *As I Saw It by Dean Rusk as Told to Richard Rusk.* New York: Norton.

Poole, M. S., and C. Baldwin. 1996. "Developmental Processes in Group Decision-Making." In R. Y. Hirokawa and M. S. Poole, eds., *Communication and Group Decision-Making,* 215–241. Thousand Oaks, Calif.: Sage.

Poole, M. S., and J. Doelger. 1986. "Developmental Processes in Group Decision-Making." In R. Y. Hirokawa and M. S. Poole, eds., *Communication and Group Decision-Making,* 237–264. Beverly Hills, Calif.: Sage.

Poole, M. S., and M. E. Holmes. 1995. "Decision Development in Computer-Assisted Group Decision-Making." *Human Communication Research* 22: 90–127.

Poole, M. S., and J. Roth. 1989a. "Decision Development in Small Groups IV: A Typology of Group Decision Paths." *Human Communication Research* 15: 323–356.

———. 1989b. "Decision Development in Small Groups V: Test of a Contingency Model." *Human Communication Research* 15: 549–589.

Purkitt, H. E. 1992. "Political Decision-Making in Small Groups: The Cuban Missile Crisis Revisited—One More Time." In E. Singer and V. Hudson, eds., *Political Psychology and Foreign Policy*, 219–245. Boulder, Colo.: Westview Press.

Putnam, L. L. 1986. "Conflict in Group Decision-Making." In R. Y. Hirokawa and M. S. Poole, eds., *Communication and Group Decision-Making*, 175–196. Beverly Hills: Sage.

Rapoport, A. 1969. "Games as a Tool for Psychological Research." In I. R. Buchler and H. G. Nini, eds., *Game Theory in the Behavioral Sciences,* 122–135. Pittsburgh: University of Pittsburgh Press.

Rhodes, R. A. W., and P. Dunleavy, eds. 1995. *Prime Minister, Cabinet and Core Executive.* New York: St. Martin's Press.

Riker, W. H., and P. C. Ordeshook. 1973. *An Introduction to Positive Political Theory.* Englewood Cliffs, N.J.: Prentice-Hall.

Rosati, J. A. 1980. "Developing a Systematic Decision-Making Framework: Bureaucratic Politics in Perspective." *World Politics* 33: 234–252.

Rosenau, J. N. 1966. "Pre-Theories and Theories of Foreign Policy." In R. B. Farrel, ed., *Approaches to Comparative and International Politics,* 27–92. Evanston, Ill.: Northwestern University Press.

Rosenthal, U., H. G. Geveke, and P. 't Hart. 1994. "Beslissen in een Competitief Overheidsbestel: Bureaupolitiek en Bureaupolitism nader Beschouwd." *Acta Politica* 3: 309–334.

Saris, W. E., and I. N. Gallhofer. 1975. "L'Application d'un Modèle de Décision a des Données Historiques." *Revue Française de Science Politique* 25: 473–501.

Scharpf, F. W. 1989. "Decision Rules, Decision Styles and Policy Choices." *Theoretical Politics* 1: 149–176.

Schlesinger, A. M., Jr., 1967. *A Thousand Days: JFK in the White House.* Boston: Houghton Mifflin.

Simon, H. A. 1957. *Models of Man: Social and Rational.* New York: Wiley.

———. 1985. "Human Nature in Politics: The Dialogue of Psychology with Political Science." *American Political Science Review* 79: 293–304.

Sked, A. 1992. *The Decline and Fall of the Habsburg Empire, 1815–1918.* London and New York: Longman.

Smit, C. 1950. *Diplomatieke Geschiedenis van Nederland, in Zonderheid sedert de Vestiging van het Koninkrijk.* The Hague: Nijhoff.

———. 1962. *De liquidatie van een Imperium: Nederland en Indonesië 1945–1962.* Amsterdam: Arbeiderspers.

———, ed. 1962. *Documenten betreffende de buitenlandse politiek van Nederland, 1848–1919.* Vol. 4. The Hague: Nijhoff.

———. 1972. *Nederland in de Eerste Wereldoorlog (1899–1919).* Groningen: Wolters-Noordhoff.

Snyder, R. C., H. W. Bruck, and B. Sapin. 1962. *Foreign Policy Decision-Making: An Approach to the Study of International Politics.* New York: Free Press.

Stapel, F. W. 1943. *Geschiedenis van Nederlands Indië.* Amsterdam: Meulenhoff.

Steinbruner, J. D. 1974. *The Cybernetic Theory of Decision.* Princeton: Princeton University Press.

Steiner, J., and R. H. Dorff. 1980a. "Decision by Interpretation: A New Concept for an Often Overlooked Decision Mode." *British Journal of Political Science* 10: 1–13.

———. 1980b. *A Theory of Political Decision Modes. Intraparty Decision-Making in Switzerland.* Chapel Hill: University of North Carolina Press.

Stikker, D. 1966. *Mémoires: Herinneringen uit de Lange Jaren waar Ik Betrokken was bij de Voortdurende Wereldcrisis.* Rotterdam: Nigh van Ditmar.

't Hart, P. 1990. *Groupthink in Government: A Study of Small Groups and Policy Failure.* Rockland, Mass.: Swets & Zeitlinger.

Thiébault, J. L. 1988. "France." In J. Blondel and F. Müller-Rommel, eds., *Cabinets in Western Europe,* 86–101. London: MacMillan.

Timmermans, A., and W. E. Bakema. 1990. "Conflicten in Nederlandse Kabinetten." In R. B. Andeweg, ed., *Ministers en Ministerraad,* 175–192. The Hague: SDU Uitgeverij.

Toirkens, S. J. 1990. "De Minister van Financiën: In het Spanningsveld van Financiële Wensen en Mogelijkheden." In R. B. Andeweg, ed., *Ministers en Ministerraad,* 127–145. The Hague: SDU Uitgeverij.

Tversky, A., and D. Kahneman. 1974. "Judgement under Uncertainty: Heuristics and Biases." *Science* 185: 1124–1151.

———. 1988. "Rational Choice and the Framing of Decisions." In D. E. Bell, H. Raiffa, and A. Tversky, eds., *Decision-Making: Descriptive, Normative and Prescriptive Interactions,* 167–192. Cambridge: Cambridge University Press.

Van den Berg, J. T. J. 1990. "De Ministerpresident." In R. B. Andeweg, ed., *Ministers and Ministerraad,* 97–122. The Hague: SDU Uitgeverij.

Van Kleffens, E. N. 1983. *Belevenissen.* Vols. 1 and 2. Alphen aan den Rijn: Sijthoff.

Vertzberger, Y. Y. I. 1990. *The World in Their Minds: Information Processing, Cognition and Perception in Foreign Policy Decision-Making.* Stanford: Stanford University Press.

Von Neumann, J., and O. Morgenstern. 1947. *Theory of Games and Economic Behavior.* 2nd ed. Princeton: Princeton University Press.

Voorhoeve, J. C. 1979. *Peace, Profits, and Principles: A Study of Dutch Foreign Policy.* The Hague: Nijhoff.

Watson, S. R., and D. M. Buede. 1987. *Decision Synthesis: The Principles of Decision Analysis.* Cambridge: Cambridge University Press.

Wilkenfeld, J., G. W. Hopple, P. J. Rossa, and S. J. Andriole. 1980. *Foreign Policy Behavior: The Interstate Behavior Analysis Model.* Beverly Hills, Calif.: Sage.

Wilson, G. L., and M. S. Hanna. 1990. *Groups in Context: Leadership and Participation in Small Groups.* New York: McGraw-Hill.

DOCUMENTS

Dutch Documents

Maintenance of neutrality during World War I
Council of Ministers. October 1 and 3, 1914. Minutes. In C. Smit, ed., *Documenten be-treffende de Buitenlandse Politiek van Nederland, 1848–1919,* vol. 4, no. 171, pp. 145–160. The Hague: Nijhoff, 1962.

Peace efforts with Hitler
Council of Ministers. July 12, 1940. Minutes. In A. F. Manning and A. E. Kersten, eds., *Documenten betreffende de Buitenlandse Politiek van Nederland, 1940–1945,* vol. 1, no. 168, pp. 170–172. The Hague: Nijhoff, 1976.
Council of Ministers. July 24, 1940. Minutes. Ibid., no. 199, pp. 214–222.

To lend Dutch gold stocks to the British for the war efforts
Council of Ministers. October 29, 1940. Minutes. In A. F. Manning and A. E. Kersten, eds., *Documenten betreffende de Buitenlandse Politiek van Nederland, 1940–1945,* vol. 1, no. 465, pp. 541–543. The Hague: Nijhoff, 1976.
Council of Ministers. December 20, 1940. Minutes. Ibid., no. 118, pp. 152–156.

Transference of the seat of the Dutch government in exile to the East Indies
Council of Ministers. January 18, 1941. Minutes. In A. F. Manning and A. E. Kersten, eds., *Documenten betreffende de Buitenlandse Politiek van Nederland, 1940–1945,* vol. 2, no. 170, pp. 215–220. The Hague: Nijhoff, 1977.

Border corrections with Germany
Council of Ministers. October 17, 1948. Minutes. Archives of General Affairs, record no. 246.

Western European Union / North Atlantic Treaty Organization
Council of Ministers. January 21, 1949. Minutes. Archives of General Affairs, record Minutes of the Council of Ministers.

European Political Community
Council of Ministers. April 29, 1953. Minutes. Archives of General Affairs, record Minutes of the Council of Ministers.

First police action in Indonesia
Council of Ministers. July 7, 1947. Minutes. In P. J. Drooglever and M. J. van Schouten, eds., *Officiële bescheiden betreffende de Nederlands Indonesische betrekkingen, 1945–1950,* vol. 9, no. 300, pp. 611–621. The Hague: Nijhoff, 1981.
Council of Ministers, July 17, 1947. Minutes. Ibid., no. 355, pp. 710–719.

First intervention of the Security Council in Indonesia
Council of Ministers. July 30, 1947. Minutes. In P. J. Drooglever and M. J. van Schouten, eds., *Officiële bescheiden betreffende de Nederlands Indonesische betrekkingen, 1945–1950,* vol.10, no. 77, pp. 115–123. The Hague: Nijhoff, 1982.
Council of Ministers. August 2, 1947. Minutes. Ibid., no. 133, pp. 201–208.
Council of Ministers. August 13, 1947. Minutes. Ibid., no. 259, p. 384.
Council of Ministers. August 14, 1947. Minutes. Ibid., no. 272, pp. 397–407.
Council of Ministers. August 15, 1947. Minutes. Ibid., no. 285, pp. 426–428.

Council of Ministers. August 18, 1947. Minutes. Ibid., no. 315, pp. 484–497.
Council of Ministers. August 27, 1947. Minutes. Ibid., no. 410, pp. 657–670.
Council of Ministers. September 4, 1947. Minutes. In P. J. Drooglever and M. J. van Schouten, eds., *Officiële bescheiden betreffende de Nederlands Indonesische betrekkingen, 1945–1950*, vol. 11, no. 16, pp. 18–29. The Hague: Nijhoff, 1983.

Second police action in Indonesia
Council of Ministers. October 26, 1948. Minutes. In P. J. Drooglever and M. J. van Schouten, eds., *Officiële bescheiden betreffende de Nederlands Indonesische betrekkingen, 1945–1950*, vol. 15, no. 259, pp. 515–525. The Hague: Nijhoff, 1989.
Council of Ministers. November 15, 1948. Minutes. Ibid., no. 328, pp. 662–670.
Council of Ministers. November 17, 1948. Minutes. Ibid., no. 341, pp. 689–691.
Council of Ministers. December 9, 1948. Minutes. In P. J. Drooglever and M. J. van Schouten, eds., *Officiële bescheiden betreffende de Nederlands Indonesische betrekkingen, 1945–1950*, vol. 16, no. 41, pp. 73–82. The Hague: Nijhoff, 1991.
Council of Ministers. December 13, 1948. Minutes. Ibid., no. 73, pp. 114–119.
Council of Ministers. December 14, 1948. Minutes. Ibid., no. 85, pp. 132–138.
Council of Ministers. December 15, 1948. Minutes. Ibid., no. 96, pp. 150–164.
Council of Ministers. December 17, 1948. Minutes. Ibid., no. 123, pp. 191–194.
Council of Ministers. December 18, 1948. Minutes. Ibid., no. 141, pp. 219–222.

Second intervention of the Security Council in Indonesia
Council of Ministers. January 28, 1949. Minutes. In P. J. Drooglever and M. J. van Schouten, eds., *Officiële bescheiden betreffende de Nederlands Indonesische betrekkingen, 1945–1950*, vol. 16, no. 175, pp. 263–267. The Hague: Nijhoff, 1991.
Council of Ministers. January 31, 1949. Minutes. Ibid., no. 203, pp. 310–317.
Council of Ministers. February 7, 1949. Minutes. In P. J. Drooglever and M. J. van Schouten, eds., *Officiële bescheiden betreffende de Nederlands Indonesische betrekkingen, 1945–1950*, vol. 17, no. 263, pp. 439–452. The Hague: Nijhoff, 1993.
Council of Ministers. February 10, 1949. Minutes. Ibid., no. 283, pp. 489–498.

Rhine navigation dispute
Council of Ministers. May 25, 1954. Minutes. Archives of General Affairs, record Minutes of the Council of Ministers.

Greece's and Turkey's admission to NATO
Council of Ministers. July 7, 1951. Minutes about Greece's and Turkey's admission to NATO. Archives of General Affairs, record Minutes of the Council of Ministers.

American Documents

Executive Committee Meeting. October 16, 1962. Minutes. In L. Chang and P. Kornbluh, eds., *The Cuban Missile Crisis, 1962: A National Security Archives Documents Reader*, no. 15, pp. 85–96. New York: Free Press, 1992.
Executive Committee Meeting. October 16, 1962. Minutes. Ibid., no. 16, pp. 97–113.
Executive Committee Meeting. October 19, 1962. Minutes. Ibid., no. 21, pp. 123–127.
Notes on the meeting of October 25 with the president. Ibid., no. 25, pp. 144–145.

Austrian Documents

Common Council of Ministers of the Austro-Hungarian Monarchy. July 7, 1914. Minutes. In M. Komjáthy ed., *Protokolle des Gemeinsamen Ministerrates der Österreichisch-Ungarischen Monarchie (1914–1918)*, no. 1, pp. 141–158. Budapest: Akadémiai Kiadó, 1966.

Common Council of Ministers of the Austro-Hungarian Monarchy. July 19, 1914. Minutes. Ibid., no. 2, pp. 144–145.

German Documents

Hitler, Adolf. August 22, 1939. Address to the supreme commanders. In *Akten zur Deutschen Auswärtigen Politik, 1918–1945*, Serie D (1937–1945), vol. 7, no. 192, pp. 167–172. Baden-Baden: Imprimerie Nationale, 1956.

Subject Index

Name Index

About the Authors

IRMTRAUD N. GALLHOFER is Senior Researcher at the Sociometric Research Foundation of Amstelveen.

WILLEM E. SARIS is Professor of Statistics and Methods at the University of Amsterdam.

ISBN 0-275-96029-3

90000>

9 780275 960292

HARDCOVER BAR CODE